D1087781

R ESILIENT IDENTITIES

Self-Relationships

and the Construction

of Social Reality

William B. Swann, Jr.

BASIC
BOOKS

A Member of the
Perseus Books Group

Copyright © 1999 by Basic Books,
A Member of the Perseus Books Group.

First published in 1996 by W. H. Freeman and Company

Interior design by Blake Logan

Library of Congress Cataloging-in-Publication Data
    [Self-traps: the elusive quest for higher self-esteem]
    Resilient identities : Self-relationships and the
construction of social reality / William B. Swann, Jr.
        p.   cm.
    Originally published: Self-traps : the elusive quest for
higher self-esteem. New York : W. H. Freeman and
Company, 1996.
    Includes bibliographical references and index.
    ISBN 0-8133-9118-0 (pbk.)
    1. Self-esteem.   2. Self-defeating behavior.   I. Title.
BF697.5.S46S83   1996
155.2—dc20   96-5265
                                                                  CIP

99 00 01 ❖ / RRD 10 9 8 7 6 5 4 3 2 1

For
my parents and
Hazeo, Nicki, and Lily

CONTENTS

WITHDRAWN

PREFACE

Proper self-esteem [is] a state of mind that ought to be. Those,
moreover, who estimate their own worth correctly, do so on the
basis of their past deeds, and so, what they have done, they dare
to try again. Those who estimate their worth too highly, or who
pretend to be what they are not, or who believe flatterers, become
disheartened when dangers actually confront them.

—Thomas Hobbes, *De Homine*

Although he wrote in 1658, Hobbes's reflections on self-esteem
have a surprisingly modern feel. We still believe, for example,
that self-esteem is a "state of mind that ought to be," and that,
in principle, it faithfully summarizes our past accomplishments. And we still believe that in matters of self-esteem, too
much is as problematic as too little.

Yet our contemporary understanding of self-esteem contrasts
sharply with that of Hobbes in at least one respect. Whereas he
conceptualized self-esteem as something that was regulated by
the internal workings of "animal spirits," contemporary thinkers
emphasize the manner in which self-esteem is regulated by, and
helps to regulate, events in the external world. In fact, the primary reason that self-esteem has assumed such a prominent
role in recent discussions of psychological health, educational
practices, and public policy is that it is widely believed that self-
esteem is the root cause underlying our personal and social
problems. This conviction has not only sparked the emergence
of a multimillion dollar self-help industry devoted to raising
self-esteem but has also given rise to a self-esteem movement

that is shaping public policy and altering some of the basic tenets of our educational system.

As a researcher who has devoted the greater part of the last two decades to the study of self-esteem and related phenomena, I have viewed the emergence of the self-esteem movement with a mixture of satisfaction and alarm. Low self-esteem is clearly a source of enormous suffering, and it is gratifying that some well-intentioned people are grappling with ways to alleviate it. I fear that the movement has raised many false hopes, however. The research that I and others have conducted in recent years shows that raising self-esteem is not as easy as it is often made out to be, nor is it a cure-all for the myriad ills that plague our society.

Yet if the self-esteem movement cannot deliver on its promises, perhaps it will at least help to focus attention on an important set of social and personal issues, and on a fascinating story that has, until now, remained hidden in the scientific journals, away from public view. That story concerns the processes that make self-esteem so resistant to change. Why, for example, do people with low self-esteem sometimes act in ways that undermine their confidence in themselves—even though they are clearly suffering as a result of their negative self-views? What childhood events promote low self-esteem and what later events maintain it? And what can be done to raise self-esteem? I address these and related questions in this book.

My interest in self-esteem sprang from the many encounters I have had with people with terrible self-esteem. What intrigued me most about these people was their paradoxical tendency to create the very conditions that perpetuated their unhappiness. I noticed, for instance, that some entered into and maintained relationships with people who exploited or otherwise abused them. What strange logic compelled their choice of partners, I wondered. To find out, I embarked upon the intellectual journey that eventually gave rise to this book.

My travels began in my own psychological laboratory at the University of Texas at Austin, where I supervised dozens of experiments, field studies, and surveys. As the findings poured in, however, I gradually realized that the participants in my studies could not hope to provide me with all the answers I needed. I thus made forays into many diverse literatures, many of which have found their way into the discussions in this book. As a result, although the core argument rests on theory and research from psychology and sociology, the contributions of psychoanalysts, historians, anthropologists, philosophers, speech pathologists, opthamologists, and neurologists are sprinkled throughout.

If there is a central question in this book, it is this: Why are so many of us unable to attain higher self-esteem despite our best efforts to do so? My answer is that we periodically fall into various traps that make it impossible to enjoy higher self-esteem. Some of these self-traps grow out of a deeply rooted human desire for self-verification, a desire that causes people to resist substantial improvements in their self-views. People with low self-esteem, for example, pay more attention to negative evaluations, remember them better, and interpret information in ways that guarantee the survival of their negative self-views. To overcome these systematic biases, they must encounter evidence that offers unequivocal support for new, more positive self-views. Unfortunately, they rarely encounter such evidence because they gravitate toward partners who evaluate them negatively, thus sabotaging improvements in their self-views.

To be sure, some people manage to escape the clutches of rejecting partners. Yet even they may fall into self-traps that are inherent in the norms and values of the larger society. Some of these self-traps, for example, involve beliefs that encourage people to pursue self-esteem in ways that are counterproductive and self-deflating.

In the course of describing various self-traps, I attempt to explode several myths about the nature of self-esteem. For instance, no one is born with qualities that lead inevitably to the development of low self-esteem. In addition, many of the practices of individuals and the larger society that are commonly thought to increase self-esteem may, in reality, promote low self-esteem. For example, both indiscriminately praising children and being extremely hard on them diminishes rather than improves self-esteem. Similarly, although taking anti-depressant drugs, such as Prozac, may provide temporary relief from depression, there is little reason to believe that these drugs produce a permanent increase in self-esteem. And many of our common assumptions about the most effective strategies for achieving high self-esteem—such as the notion that we can improve ourselves through romantic relationships or by acquiring material goods and other markers of success—often systematically undermine self-esteem. Yet there is a hopeful message here, for as I discuss in the final chapter, many of these self-traps can be avoided as we become aware of them and change our behavior or the appropriate social institutions.

Acknowledgments

The National Institute of Mental Health and the National Science Foundation have generously funded my research on the self over the last decade and a half. Equally crucial to this work have been the many students and colleagues who have worked with me on the research that provides the empirical backbone of the book: Camille Buckner, Chris De La Ronde, Robin Ely, Brian Giesler, Daniel Gilbert, John Griffin, Craig Hill, Gregory Hixon, Douglas Krull, Shawn McNulty, Brett Pelham, Elizabeth Pinel, Stephen Predmore, Stephen Read, Daniel Schroeder, Al Stein-Seroussi, Romin Tafarodi, and Richard Wenzlaff. In less direct ways, several people helped make the book possible by providing me with encouragement and sound advice at critical junctures. I am especially indebted to Bruce Campbell, Daniel Gilbert, Thane Pittman, David Schneider, Berna Skrypnek, Daniel Wegner, and Richard Wenzlaff. Several assistants have also played a vital role in gathering materials for this book and performing various other tasks, especially Michel Arneson, Heidi Mumford, Carrie Proske, and Alana Voss.

A legion of generous colleagues, friends, and students commented on earlier drafts of the manuscript, including Cary Booker, Jennifer Bosson, Kelly Brennan, Ryan Brown, Camille Buckner, Stephen Finn, Michael Gill, Ted Huston, Deborah Jacobvitz, Ned Jones, Robert Josephs, Kathryn Morris, Elizabeth Pinel, Jeffrey Polzer, Oliver Sacks, and Daniel Wegner.

A special thanks to the reviewers for this book, Brett Pelham, David Schneider, Robert Scott, and two anonymous commentators, and to Laurie Milton, who painstakingly read and re-read the entire manuscript and shared her wisdom about countless issues. Nancy Hazen did all the foregoing and more, cheerfully enduring my ceaseless musings and ruminations about the contents of the book, offering incisive comments at every turn, and bringing new meaning to the phrase "moral support."

Throughout the early stages in the writing of this book, I was reassured by the conviction that my editor, Jonathan Cobb, had an exceptionally clear vision of where the book was going, clearer even than my own vision. As the book approached completion, I realized that Jonathan had been reassuring himself that I was the one enjoying this exceptionally clear vision. He may have been correct all along, but I am sure that I would never have been able to translate this vision into this book without his sage advice along the way. I am very grateful to him, and also to Katherine Ahr, the project editor, and Diana Siemens, the copy editor, for innumerable helpful suggestions. Thanks also go to Blake Logan for her elegant design, to Julia DeRosa for coordinating the book's production, and to Susan Cory for her deft page makeup.

"Only in man does man know himself," Goethe once observed. Our self-views are, in a very profound sense, gifts from our fellow human beings. Each time someone favors us with a loving embrace, an understanding glance, or any sign that they recognize us for what we are, we know a tiny bit more about our place in the universe, and hence, a little more about who we are. Although these self-sustaining gifts come from many quarters, our most important benefactors are often the members of our immediate families, for it is they who play the biggest role in confirming and sustaining us. In this respect, I owe my greatest debt to Hazeo, Nicki, and Lily, whose gifts of love have been enough to sustain a hundred men.

William B. Swann, Jr.
Austin, Texas
February 1996

1 THE HOLY GRAIL OF SELF-ESTEEM

I am a 35-year-old housewife and mother of two. From my first boyfriend (who married me five years later and fathered my child), throughout my dating history, and up to my present husband, I have been attracted to verbally, mentally and emotionally abusive men. I have spent hundreds of dollars on self-help materials trying to find out why this has happened to me all my life.

I am not unattractive. I know how to dress well and look good, although present finances prevent my doing this to the degree that I am capable. I consider myself well-rounded in travel and life experiences. I am conscientious about health and personal hygiene. On the other hand, my social skills seem to have come to a dead stop in the past few years. I am withdrawn, introverted and self-conscious to an extent I've never known before. I have never learned to be assertive, although I know what it means. I have allowed overbearing people to force their will on me. . . . Also, during the eight years I have been with my present husband, I put on extra weight that I cannot seem to lose. I am one of those women who chose to stay at home to see that her child has some semblance of stability. I have been threatened with divorce for not having a job, for not cleaning house (I cleaned seven others for pay at that time) and because my husband thought I was not happy with him.[1]

S tories like Katherine's are all too familiar. Convinced that they are worthless, people like Katherine—both men and women—often add to their misery by paradoxically thinking and acting in ways that preserve their negative thoughts and feelings about themselves. Although hers is an extreme case, Katherine's choice of partners who belittle or even abuse her is common among people with quite negative self-views.

Katherine's strategy for remedying her situation is also typical: she has sought to overcome her pattern of troubled relationships by spending hundreds of dollars on self-help books and related materials. Yet these materials have done little to free her from the relationship traps into which she has repeatedly fallen. Instead, following the simplistic advice of the self-help literature has left her even more distraught and discouraged than before. Katherine, like so many others, is thus a double victim: first of the partners whom her low self-esteem led her to choose and second of the naive "quick fixes" to which she has turned hoping to raise her self-esteem.

The suffering of people like Katherine is very real and surprisingly widespread. Yet the choices they make are puzzling, for they seem to defy some long-standing assumptions about human nature, particularly the notion that everyone is motivated to seek praise and encouragement from their friends, coworkers, lovers, and others. In this book, I attempt to lay bare the mechanisms underlying the seemingly paradoxical behaviors of people with negative self-views. Drawing upon more than a decade of research on low self-esteem and depression, I examine the nature of low self-esteem, where it comes from, and how one can overcome it and the suffering it fosters.

Unfortunately, the suffering associated with low self-esteem and the difficulty of overcoming it have recently been overshadowed by the phenomenal growth of what has become known as the self-esteem movement. The movement has claimed that a myriad of problems grow out of low self-esteem and has asserted that these problems can be remedied by implementing a set of simple remedies designed to raise self-esteem. Yet as the experiences of Katherine illustrate, quick fixes typically not only fail to raise self-esteem but also raise false hopes and thus add to the anguish of victims of low self-esteem.

The "remedies" that Katherine tried represent only a few of the legion of programs developed and endorsed by the self-esteem movement. The movement has targeted its programs at people of both sexes and all ages, races, and socioeconomic backgrounds and has even suggested that strategies for raising self-esteem be incorporated into public policy. Despite all the hype, however, these programs are doomed to failure. To understand why, and to appreciate the difficulties of people like Katherine and the larger problems of self-esteem in our society, it's important to consider the self-esteem movement's guiding ideas.

The Self-Esteem Movement

A few years ago, my daughter arrived at the breakfast table sporting a bright new T-shirt with "I'm lovable and capable" emblazoned across the front. Feeling vaguely uneasy, I asked who'd given it to her. All the kids in her kindergarten had one, she replied; it was "the thing" to wear them on Fridays. The school counselor thought the slogan so important that she had the class recite "I'm lovable and capable" before every discussion session. My daughter fell silent for a moment and then, with a quizzical expression, asked, "Daddy, all the kids are wondering, what does 'capable' mean?"

The slogan, or "affirmation," that my daughter was required to recite was developed in the 1980s by a Californian named Jack Canfield. A former schoolteacher, he became a player in the movement when he founded Self-Esteem Seminars in Los Angeles. Endless variations on his techniques for raising self-esteem are now used throughout the country.

Affirmations and T-shirts are just two of many manifestations of the self-esteem movement. As educators have become convinced that building the confidence and self-esteem of elementary and high school students should be their paramount concern, they have dramatically shifted their approach to education. To protect their students from the possibly esteem-deflating effects of negative evaluations, many administrators have begun to water down school curricula and grading requirements so that children are less likely to fail. Many teachers are also being increasingly generous with praise and tokens and giving less corrective feedback. Proponents of this shift believe that it will pay off in the long run, because children who feel good about themselves cannot help but be better learners.[2]

Schoolchildren are not the only ones the self-esteem movement seeks to benefit. Tune in to talk shows such as "Oprah,"

"Geraldo," or "Sally Jesse Raphäel," browse the self-help section of your local bookstore, or look into the seminar offerings in your city and you'll quickly realize that low self-esteem has become a favorite explanation not only for various forms of unhappiness but also for a wide array of deviant behaviors. Even members of the clergy are using low self-esteem to rationalize behaviors that they once would have condemned as immoral. When Peewee Herman was arrested for masturbating in a movie theater a few years ago, Jesuit scholar William O'Malley observed that "masturbation isn't the problem, it's low self-esteem." If O'Malley is correct, many more of us have low self-esteem than anyone ever imagined.

The widespread conviction that self-esteem deficits lie at the heart of countless dysfunctional behaviors has catapulted the quest for self-esteem into something of a modern-day search for the Holy Grail. A dizzying array of programs now promise to raise self-esteem, sometimes in as little as 10 days. Even though many of the programs specifically target adults and involve such exhortations as "Recall all the successes in your life since you were a child," their content is surprisingly similar to the programs aimed at schoolchildren. Using simple assertions ("No one deserves to have low self-esteem!"), challenges ("What do you mean when you say you are too old or too fat? Too old for what? Fatter than whom?"), and visualization ("If you think you are unworthy and undeserving, practice visualizing yourself as a valuable, worthy individual making an important contribution to the world"), the approach is first to tell readers that they shouldn't have low self-esteem and then to urge them to "tell themselves the same thing—over and over again—"until their unconscious gets the message."[3]

To be sure, the programs that target adults are generally bolder than those aimed at children, presumably because adults who are desperate to improve their self-esteem will do things that most children would never dream of doing. Nathaniel Branden, author of the best-selling *Six Pillars of Self-Esteem*, advises readers that some affirmations are most effective if performed while naked. The procedure is simple enough. First, get naked. Then gaze into a full-length mirror and recite: "Whatever my defects or imperfections, I accept myself unreservedly and completely." Branden acknowledges that people may see something they don't like in the mirror and thus balk at the idea of accepting themselves "unreservedly and completely." Not to worry; Branden asserts that even if you come away from this exercise feeling disgusted with your body, your self-esteem will improve. Why? Because, he tells us, the key to self-esteem is *accepting* yourself, and accepting yourself is really nothing more than *recognizing* yourself: "accepting that the face and body in the mirror are your face and body" and that "they are what they are." Once people learn to "respect reality," they will "enter a more harmonious relationship with themselves" and enjoy higher self-esteem.[4]

Branden provides no systematic evidence for his assumption that people with low self-esteem are plagued by an inability to recognize their own reflections. Nor does he offer any hard evidence that affirmations uttered into the mirror while contemplating your nakedness have beneficial effects. No matter; Branden is convinced that his esteem-enhancing techniques will eradicate an impressive list of personal and social ills:

> *I cannot think of a single psychological problem—from anxiety to depression, to under-achievement at school or at work, to fear of intimacy, happiness, or success, to alcohol or drug abuse, to spouse battering or child molestation, to co-dependency and sexual disorders, to passivity and chronic aimlessness, to suicide and crimes of violence—that is not traceable, at least in part, to the problem of deficient self-esteem.[5]*

Countless thousands of Americans have come to believe such extraordinary assertions, and over the past decade the self-esteem movement has swelled from a trickle into a torrent. The most visible symbol of the country's commitment to improving self-esteem is California's Task Force to Promote Self-Esteem and Personal and State Responsibility.[6] Developed during the 1980s by a group of politicians and health professionals, the task force was predicated on the assumption that raising self-esteem could help to remedy virtually all of the problems just mentioned, *plus* welfare dependency, teen-age pregnancy, academic failure, and recidivism. Members embraced their mission with evangelical zeal; one exclaimed breathlessly, "I feel like I'm sitting in on the meetings that were held to draw up the Declaration of Independence."[7] Such unabashed enthusiasm has since swept the continent. Millions of Americans now believe in their hearts that high self-esteem is right, it is good, and it is something that all Americans are entitled to have. High self-esteem has become part of the American Dream.

The Movement's Critics

The messianic fervor of its proponents notwithstanding, the self-esteem movement has come under fire of late. Brown University psychologist William Damon has expressed deep concerns about the impact of the self-esteem movement on school programs. He has deplored the growing reluctance of teachers to deliver corrective feedback to students and suggests that the removal of difficult material from school curricula has compromised academic programs.[8] In a similar vein, *Newsweek* magazine comments:

> *Think of Halsey Schools [in Woodland Hills, California], where the word "bad" is never spoken, where everyone gets an award every year, where kindergarten students learn to count by being handed pictures of objects and told how many there are instead of figuring it out themselves. Ask yourself: wouldn't it be nice if life were really like this? And what's going to happen to those kids when they find out it's not?[9]*

Others have questioned the extravagant claims of the self-esteem movement. The researchers who assessed the feasibility of the objectives of the California task force, for example, reluctantly concluded that self-esteem was not consistently related to any of the key variables they examined.[10] Obviously, if self-esteem is not related to such problems as academic failure, welfare dependency, and the like, then improving it will not remedy these difficulties.

Even if researchers had discovered strong and consistent relationships between self-esteem and the social ills that the task force set out to remedy, the approach tempts people to think of such ills as isolated problems that can be solved by arranging for the treatment of those who have "it" (that is, low self-esteem). In reality, many of the problems that the task force identified arose from the failure of *public institutions* to provide services that they could no longer afford to offer. In California and throughout the nation, budget cuts have resulted in schools that don't educate, police that can't control crime or curb drug abuse, prison systems that release prisoners before rehabilitating them, a public welfare system that doesn't enable people to escape poverty, and a health care system that provides adequate treatment only for those wealthy enough to afford it. Even if one were able to raise the self-esteem of those living under such conditions, at best it would help them to cope with their harsh surroundings; it would do nothing to alter those surroundings directly. Real social problems cannot be reduced simply to personal psychopathology.

The absurdity of the task force's claims becomes particularly evident when one closely examines the primary weapons deployed in the war against low self-esteem. No one has pilloried these techniques more effectively than Al Franken, writer for the television program "Saturday Night Live." Franken parodies esteem-affirmation exercises by having Stuart Smalley, one of the show's characters, gaze tentatively into a mirror, smile, and then carefully recite, "I'm good enough, I'm smart enough, and doggone it, people like me." The newly esteemed Stuart then beams with satisfaction.[11]

Stuart's affirmation exercises are so hilariously naive and the claims of groups like the California task force so extravagant that it is tempting to dismiss anything even vaguely associated with efforts to increase self-esteem. Yet to do so would be a tragic mistake. We all know people who feel incompetent no matter how momentous their accomplishments and unloved no matter how much devotion they inspire. We have all met people who somehow manage to bring out the worst in everyone they encounter or who, like Katherine, wander into one deflating or abusive relationship after another. Indeed, research suggests that low self-esteem is a serious problem that afflicts at least a quarter of Americans. Moreover, the feelings of worthlessness that are the hallmark of low self-esteem may set the stage for clinical depression and suicide.[12] Surely no one would deny that these are deep and troubling forms of human misery. Nor are all efforts to improve self-esteem as useless and inane as those lampooned by Stuart Smalley. Although the path to high self-esteem is often a steep and rocky one, as I discuss in Chapter 7, it can be traveled.

The Self-Esteem Movement's Mistaken Assumptions

If ways of improving self-esteem *do* exist, what has caused the task force and related programs to miss them? Part of the problem is the task force's misunderstanding of the nature of self-esteem indices, as in their assertion that self-esteem is the cause of every personal and social ill imaginable. As I mentioned, researchers have found that self-esteem isn't consistently related to any of the phenomena that the task force tried to remedy. Nor should it be. Self-esteem is a very general concept, and general concepts tend to be associated with similarly general concepts rather than with specific ones. For example, the gross national product of the United States, a general index of economic health, ought to be related to other general indices of affluence, such as the average annual income of American workers; no one would expect the GNP to be related to a highly specific indicator of affluence such as the number of New Jersey chicken farmers who drive Lexuses. Likewise, self-esteem should be and is related to general reactions to the self, such as whether people are satisfied with themselves or depressed, but it should not necessarily be related to the multitude of specific behaviors that the task force examined. If one wants to predict whether teenagers will become pregnant or whether people will perform well in academic or professional settings, one should use appropriately specific indices, ones that directly tap people's feelings and beliefs about the particular behaviors under scrutiny.[13]

Even if the task force had discovered that indices of self-esteem *were* related to many social problems, such evidence alone would not have established that low self-esteem *causes* these problems. Suppose, for example, you found that self-esteem is lower among people who flunk out of high school than it is among those who graduate. Although this finding could reflect a tendency for low self-esteem to lead to failing grades, it could also reflect a tendency for failing grades to diminish self-esteem. If low self-esteem didn't cause academic failure in the first place, raising it would do little to solve the problem.

If such concerns rule out the possibility that bolstering self-esteem will save our society from countless difficulties, they leave open a second possibility. Imagine that it could be estab-lished that some specific self-view, such as the confidence of students in their academic abilities, does indeed play a causal role in some social problem, such as the high school dropout rate.[14] In principle, this would raise the possibility that programs could be developed to improve the specific self-views associated with such problems. Yet, in practice, developing programs that are effective in changing self-views may be exceedingly difficult. Why? The answer centers around three crucially important assumptions about the nature and function of self-knowledge. Although these assumptions are widely held by people in our society and by the leaders of the self-esteem movement, they are wrong.

The first and most deeply entrenched assumption is that all people are consumed by an overwhelming desire to think well of themselves. At some level, we undoubtedly *do* want to feel good about ourselves. Yet we are also motivated by a desire to confirm our existing self-views—even if those self-views are negative. Our self-views reside at the center of our knowledge system. They serve as the lens through which we observe reality; they organize our experiences and allow us to predict and control important events in our lives. So important are our self-views to psychological survival that we feel enormously threatened by the prospect of a world in which things are different from the way our self-views have led us to expect them to be. So we work to preserve our self-views, even if they are negative. The research I will describe later shows that people with negative self-views, like Katherine, may work to preserve these self-views by seeking people who are critical of them and avoiding those who praise them.

The second erroneous assumption made by the self-esteem movement is that all people feel entitled to praise and feel good when they receive it. Recent research indicates that when people who think poorly of themselves encounter favorable evaluations, they initially feel good, but their elation soon gives way to the perception that something must be amiss and that the real truth will soon emerge. Such discomfort may be so intense that they subsequently avoid favorable evaluations.

The third erroneous assumption is that relationship part-ners (spouses, friends, coworkers, and so forth) and the larger society will support an individual's quest for higher self-esteem.

One problem with this assumption is that it overlooks a basic fact of social life: we all depend on one another to honor the identities that we have negotiated in the past and to "be" the people we have agreed to be. Those who fail to conform to the identities that are expected of them may come under attack. Consider, for example, the turmoil that may result if a man sells his business and devotes himself to raising his children while his wife continues her demanding career. Although the wife may be pleased that her children are spending time with their father, she may resent the loss of income and fear that her husband's decision makes her seem like a neglectful parent by comparison. So she may criticize her husband's choice and urge him to return to a full-time job. His former coworkers, his relatives, and his friends may also challenge his decision because it threatens their traditional values. In a related but often more subtle fashion, members of minority groups may find that the dominant group frowns upon their entry into certain well-paying and socially valued professions, and thus they may feel compelled to find other pathways to high self-esteem.

The norms and values of the larger society may not only discourage people from using certain routes to enhance their self-esteem but also encourage them to pursue dead-ends. From childhood we learn that one of the keys to self-esteem is to become romantically involved with someone, for example. Unfortunately, much of what we learn draws on the romantic ideal, a belief system that fosters discordant, self-deflating relationships rather than mutually satisfying, esteem-enhancing ones. Those of us who look to our work as a source of self-esteem are often no better off, for our values and norms encourage us to see work as a means of acquiring material wealth rather than as an intrinsically gratifying activity in its own right. Work may thus foster feelings of alienation rather than feelings of self-worth. The upshot is that although both love and work may occasionally yield short- and even long-term gains in self-esteem, neither of these outcomes is inevitable. People who rely on these strategies to improve their self-esteem may find themselves worse off than they were to begin with.

Thus, several distinct processes operate to make self-esteem very difficult to improve. Some of these impediments to higher self-esteem involve people's own thoughts and behaviors; others concern the reactions of those with whom they form relationships; still others involve the responses of the larger society. In this book, I use the term *self-traps* to refer to these impediments to high self-esteem.

Self-Traps

The simplest and most straightforward self-traps are associated with our responses to personal evaluations. People with low self-esteem, for example, rarely seem to be listening when others praise them but are all ears when someone has something derogatory to say. If they happen to hear a compliment, they either forget it quickly or attribute it to some ulterior motive on the evaluator's part. Other self-traps involve behavior. If offered a choice between talking with someone who thinks well of them and talking with someone who does not, people with negative self-views often pick the person who thinks poorly of them. And if they end up in relationships with people who think well of them, such people will often attempt to bring their partner to see them as they see themselves. Failing this, they may simply withdraw from the relationship. In these ways, people may create—either in their own minds or in reality—idiosyncratic worlds that confirm and sustain their negative self-views.

This is why it is misguided to conceptualize self-esteem as a structure that exists "inside" a person like the heart, lungs, or liver. Self-esteem is more than a feeling that is disconnected from all other aspects of experience; it encompasses an entire manner of relating to the world—a set of strategies for setting goals, reacting to challenges, and dealing with setbacks.

Many of the crucial elements that make up an adult's self-esteem spring from experiences that happened years before and are remembered only dimly, if at all. Virtually all the essential aspects of self-esteem are tied to the ways in which the world has related to us in the past and is currently relating to us. People who *feel* downtrodden sometimes *are* downtrodden. For this reason, merely changing people's ways of feeling about themselves may create an illusion that will vanish in the harsh light of reality. For these and many other reasons, improving self-esteem is fraught with difficulty; quick fixes like the self-help materials purchased by Katherine just won't work.

The limitations of quick fixes are also apparent when one examines the effects of Prozac and other antidepressants. There is no doubt that altering the brain's biochemistry through antidepressants can make people feel less despondent about their problems and temporarily lift them out of the depressive mood states that are often associated with low self-esteem. For some people, temporary relief from depression may provide a window of opportunity during which they can begin to take steps toward rebuilding their sense of self-worth. Eventually, this process may culminate in higher self-esteem. Yet there is no guarantee that it will do so, because self-esteem is a relatively stable belief system that is deeply woven into the fabric of our interactions with our world. In itself, improving mood states through the use of antidepressants does nothing to alter that fabric, at least not directly. For this reason, it is misleading to suggest that changing the mood state of depression through Prozac, say, can *of itself* alter self-esteem.[15] This is why most responsible therapists deplore the practice of general practitioners prescribing antidepressants (sometimes less than three minutes into the visit!) without recommending therapy.

The ponderings of Elizabeth Wurtzel are revealing here. Wurtzel wrote *Prozac Nation* after taking the drug for seven years, perhaps longer than anyone else on the planet. Looking back on her struggle with depression, she credited Prozac with saving her life but still asserted that it was a partial and incomplete solution to her difficulties:

> *Years and years of bad habits, of being attracted to the wrong kinds of men, of responding to every bad mood with impulsive behavior (cheating on my boyfriend or being lax about my work assignments), had turned me into a person who had no idea how to function within the boundaries of the normal, nondepressive world. I needed a good therapist to help me learn to be a grownup, to show me how to live in a world where the phone company doesn't care that you're too depressed to pay the phone bill, that it turns off your line with complete indifference to such nuances.*[16]

Wurtzel's ingrained modes of thinking and behaving, the *self-traps* in which she had become ensnared, were far too dense to be touched by Prozac's "cosmetic pharmacology" or any other quick fix.[17] In this, Wurtzel is not alone.

Therapy is not for everyone, of course. But no matter what path people decide to venture down in the quest for higher self-esteem, it is important to bear in mind that negative self-views cannot be changed at the drop of a hat. One reason is that people possess a deep-seated desire for self-confirmation. Thus, when people with negative self-views contemplate positive change, they experience extreme ambivalence; they find themselves caught in a psychological crossfire in which the warmth produced by favorable evaluations is chilled by incredulity, and the feelings of reassurance produced by unfavorable evaluations are tempered by sadness that the "truth" could not be kinder.

One of the primary goals of this book is to illuminate the nature and origin of the negative self-views that result in such extreme ambivalence. I examine, for example, the practices of parents that promote low self-esteem and how children with low self-esteem later go on to re-create the conditions that caused their low self-esteem to begin with. In this sense, this book addresses many of the concerns that inspired the self-esteem movement. In contrast to the self-esteem movement, however, I argue that we can never truly understand either the nature of self-esteem or how it can be increased without first understanding the processes that make self-esteem stubbornly resistant to change.

One reason that self-esteem is so difficult to change is that it arises in no small part from social circumstances. To understand why some people develop and maintain negative self-views requires understanding the values and norms of the larger society as well as the idiosyncratic experiences of the individuals who make up that society. More generally, problems of low self-esteem are not just isolated personal problems that are "all in the head"; they involve phenomena of broad social significance.

There is yet another sense in which problems associated with self-esteem are of wide significance: few people escape them. Although people with low self-esteem suffer the most from negative self-views, virtually everyone has periods in their lives during which their negative beliefs and feelings about themselves cause them great anguish. Because no one's self-views are written in stone, even those who usually enjoy high self-esteem occasionally feel the need to shore up a flagging sense of self-worth. This book, therefore, is not just about how people with enduring negative self-views deal with their isolated personal problems. It is about all of us and our struggle to make a better life for ourselves.

2 GROUCHO'S PARADOX

I just don't want to belong to any club that would have me as a member.

—Groucho Marx, explaining why he was dropping out of the Hollywood chapter of the Friar's Club

Groucho's quip is beguiling because it doesn't quite make sense. It would seem that we humans will do almost anything to win the praise and adoration of others. The idea that we love to be loved is not only a pearl of cultural wisdom, it is a bedrock assumption of virtually every theory of human conduct. And indeed, it is often borne out, for social scientists have shown that people will fight like tigers for the smallest scrap of praise and accept even the most richly undeserved of compliments.[1]

Was Groucho just kidding, then? Perhaps. Here was a man who spent most of his film career chasing women and out-smarting men—and who was not above stretching the truth along the way. Yet we should not dismiss his comment too quickly. His son once confided that underneath his cocky, wildly irreverent exterior, Groucho suffered from an enormous inferiority complex.[2]

Whether or not Groucho really meant what he said, most of us have known people who have said similar things and *did* mean them. In general, such people share two characteristics. First, they suffer from persistent negative self-views (negative thoughts and feelings about themselves). Second, they think and behave in ways that tend to preserve their self-views. It is particularly troubling that such people tend to shy away from those who think well of them in favor of those who belittle or even abuse them.

Katherine: The Repetition of Abuse

A case in point is Katherine, whose story opened Chapter 1. She reinforces her negative self-image by entering relationships with one abusive partner after another. Why would an intelligent woman repeatedly choose partners who mistreat her? One thing is certain: such people are not masochists who derive perverse pleasure from being walked on.[3] On the contrary, Katherine and others with negative self-views suffer enormously at the hands of their abusive and demeaning partners. When asked to explain their choice of partners, they become uneasy and circumspect. If pressed, they sometimes point to a vague feeling of discomfort that they experience around people who like and respect them. "It's as if they don't quite know me," they sometimes complain half-jokingly. Wary of people who view them favorably, they gravitate toward those who do not.

Frank: Fleeing Positive Relationships

Of course, not all people who suffer from low self-esteem end up being victims of abuse. They may, however, fail to cultivate relationships with people who view them favorably. Consider Frank, a 38-year-old musician from Austin, Texas. Although Frank didn't have much faith in psychotherapy, he agreed to visit a practitioner at the insistence of his girlfriend, Deborah. In part, Deborah was concerned about the periodic bouts of depression and lethargy that Frank had experienced for more than a decade. A more immediate concern, however, was her perception that their relationship was in jeopardy. The trouble seemed to have started when they had begun talking about getting married. Not long after these discussions began, she had received a Christmas card from an old flame, and Frank had responded by threatening to end their relationship. When Deborah mentioned the incident to Frank's sister, his sister revealed that he had a long history of getting "cold feet" just as his love relationships began to get serious. Frank insisted that he had bailed out because his girlfriends had been cheating on him, yet he admitted that he had never encountered any evidence to back up his suspicions.

Despite his reluctance to enter therapy, Frank seemed to benefit from it. Just when the therapist believed that dramatic progress was about to be made, however, Frank abruptly announced that he was discontinuing the sessions. The therapist expressed surprise, noting that he thought the therapy had been going quite well. Frank agreed but said that he couldn't bear to continue because he sensed that the therapist regarded him as pathetic and disgusting. The therapist was flabbergasted: he had enormous respect for Frank and had taken pains to communicate these feelings to him. He looked Frank in the eye and told him that he admired and liked him and looked forward to their sessions. To the therapist's astonishment, Frank was visibly shaken by his statement. Frank turned pale and for a moment seemed to lose his balance, spilling his coffee. When Frank had calmed down, the therapist asked, "What's wrong, Frank? Didn't you believe me when I said how I felt?" Frank slowly replied, "The trouble was that I *did* believe you. It just makes me anxious to think about people liking me. It just never feels quite right."

Unlike Katherine, who was still having troubles the last time I heard from her, Frank seemed to recover. He remained in therapy and came to see how his feelings of insecurity were disrupting his close relationships. His discomfort caused him to break off his relationships when things got serious, which in turn fostered feelings of loneliness and depression, which then caused him to seek a new partner, at which point the cycle repeated itself. Once Frank could recognize this vicious circle, he was able to reevaluate his relationship with Deborah, and they got back together.

Katherine and Frank illustrate two distinct ways that negative self-views may express themselves. Whereas Katherine endured one abusive partner after another, Frank avoided relationships in which he was apt to receive praise. By choosing these particular examples, I do not mean to imply that members of either gender are more likely to have one type of experience rather than the other. In fact, researchers' best estimates suggest that men are just as likely as women to wind up in relationships in which they are subjected to verbal, emotional, or physical abuse. Because they are generally smaller physically, however, women are more likely than men to suffer serious injury.[4] Similarly, of the 25 percent of people who possess quite negative self-views, women seem to be just as likely as men to steer clear of potential partners who are favorably disposed toward them.

Sadly, adults have not cornered the market on feelings of worthlessness and the difficulties associated with them; they occur even among small children. To this day, I am haunted by the memory of one such child, a seven-year-old named Tommy.

Tommy: Campaigning for Criticism

As a college student, I spent a summer working as a counselor at a camp for underprivileged children near Philadelphia. Tommy was one of the first children I met that summer. I was immediately taken with his smile; it was so radiant that it seemed to light up the entire dining hall. As we became better acquainted, though, I noticed how rarely he smiled. I wondered why and began to observe him during my free time. What I witnessed struck me as bizarre. Wherever he went, Tommy seemed to be actively seeking the distinction of being the camp's most unpopular child. With the counselors, he constantly denigrated himself; with his peers, he vacillated between being distant and being disruptive.

Most puzzling was Tommy's relationship with another little boy whom the counselors had dubbed "Crazy Louis." Louis was a mean-spirited bully. This fact was not lost on the other children, who quickly learned to steer clear of him. Not Tommy. On the contrary, Tommy routinely sought him out, and Louis obliged by subjecting him to a wide array of verbal and physical abuse. Although Tommy clearly suffered at the hands of Louis, something about the relationship seemed strangely reassuring to him.

Tommy thus seemed to structure his life so that his feelings of worthlessness would remain unchallenged. Why? Such behavior has puzzled clinical psychologists and others for decades. Psychologist Orval Mowrer wrote nearly half a century ago:

> *Common sense holds that a normal, sensible man, or*
> *even a beast to the limits of his intelligence, will weigh*

and balance the consequences of his acts: if the net effect is favorable, the action producing it will be perpetuated; and if the net effect is unfavorable, the action producing it will be inhibited, abandoned. In neurosis, however, one sees actions which have predominately unfavorable consequences; yet they persist over a period of months, years, or a lifetime.[5]

Whether or not one considers Tommy's behavior neurotic, it is clear that it is not unique. Tommy sought out Crazy Louis, Katherine stayed in relationships even when she knew they were abusive, Frank left the women who loved him, and Groucho quit his club.

Some psychologists and psychiatrists have suggested that negative self-views play a key role in such paradoxical behavior. Psychologist Thomas Widiger offers an example of a woman who

felt that she should be paying more for her therapy sessions and offered to either pay more or type the therapist's progress notes to "do her fair share." In fact, she at times would wait outside the clinic, well beyond the beginning of her hour, because she thought that the previous patient needed more time. Now this sacrifice wasn't really simply altruistic. The therapist's failure to go out and find her, or to then give her additional time for the time that she lost, reaffirmed in her mind that he devalued her. . . . The past relationships [of such patients] have so cruelly distorted their self-image and expectations that they are really unable to recognize opportunities that they have in life or to resist further victimizations and failures. They simply accept denigration and abuse as their fate. As one patient put it, "I was born under a bad star."[6]

The tendency for people with negative self-views to accept denigration and abuse as their fate is inconsistent with the assumption that all people possess a basic human preference for favorable evaluations. If a deep-seated need for praise and adulation is a basic feature of our emotional architecture, why is it that people with negative self-views seem to systematically refrain from filling this need? After all, it would seem that having negative self-views should *accentuate* a person's craving for praise in much the same way that being on a diet should accentuate a person's craving for food. Why do people with negative self-views seem to be an exception to this rule?

In the hope of finding an answer to this question, I began a series of experiments and surveys at the University of Texas nearly two decades ago. As the results from our own laboratory and those of other researchers poured in, a finding began to emerge that has been completely overlooked by the self-esteem movement. In study after study, people made it clear that although they do indeed enjoy praise and adoration, they also want *self-verification* in the form of evaluations that confirm and validate their own views of themselves. Because most people have predominantly positive self-views, they experience no conflict between their desire for positive evaluations and their desire for self-verifying ones. Instead, for most people, the two motives work in concert to create a powerful preference for favorable evaluations.[7]

People with negative self-views, however, find themselves caught between their desire for positive evaluations and their desire for evaluations that confirm their firmly held views of themselves. Such people are deeply *ambivalent:* to the extent that they are governed by their desire for positive feedback, they want favorable evaluations; yet to the extent that they are governed by their desire for self-verification, they want unfavorable evaluations. Therefore, it is too simple to say that people with negative self-views want either favorable *or* unfavorable evaluations alone. They want both and are thus caught in a self-trap.

People like Katherine, Frank, and Tommy are not the only ones whose lives are touched by a desire for self-verification. The desire for self-confirmation is quite widespread, and it shapes our lives whether we have high or low self-esteem. In fact, it does not matter whether our self-views are positive or negative, well-founded or erroneous, or based on something that happened during the previous year or on events in the distant past. As soon as people become confident of their self-views, they work to preserve them. The need for self-verification even offers an explanation for the baffling reactions of the intended beneficiaries of "miracle cures," who cannot endure dramatic changes to their identities, despite their high self-esteem.

Miracle Cures

In the 1960s, an Italian surgeon named Benedetto Strampelli developed a procedure for restoring sight to people who had problems with the lenses of their eyes. By carefully grafting an acrylic lens onto the eye, surgeons were able to restore sight to patients who had been blind for decades. Strampelli expected that potential beneficiaries of his new procedure would line up at their doctors' doors and that their newly acquired sightedness would vastly improve the quality of their lives. This did not always happen, however, as illustrated in a case reported by sociologist Robert Scott.

The patient was a middle-aged woman who had been without sight since the age of six. Although blind, she had coped valiantly with her disability, graduating from high school and college with honors and obtaining a postdoctoral degree. When Scott met her, she was living a very active and satisfying life. Not only was she the head of a major rehabilitation clinic in New York, she had a happy marriage and was the devoted mother of two teenage daughters.[8] Then a "miracle" occurred; she underwent surgery that restored her sight. Immediately after the operation, she and her family were euphoric. Convinced that she was on the threshold of a much richer life, she eagerly embraced the world of visual images that had been denied her since childhood.

As the full implications of her newfound sightedness sank in, however, her euphoria gradually gave way to ambivalence and then to depression. Her life began to unravel. Her husband filed for divorce, her employer demanded that she take a leave of absence, and her children and friends became disaffected with her. When Scott last heard from the woman, her life was continuing to deteriorate.

Scott's careful analysis led him to conclude that her efforts to take on the identity of a sighted person (the self-views, roles, and so forth) were stymied by obstacles that no one had anticipated. After her operation, she sensed that people expected her to act differently. Unfortunately, she couldn't figure out precisely what she was supposed to do; she didn't know how to "act sighted." In a very profound sense, she was forced to relearn the world around her, painstakingly translating every detail of the tactile world that she knew so well into the bright and colorful images of a perplexing new visual sphere. In many ways, she felt childlike and naive, thrust into an environment that she only dimly comprehended.[9] The result was the nagging sense that she had lost something that was terribly important to her. She constantly complained that her life now lacked a feeling of coherence and that her old confident sense of self had deserted her. When asked to describe herself, she used such terms as "hollow," "vacuum," and "nothingness."

This woman's experience defies the common assumption that all people want, and will eagerly embrace, certain "objectively" desirable states. Her reactions parallel those of people who enter psychotherapy in the hope of raising their self-esteem. Although such patients clearly want at some level to believe the best about themselves, they often become deeply distressed when they confront information that challenges their negative self-views.

Because the intended beneficiaries of miracle cures typically have high self-esteem before treatment, their postoperative experiences suggest that all of us may have difficulty accommodating radical changes in ourselves, regardless of our level of self-esteem. The experiences of John Howard Griffin lend further support to this conclusion. A Caucasian who was born and raised in Texas some 50 years ago, Griffin became deeply interested in racism and the experiences of African Americans. To gain firsthand knowledge of their experiences, he dyed his skin and traveled through the deep South in the late 1950s. In his book *Black Like Me,* he eloquently described the enormous toll that his newly altered physical appearance took on his self-views:

> *The completeness of this transformation appalled me. . . .*
> *I felt the beginnings of great loneliness, not because I was*
> *a Negro but because the man I had been, the self I knew,*
> *was hidden in the flesh of another. If I returned home to*

*my wife and children they would not know me. They
would open the door and stare blankly at me. My children
would want to know who is the large, bald Negro. If I
walked up to my friends, I knew I would see no flicker
of recognition in their eyes. . . . I had tampered with the
mystery of existence and I had lost the sense of my own
being.[10]*

Two aspects of Griffin's account are noteworthy. First,
he felt that he had lost his sense of self, which grieved
him deeply. Second, the aspect of this loss that concerned him
most was the feeling that he had severed connections with his
wife, his children, and his friends. If they no longer recognized
him, he had, in a sense, ceased to exist. Griffin thus turned
Descartes on his head. Rather than "I think, therefore I am,"
Griffin suggested that "they no longer think I am, therefore I
no longer am."

But what do Griffin's ponderings have to do with Katherine,
Frank, and Tommy? One link is that Griffin was intensely
uncomfortable with the dramatic self-change that he underwent. If all people are upset by abrupt self-change, his reactions
may offer insight into why people strive to preserve negative
self-views that form their sense of identity, even though by
doing so they avoid a shift to more positive self-views. Second,
Griffin's sinking feeling that if his family and friends no longer
recognized him *he* would cease to exist suggests that the evaluations people receive from others play a key role in sustaining
their self-views, regardless of whether those views are positive
or negative. This idea fits well with the analyses of several
prominent turn-of-the-century thinkers as well as with much
subsequent research on self and society.

The Roots of Self-Knowledge

The sociologists Charles Horton Cooley and George Herbert
Mead argued that we don't just "know" who we are; we infer
our self-views from our experiences with others. The road to
self-knowledge is thus a rather circuitous one that we travel
perpetually throughout our lives.[11] One important source of

self-knowledge is the treatment we receive from others. We infer that we *deserve* the treatment we receive, particularly from others who are important to us and whose opinions we trust.[12] In addition, we learn about ourselves by comparing ourselves to other people and by observing our own behavior in various situations.

The idea that the reactions of others provide the basis for our self-views has gradually gained widespread acceptance within the social sciences. Some of the strongest support for this idea comes from evidence that parents shape the self-views of children, as I will discuss in Chapter 4. At first, children know very little about themselves and hence are exceptionally impressionable. They generally believe (at least until they reach adolescence) that their parents and teachers know what they are talking about.[13] But even adults continue to rely on the evaluations of others to nourish their self-views. Studies have shown that over the course of a single semester, college students tend to bring their self-views (of academic and athletic ability, sociability, and so forth) into accord with the impressions that their roommates had of them at the term's outset.[14]

The tendency to infer who we are from our social context is so general that it appears even in other species. In a fascinating study, researchers required a female chimpanzee who had been raised as a member of a human family to sort a series of pictures of humans and animals into two stacks. Without fail, the chimp placed pictures of humans in one stack and pictures of animals (including other chimps) in a second stack. When she came to a picture of herself, however, she placed it in the stack of humans. Apparently, a lifetime of being *treated* like a human caused her to conclude that she belonged in the same category as humans.[15]

Although relatively little is known about the self-views of apes, researchers have learned a great deal about the self-views of humans. Three distinctions that psychologists have made are especially important to understanding self-esteem.

First, the two basic components of self-esteem are a feeling of being lovable (often sustained by relationships with others) and a feeling of being competent (often sustained by performance in educational or work settings). Like height and weight, these central aspects of self-esteem are related but distinct. One implication of the relative independence of these two components is that different people can rely on vastly different strategies to improve their self-esteem. Later, I will discuss how some people strive to bolster their feelings of lovability through romantic love (Chapter 5), others attempt to bolster their feelings of competence through work (Chapter 6), and still others employ both strategies.

Second, low self-esteem is related to, but distinct from, depression. Like people with low self-esteem, people who are depressed tend to rate themselves quite negatively.[16] One important difference, however, is that self-esteem tends to remain stable, whereas depression is more apt to fluctuate. Also, severe depression is characterized by profound lethargy, memory losses, and physical symptoms that people with low self-esteem do not ordinarily manifest. And people can slip into depression for reasons that have nothing to do with their self-esteem (for example, your house could burn down or your computer could crash).

Third, variations in the *certainty* of self-views can be an important determinant of how people behave and how they respond to threats to self-worth. In general, people are reluctant to relinquish firmly held self-views. The would-be miracle cure discussed earlier, for example, went sour because the supposed beneficiary could not bear the stress of changing an identity that she held quite firmly (that is, "blind person"). In contrast, when people are extremely *un*certain of valued self-views, they may worry constantly about losing them. Such uncertainty gets at the heart of the difference between people with truly high self-esteem and those with defensively high self-esteem or narcissism. People with truly high self-esteem believe that they are competent and lovable; narcissists claim to have very positive self-views but are actually uncertain of their self-worth. Consequently, narcissists feel compelled to shore up their positive self-views through unhealthy compensatory activity. Unsure that they can *earn* self-esteem by developing skills or by establishing mutually satisfying relationships, narcissists often compensate for their self-doubts by trying to put other people down.[17]

Identity Negotiation and the Desire for Self-Stability

Once people form self-views, they usually make deliberate efforts to "act the part." Their actions, in turn, will influence how others respond to them, which will then influence their own responses, and so forth. This process of mutual give-and-take is called identity negotiation.

Imagine, for example, that you have just moved into a new neighborhood and are preparing to attend a block party held in your honor. If you care what your new neighbors think of you, you will help them along in their efforts to figure out who you are.[18] Whether you see yourself as an intellectual, an athlete, or a budding politician, you will be careful to wear the "right" clothes, say the "right" things, and even hold yourself and smile in the "right" manner. Your new neighbors will (consciously or unconsciously) enact parallel efforts to bring *you* to see *them* as they see themselves. Although these efforts may never be completely successful, usually you and your neighbors will arrive at satisfactory agreements about the identities that everyone will assume in their respective relationships.

After people establish their mutual identities, the process of identity negotiation slips from center stage so that everyone can turn their attention to the tasks or pastimes that brought them together. Nevertheless, the *fruits* of the identity negotiation process (that is, the implicit agreements about who is who) continue to define the relationships. This becomes apparent when someone fails to honor a previously negotiated identity. Witness, for example, the furor that often results when a spouse unexpectedly chooses to experiment with an open marriage. Similarly, the relationships between parents and their adolescent children are often strained when the children strike out in new directions and refuse to honor identities (for instance, the obedient or respectful child) that they have negotiated in the past. Although some identities can be renegotiated more readily than others, any such negotiation is disruptive to a relationship, even if only temporarily.

The principles of identity negotiation apply to all kinds of relationships, from the relatively trivial, fleeting transaction between a cashier and a customer to the highly consequential, enduring relationship between a wife and her husband of 50 years. In both cases, the process through which people recognize and verify each other's identities serves as the "thread" that weaves the fabric of social interaction.

Yet there is one sense in which the identities being negotiated in casual as compared to intimate relationships are fundamentally different. The identities that a cashier and customer usually negotiate are apt to involve relatively superficial qualities that neither person cares much about. In contrast, the identities that spouses negotiate often involve relatively deep qualities associated with their most important, or core, self-views. Philosopher Martin Buber seems to have had these core self-views in mind when he suggested that the process of self-confirmation represents the essence of being human:

> *The basis of man's life with man is twofold, and it is one—the wish of every man to be confirmed as what he is . . . and the innate capacity of man to confirm his fellow man in this way.*[19]

When Buber spoke of the wish of every person to be confirmed as "what he is," he referred to a desire to validate the relatively stable, core self-views through which people make sense of their world.[20] For Buber, the process of identity negotiation does much more than merely grease the wheels of social interaction; it provides the "glue" that holds together people's perceptions of reality and gives them a vital sense of *psychological coherence.*

Although Sigmund Freud was not concerned explicitly with the search for psychological coherence, he did believe that maladaptive patterns of thinking and behaving tend to take on a life of their own:

> *When we undertake to cure a patient, to free him from the symptoms of his malady, he confronts us with a vigorous, tenacious resistance that lasts during the whole time of the treatment. This is so peculiar a fact that we cannot expect much credence for it. . . . Just consider, this patient suffers from his symptoms and causes those about him to suffer with him . . . and yet he struggles, in the very interests of his malady, against one who would help him. How improbable this assertion must sound!*[21]

Freud assumed that the resistance of his patients resulted from an unresolved emotional conflict from early childhood.[22] I concur with Freud that resistance is often associated with the clash of powerful motives, but I believe that the conflicting motives are the desire for positive evaluations and the desire for self-verification.[23] The fervent desire of people with negative self-views to satisfy both of these motives simultaneously places them in a self-trap marked by ambivalence.

One advantage of my conceptualization is that it sidesteps some recent criticisms of classical psychoanalysis. Psychologist Paul Wachtel, for example, has complained that Freud's preoccupation with patients' distant pasts led him to assume that early experiences are preserved *in spite of* experiences that occur later in life.[24] In contrast, Wachtel emphasizes the ways in which people's beliefs cause them to recreate their pasts in the present, preserving their early experiences *through* their later experiences. Rather than assume that Katherine moved from one bad relationship to the next because she couldn't get over a turbulent relationship with her father, for example, Wachtel might examine the ways in which her tendency to settle for abusive men was perpetuating her negative self-views.

Of the other psychoanalytic theorists whose writings are compatible with the assumption that people have a powerful desire for self-stability, the position of psychiatrist Harry Stack Sullivan is probably closest to my own.[25] Sullivan believed that people seek to stabilize their self-views because such stability makes their social relations manageable and anxiety-free. He also noted that the desire for self-stability is so powerful that people may even pass up positive experiences that pose a threat to their self-views.

Although Sullivan, a psychiatrist, seems not to have realized it, a little-known American psychologist named Prescott Lecky reached many of the same conclusions nearly two decades earlier (regrettably, psychiatrists and academic psychologists typically don't read one another's work). Noting that people strive for order and symmetry in their perceptions of the physical world, Lecky extended this idea to perceptions of the social world. He proposed that a person is motivated to live "in a stable and intelligible environment in which he knows what to do and how to do it. In a world which is incomprehensible, no one can feel secure." Lecky's position was even more radical than that of Sullivan and other psychoanalysts, for he challenged the prevailing view that the desire for love and pleasure is the most basic of all motives. Lecky suggested instead that the desire for self-confirmation is the fundamental human motive.[26]

Lecky reasoned that because all self-views foster a sense of psychological coherence and unity, people would work to stabilize even their *negative* self-views.[27] Nearly two decades later, two creative social psychologists—Elliot Aronson and Merrill Carlsmith—tested a variant of Lecky's hypothesis. They began by attempting to lower the self-views of a group of students by giving them unfavorable feedback. Then they observed the students' subsequent behavior. The results offered tantalizing support for Lecky's hypothesis: students who had presumably come to think badly of themselves later sabotaged their own performance.[28]

Unfortunately, most subsequent researchers were unable to repeat Aronson and Carlsmith's provocative findings, apparently because of subtleties of their experimental design. This in itself would have been bad news for Lecky's idea that people with negative self-views work to preserve those views. The fact that Lecky's hypothesis contradicted the widely accepted belief in the predominance of the desire for positive evaluations made matters worse. After a decade of failures to uncover consistent support for Lecky's hypothesis, many researchers consigned it to that scientific Valhalla reserved for phlogiston, ether, and the four humors.[29]

In hindsight, the abandonment of Lecky's hypothesis seems to have been premature, because many psychologists now recognize that the design of the Aronson and Carlsmith study provided a weak test of Lecky's idea.[30] Nevertheless, the study left a legacy that was still alive when I began to wonder if people with negative self-views might work to confirm such self-views. I had no inkling how intensely skeptical other psychologists were of this idea until I casually told one of my colleagues about the letter I had received from Katherine. After I described the letter, my colleague asked whether I thought that Katherine was just some sort of weirdo or if her behavior reflected a more general psychological principle. I replied that I believed the phenomenon to be a general one and that anyone who had firmly held negative self-views would behave as Katherine did. An expression of incredulity swept across my colleague's face. In a voice dripping with sarcasm, he asked: "You mean to say that if you were to go down to the shopping mall right now and ask people how they felt about their husband or wife, the ones with negative self-views would be most enamored with spouses who evaluated them unfavorably?" I was about to nod yes, but he was already out the door, chuckling in disbelief. Like most behavioral scientists, my colleague was a firm believer in the idea that, above all else, everyone loves to be loved.

Not long afterward, two of my students (Greg Hixon and Chris De La Ronde) and I decided to take up my colleague's mocking suggestion. We designed a study that resembled his hypothetical one.

The Marital Bliss Study

In the first phase of the study, we took my colleague's challenge quite literally. We marched down to a local shopping mall in Austin, Texas, and recruited a group of married couples. As a check that any findings we obtained were not unique to shoppers, we soon added a sample of couples who were enjoying an afternoon's horseback riding at a ranch in neighboring Bee Caves, Texas.[31]

We approached couples one at a time and asked if they would participate in a study of "the relation between personality and close relationships." If they expressed interest, we had both members of the couple complete a series of questionnaires. First came the SAQ (Self-Attributes Questionnaire), a questionnaire that psychologist Brett Pelham and I had devised several years earlier. It assesses people's self-views on five attributes that most Americans regard as important: intelligence, social skills, physical attractiveness, athletic ability, and artistic ability. Although the SAQ is by no means a perfect or all-inclusive measure of self-views, we have found it to be a useful index of people's sense of competence. It can be found in the appendix.

After completing the SAQ for themselves, each person completed it again, this time rating his or her spouse. Finally, participants filled out a questionnaire measuring their commitment to the relationship (their desire and expectation that the relationship would last, as well as how much they disclosed intimate matters to their partner and spent time with him or her). While each person completed this questionnaire, his or her spouse completed the same one. Thus, we had indices of what everyone thought of themselves, what their spouses thought of them, and how committed they were to the relationship.

We were interested in how people would react to favorable or unfavorable evaluations from their spouses. We expected that people with positive self-views would respond in the intuitively obvious way—that is, they would be more committed to spouses who evaluated them favorably. On the other hand, we anticipated that people with negative self-views would be most committed to spouses who derogated them.

Just such a pattern of results emerged. Participants with positive self-views were more committed to spouses who thought well of them, whereas those with negative self-views were more committed to spouses who thought poorly of them. Those with moderate self-views were equally committed to spouses who rated them favorably or unfavorably. Gender was unimportant: men and women were equally inclined to display more commitment toward spouses whose evaluations confirmed their self-views.

There was an especially interesting twist to these findings. It was not just people with negative self-views who eschewed overly favorable evaluations; even people with positive self-views displayed less commitment to spouses whose evaluations were *extremely* favorable (relative to the evaluations by other spouses in the study).[32] This finding suggested that the effect was not peculiar to people with negative self-views; rather, anyone who sensed that his or her spouse appraised him or her in an unduly favorable manner tended to withdraw from the relationship.

We and other researchers later conducted several related studies. Again and again, a preference for self-verifying partners emerged. Furthermore, this preference was equally strong whether participants were men or women, whether they had positive or negative self-views, whether they resided in any of several U.S. cities, and regardless of the specific procedures and measures used. Similarly, it did not matter whether the research participants were volunteers from the community or university students. Differences in the social class and ethnicity of participants also seemed not to matter.[33]

It appears that Prescott Lecky was right after all. People *do* seem to prefer relationship partners who confirm their self-views, even when it means passing up relationships with people who perceive them favorably. This preference for self-verifying partners could thwart attempts to increase self-esteem. Imagine a wife suffering from low self-esteem who gets a terrible evaluation from her boss. Devastated, she goes home and relates the bad news to her husband. If she is convinced that her husband believes in her abilities, her conversation with him may neutralize the threat to her esteem posed by her boss's cruel comments. In contrast, if she knows that her husband is just as doubtful of her abilities as her boss is, talking to him may do little to repair her feelings about herself.

How Partners Stabilize Our Self-Views

Stephen Predmore and I explored this possibility by recruiting college-age couples who had been dating each other exclusively for an average of 18 months.[34] The crucial point in the procedure came when an experimenter posing as a clinician gave one member of the couple some "test results." Although the experimenter indicated that these test results were based on responses that the recipient of the feedback had made earlier in the session, in reality they had been prepared in advance so that they always challenged the recipient's self-views. For example, if the recipient saw himself as socially competent, the test results indicated that he was uncomfortable around people he didn't know well and sometimes didn't handle social interactions adeptly. In contrast, if the recipient saw himself as socially incompetent, the test results indicated that he was comfortable around people he didn't know well and handled social interactions gracefully.

After delivering the test results, the experimenter withdrew, leaving the couple alone to discuss anything they wanted to for five minutes. (In virtually all cases, they spontaneously discussed the test results.) At the end of this period, the experimenter returned to measure the effect of the bogus test results on the self-views of the recipient of the feedback.

We were interested in whether the mere presence of dating partners would buffer recipients against the challenging feedback. It did, presumably because the dating partners of feedback recipients saw them as they saw themselves. The buffering effect of the dating partners was evident in that recipients who received the feedback in the presence of their partner changed their self-views less than those who received the feedback in the presence of a complete stranger. Exactly what dating partners said to the feedback recipients during the five-minute discussions seemed not to matter; the important thing was that they sat there with them. Also, dating partners were especially effective in buffering their mates against the feedback if their impressions of the recipient closely agreed with the recipient's self-views.

Surprisingly, perhaps, being with a dating partner tended to neutralize the feedback regardless of the positivity of the feedback. Just as being with a partner tended to buffer people who saw themselves as socially competent against unfavorable feedback, so too did being with a partner buffer people who saw themselves as socially incompetent against *favorable* feedback. The latter finding is troubling, because it suggests that the tendency for people with low self-esteem to maintain relationships with intimates who confirm their self-views may block improvements to their own self-esteem. Even if their friends or therapists begin to convince them that they are worthwhile human beings, they may be quickly *unconvinced* if they return home to a self-trap armed with a partner who is contemptuous of them.

Worse yet, people with low self-esteem may be victimized in more direct and obvious ways. In one recent study, we sought to discover the types of men that women with low self-esteem date and marry. We gave a series of questionnaires to a sample of couples who were shopping at a flea market. Most were from the lower or middle class.[35] Women with low self-esteem were apt to be in relationships with men whose responses to a personality test revealed them to be hostile, arrogant, and intolerant. Further, men who possessed these qualities were especially likely to abuse their partners verbally and physically, as reported by the women themselves.

Most outsiders find it difficult to understand why anyone might want to remain in an abusive relationship. Although many factors contribute to such decisions, family therapists and family-systems theorists have offered some particularly useful insights into the dynamics that underlie such relationships. William Fry, for example, notes that husbands and wives who enter therapy have often established implicit contracts about the roles each is to play. Often, the husband is assigned the role of the healthy, competent person and the wife the role of the sick, dependent person. Once these implicit contracts are established, both parties work actively to honor them, even if it requires that the wife bear the responsibility for a debilitating pathology that is as much her husband's as her own:

> *The spouses reveal, upon careful study, a history of symptoms closely resembling, if not identical to, the symptoms of the patient. Usually they are reluctant to reveal this history. For example, a wife was not only unable to go out alone, but even in company she would panic if she entered a brightly lighted and/or crowded place or had to stand in line. Her husband disclaimed any emotional problems of his own at first, but then revealed he experienced occasional episodes of anxiety and so avoided certain situations. The situations he avoided were: Being in crowds, standing in line, and entering brightly lighted public places. However, both marriage partners insisted the wife should be considered the patient because she was more afraid of these situations than he was.*

In another case the wife was labeled the patient because she was afraid of enclosed places and could not ride in elevators. Therefore, the couple could not visit a cocktail lounge on the top of a tall building. It was later revealed, however, that the husband had a fear of high places which he never needed to face because of the marital agreement that they never went to the tops of buildings because of the wife's fear of elevators.[36]

Outsiders often fail to recognize that the seemingly dominant partner in such relationships is often extraordinarily dependent on the "dependent" partner. As a result, the superficially dominant partner may struggle vigorously when the weaker one tries to break away. A case in point is the relationship between Mrs. Field and her daughter June. June was born with a dislocation of her hip that severely curtailed her activities. Paradoxically, her mother recalled June's predicament in a manner that bordered on the jovial:

> *Mother: Oh yes, she was always with me, always. Well, naturally I wouldn't leave her because of her irons in case she fell on anything. She did fall as a matter of fact, she knocked her front teeth out. . . . She had good leather straps on because she's always been a very strong child and I had a dog lead here and a dog lead there, then June could move freely up and down. . . . As I say, she was always a boisterous child, she's always been such a happy little girl, haven't you June?*
>
> *June: Mmm.*
>
> *Mother: Yes you have, dear.*[37]

From Mrs. Field's perspective, all went well until June went to a camp at age 14. This was the first time the pair had been separated since June was hospitalized for surgery as a 2-year-old. In this new environment, June began to realize that she was not the helpless and dependent child that her mother made her out to be. Upon returning home, June began to assert herself tentatively as an autonomous individual. Almost everyone (June's sister, father, and teacher, for example) regarded the change in June as the normal manifestation of someone who had finally come to realize that she was more than her mother's appendage. Mrs. Field, however, decided that June's emerging independence was a sign of mental illness and challenged her at every turn. The situation grew progressively more volatile until June was hospitalized after a severe mental breakdown. When June finally left therapy, she was still locked in a vicious struggle with her mother over her right to autonomy.

The mutual interdependency of the self-views of people involved in such relationships is readily apparent. Similar interdependencies may explain why, in the marital bliss study, people remained in relationships with partners who did not think much of themselves. Consider a marriage in which the husband has positive self-views, the wife has negative self-views, and both partners have self-verifying impressions of the other. The benefits of this arrangement for the husband are quite evident, for the praise that his wife heaps upon him will satisfy his desire for positivity as well as for self-verification. He may also delight in the sense of security fostered by his conviction that his spouse would not leave him no matter what he did.

And the wife? The husband's relatively unfavorable evaluations will offer her self-verification. In addition, she may derive pleasure from being in a relationship with a man she respects and admires. She may reason that although she will never be able to convince herself that she is wonderful, she can at least enjoy the fact that she had the good fortune to land a *husband* who is. In fact, she may even feel privileged to have landed such a "saintly" husband, because her negative self-views convince her that no one else would put up with her.

Whatever the precise logic underlying the behavior of partners in such relationships, the self-views and behaviors of both people are obviously part of a complex system that includes many carefully synchronized components. Although in this book I focus mostly on the self-views of victims, it is because they provide a readily accessible window on this larger system and not because they are more important than the other components in the system. One cannot separate self-views from the interpersonal contexts that sustain them. George Herbert Mead put it well:

> *No hard and fast line can be drawn between our own selves and the selves of others, since our own selves exist and enter as such into our experience only insofar as the selves of others exist and enter as such into our experience also.*[38]

In this respect, the philosophical assumptions underlying this book contrast sharply with the assumptions underlying many contemporary approaches to the self, particularly those that gave rise to the self-help industry. Whereas those approaches often assert that the only way to understand ourselves is to peer inward and discover our true selves, I argue that to truly understand ourselves we must scrutinize the relationships that sustain our conceptions of who we are.

Of the relationships that sustain our self-views, the ones we form with acquaintances, close friends, and lovers are certainly important. Nevertheless, the relationships that we form with society at large are also crucial. Membership in a particular family, community, social class, religious group, and nation not only imposes a characteristic style of life, values, and beliefs, it also makes some pathways to self-esteem seem more or less viable. Through the media and our interactions with others, we absorb cultural beliefs that tell us how members of our society in general and our subgroup in particular are supposed to seek self-worth. In this way, our gender, social class, ethnic background, and other qualities come to constrain our visions of who we are, who we can become, and how we should pursue higher self-esteem. Unfortunately, these constraints can sometimes lead us into self-traps that warp or even sabotage our efforts to attain self-esteem.

All of which is to say that although we are accustomed to thinking of impediments to self-esteem in terms of processes that occur inside people, what happens "outside" in our intimate relationships and in our interactions with the larger society may be every bit as important. Before we can understand such sociological processes, we need first to examine more closely the nature of the self-traps that gave rise to the responses of Groucho, Katherine, and others. The key to understanding their responses lies in the concept of self-verification.

3 THE VERIFIED SELF

In 1845, catastrophe struck Dawson's Landing, Missouri.[1] An epidemic of measles swept through the small town, killing dozens of children and terrifying the rest. Ten-year-old Sam Clemens—later known by his pen name, Mark Twain—was one of the distraught survivors. Awash with anxiety, he decided to take matters into his own hands:

> I made up my mind to end the suspense and settle this matter one way or the other and be done with it. Will Bowen [a playmate] was dangerously ill with the measles and I thought I would go down there and catch them. . . . I slipped through the backyard and up the back way and got into the room and into the bed with Will Bowen without being observed. . . . It was a good case of measles that resulted. It brought me within a shade of death's door.[2]

Twain's self-inflicted bout with measles may seem far afield from the apparently paradoxical tendency for people with negative self-views to embrace partners who think poorly of them and shun those who think well of them. Yet these behaviors are closely related. Both involve enduring a negative outcome to achieve a positive one: Twain infected himself to make an uncertain situation more predictable and controllable; people with negative self-views seek confirming but negative partners for precisely the same reason. Self-verification strivings therefore reflect a broader motive to predict and control the world.

Although most people can readily see the utility of seeking partners who seem predictable and controllable, some find it difficult to believe that this motive is so powerful that it could explain the "irrational" actions of those who, for example, remain in abusive relationships. Such skepticism occurs because people seldom recognize consciously the powerful role that self-views play in making our worlds predictable and controllable. Although we are seldom aware of it, our self-views lend an invaluable sense of coherence and orderliness to our lives, serving as the very foundation of our belief systems. If our self-views should waver, the integrity of the belief systems that rest upon them will be jeopardized. Rather than allow this to happen, we stand by our self-views, even if they happen to be negative.

When I suggest that people enjoy and seek predictable and coherent evaluations, critics often raise an immediate objection: "How can you say that people want predictability when everyone knows that what they really crave is *un*predictability? Novelty is the spice of life, you know." Such arguments must be taken seriously, because novelty is obviously alluring. No matter how much we like something at first—a scrumptious meal, a melodic song, or a beautiful vacation spot—when experienced repeatedly, we sooner or later conclude that enough is enough. So we pursue novelty. And we sometimes turn to novelty not because we are bored but simply because we hunger for a bit of adventure, whether it be taking up a new hobby, meeting different people, or traveling to a foreign land.[3]

How can evidence of the appeal of novelty be reconciled with evidence that people often seek predictable relationship partners? Because no partner is completely predictable, we can be confident of encountering some element of novelty in even the most routine relationship. But our enjoyment of novelty is tempered by our dislike of experiences that pose a threat to our physical or psychological well-being. Our enjoyment in meeting new neighbors would fade quickly if we learned that they had a penchant for pranks involving plastic explosives. Similarly, the exhilaration of taking a new job would vanish if we learned that our coworkers all believed that they had recently been abducted by aliens. Thus, we indulge our desire for novelty only when we can be assured of encountering it in the larger context of predictability.[4]

The Soothing Voice of Thunder

The desire for predictability is so basic to our biological functioning that it appears even in primates. Some of the earliest evidence of this desire was reported during the 1920s by Yale University psychologist Otto Tinklepaugh. He began by putting food under one of two cups as a monkey watched intently from across the room. Then a screen was briefly lowered that blocked the monkey's view of the cups, and after a delay the monkey was allowed to approach the food. The monkey raced across the room and almost invariably picked up the cup with the food and ate it.

After the monkey became accustomed to this procedure, Tinklepaugh changed the script by surreptitiously switching the type of food under the cup during the delay period. For example, if the monkey witnessed a banana being placed under the cup, Tinklepaugh replaced it with an equally desirable food, such as lettuce, while the screen was lowered. When the monkey realized that the food was not what was expected, it was not amused:

> She extends her hand to seize the food. But her hand
> drops to the floor without touching it. She looks at the
> lettuce but (unless very hungry) does not touch it. She
> looks around under the cup and behind the board. She
> stands up and looks under and around her. She picks the
> cup up and examines it thoroughly inside and out. She
> had on occasion turned toward observers present in the
> room and shrieked at them in apparent anger.[5]

People crave predictability at least as much as apes do. In fact, the rudiments of a desire for predictability appear to be wired into our neural circuitry. Analyses of the visual system of young children, for example, indicate that even newborns possess a precursor to a desire for predictability—a pre-disposition to find patterns and regularities.[6] And for good reason. Without such a predisposition, suggests philosopher Karl Popper, children would be incapable of learning:

> One of the most important of [the] expectations [that
> children are born with] is the expectation of finding a
> regularity. It is connected with an inborn propensity
> to look for regularities, or with a need to find
> regularities. . . . This "instinctive" expectation of finding
> regularities . . . is logically a priori to all observational
> experience, for it is prior to any recognition of
> similarities . . . and all observation involves the
> recognition of similarities (or dissimilarities).[7]

As children mature, their desire for regularity and predictability colors their reactions to virtually everything they encounter. It even informs musical preferences. At any particular time in history, a consensus emerges about pleasant and unpleasant interval sizes. The Greeks were partial to octaves, as evidenced by Aristotle's query, "Why is the octave the most beautiful consonance?" Centuries later, musicians began to experiment with shorter intervals. In the fourteenth century, Pope John XXII grew uneasy when he noticed that people had begun singing in thirds and promptly issued a decree against it. It was another half century before the Church finally relented and welcomed thirds into the fold.[8] Even today, people typically express considerable ambivalence when they first encounter unfamiliar tonal combinations or rhythmic variations; only when the new patterns have become predictable do people begin to enjoy them.

So powerful is the desire for predictability that it can even be used to transform an unpleasant experience into a pleasant one. Prescott Lecky, the founder of self-confirmation theory, used this logic to persuade his daughter to enjoy a terrifying thunderstorm:

> *My eldest daughter, aged 3.5, was awakened by a heavy thunder and lightning storm. . . . The whole house shook and everyone retreated into his skin. Upstairs I heard the children shrieking and yelling. I ran up and she was standing up in bed trembling like a leaf. Obviously the storm could not be stopped. So I pulled up the shade, drew a chair to the window, took her on my lap, and said: "Now every time the lightning flashes the sky goes 'Boom!' We'll play a game and see if we can say 'Boom' before the sky does!" We didn't have to wait long before the next flash. "Boom!" I yelled before the thunder came, and I pretended to be quite pleased. We sat there shouting "Boom" and soon she joined in, and inside of fifteen minutes her disturbance was entirely past.[9]*

Lecky's charming story illustrates how predictability can take the sting out of an otherwise frightening ordeal. Such anecdotal cases are never completely persuasive, however, because it is always possible that they say more about the idiosyncratic reactions of particular individuals than about any general psychological principle. For example, Lecky may have been so masterful at calming people that he could have said virtually anything to his daughter.

Fortunately, researchers have addressed such ambiguities by conducting controlled laboratory studies of the desire for predictability. In one of the first such studies, Lawrence Pervin at Princeton University examined how people react to unpredictable and uncontrollable pain.[10] He began by seating each participant (all students) in front of a board of flashing colored lights. He then strapped an electrode to the student's leg, explaining that it was connected to a shock generator that was, in turn, wired to the flashing lights. A clever observer, Pervin continued, could learn to anticipate when a shock would occur by carefully noting the order in which the lights flickered.

In reality, the shocks were delivered at random on 5 of 12 trials; the sequence of flashing was unrelated to the timing of the shocks. Convinced that there was a pattern to be detected, however, the students worked to decipher the code. Typically, after a few trials, they developed hypotheses about when a shock was coming up. The next time they thought a shock was imminent, they tensed their muscles and braced their legs against the table.

Pervin speculated that when students were lucky enough to predict that a shock was coming (lucky because there was no way for them to know), they would be less bothered by it. Sure enough, when students received shocks that they had predicted, they were almost jubilant. This reaction is not as surprising as it might seem. After all, the students' successful prediction meant that they could congratulate themselves on being correct. What's more, they now felt hopeful that they could anticipate future shocks.

Perhaps more surprising was the students' reaction when a predicted shock failed to materialize: they were clearly disgruntled. Two issues seemed to trouble them. First, anticipating the shock had made them tense and its failure to materialize left them that way. Worse yet, when the shock didn't occur, they realized that their scheme for predicting the shocks wasn't working. This was so disappointing that some students insisted that once having prepared themselves for the event, they preferred being shocked to not being shocked.

The most distressing scenario occurred when students received a shock that they had not predicted. Such unanticipated shocks represented a double whammy. Not only were the shocks themselves painful, but they also took the recipients by surprise, reminding them that the exact pattern of the presumed light-shock sequence was still unknown.

This double-whammy was so unpleasant that some students sought to avoid a recurrence by maintaining a constant state of vigilance. One student noted that he would rather brace himself for the shock every time than let it hit him by surprise.[11] The student's reaction illustrates the intricate connection between the external physical world and the internal psychological world. When people sense that events in the external world are occurring unexpectedly and capriciously, they take steps to ensure that the chaos on the outside does not create chaos on the inside; they do something, *anything*, that seems likely to restore their sense of control over the situation.

Pervin's hypervigilant students were not only trying to predict when the shocks were coming but also trying to *take control* of their experience by preparing to take a hit on every trial. Thus, prediction and control are related but distinct; although we may predict that the sun will rise in the east, we have no control over it. There are many examples of how people struggle to maintain perceptions of control. For instance, most people report feeling safer driving a car than riding as a passenger in a jet—even though, in deaths per mile, driving is roughly 10 times more dangerous than flying. Similarly, in a study of conflict resolution, participants in a mock trial were more satisfied with the fairness of the judge's decision when they felt that they had some control over how the issue was resolved, even when the ruling cost them money.[12]

Pain as an Old Friend

Mark Twain was compelled to use an extraordinary strategy for restoring a sense of control over his world because the situation he encountered (a devastating epidemic) was extraordinary. In most everyday situations, we are able to make our world seem at least somewhat predictable and controllable much more safely: we simply form beliefs and work to maintain them. Stable beliefs and the feelings of continuity they engender are as integral to our mental well-being as air is to our physical survival. As we struggle to predict and control our world, this sense of coherence is what the purr of the automobile is to the driver or the roar of the jet engine is to the pilot: a signal that all's as it should be. A sense of continuity tells us that our perceptions of reality are on the mark.

Stable beliefs give rise to a form of competence that is unlike all others. Most competencies are tied to particular tasks or domains, such as thinking quickly, talking clearly, or singing beautifully. The sense of continuity associated with stable beliefs, however, reinforces our conviction that we understand reality—social as well as physical—and can determine our relation to it. Depriving us of this special form of competence fosters a feeling of incoherence and meaninglessness that poses a colossal threat to our sense of self. We will not merely feel incompetent, we will fear that our very existence, our moorings in the world, are in jeopardy. In the most serious cases, we will fear that our sense of self lacks coherence and is fragmenting or disintegrating. Existential philosopher Rollo May explained that because such anxiety

> *attacks the foundation (core, essence) of the personality, the individual cannot "stand outside" the threat, cannot objectify it, and thereby is powerless to take steps to meet it. . . . [Such anxiety] is described on the philosophical level as the realization that one may cease to exist as a self.*[13]

Similarly, the psychoanalyst Heinz Kohut has argued that when people's desire for self-validation (or "mirroring") is frustrated, the self-concept begins to fragment, causing a sinking feeling that something is terribly wrong. Eventually, the person may experience severe disorientation and accompanying feelings of emptiness, incoherence, and worthlessness. He called this phenomenon disintegration anxiety. Like Rollo May, Kohut emphasized that disintegration anxiety is distinct from ordinary anxiety. Whereas ordinary anxiety comes from specific danger situations (such as a threat from a spouse), disintegration anxiety comes from a threat to the coherence and plausibility of one's self-concept. He carefully distinguished this form of anxiety from that produced by loss of love:

What is feared [is] psychological death. . . . It is not
fear of loss of love that is at stake here . . . even hatred—
that is, human hatred which confirms the victims'
humanness—is sustaining.[14]

Disintegration anxiety, then, grows out of the perception that one or more central self-views lack support. Threats to a central self-view do much more than merely challenge that particular view of ourselves; they challenge the effectiveness of the very way we perceive the world. For this reason, those who suffer from disintegration anxiety may fear that they are losing their grip on reality.

Victor Hugo presents a particularly poignant illustration of disintegration anxiety in *Les Miserables*. A central antagonist in the story is Javert, a law-and-order chief detective who devotes his life to fighting crime. His fervor for his job is fueled by a deep conviction that members of the criminal class are inherently base and immoral. This belief is shattered when Jean Valjean, an escaped convict he has hunted for many years, saves his life. Jean Valjean's selfless behavior shakes the very foundations of Javert's belief system, causing him to question not only his values but the very meaning of his life:

All the axioms which had served him as points of support
all his life long, had crumbled away in the presence of
this man. Jean Valjean's generosity towards him, Javert,
crushed him. Other facts which he now recalled, and
which he had formerly treated as lies and folly, now
recurred to him as realities. . . . A convict was his
benefactor. . . . His supreme anguish was the loss of
certainty. He felt that he had been uprooted. . . . A whole
order of unexpected facts had cropped up and subjugated
him. A whole new world was dawning on his soul:
kindness accepted and repaid, devotion, mercy,
indulgence, violence committed by pity on austerity,
respect for persons. . . . He was forced to admit that
goodness did exist. . . . He felt himself emptied, useless,
put out of joint with his past life, turned out,
dissolved. . . . He no longer had any reason for
existing.[15]

People also experience disintegration anxiety when they undergo some fundamental change in themselves. I presented one example in Chapter 2—the blind woman who suddenly regained her sight. But there are many other examples. Consider men whose voices fail to change as they pass through puberty.[16] Although there are obvious social costs associated with the falsetto (that is, unusually high) voices that result, in many cases the men affected become quite attached to them:

> *Often, after hearing my voice, people tacked on behavior traits to me as well. They expected me to act gimpy, since I talked gimpy. I don't know if anyone else can understand how all-encompassing my voice was to me. . . . It was not part of my life, it was my life. Every action I made, every decision, opinion, all of my behavior was what it was because of my voice.[17]*

The treatment for such falsetto voices is both quick and effective. Yet some men forgo it, apparently because they, like the intended beneficiaries of miracle cures, are afraid of forfeiting a central aspect of their identity. The speech pathologist William Ickes described a 35-year-old man who sought treatment after speaking with a falsetto voice for his entire life. After a brief examination, Ickes explained that there was no anatomical reason the man could not speak in a normal (that is, baritone) voice. He instructed the patient to go home and perform a series of very simple exercises (for instance, speaking while clearing his throat). Two weeks later, the patient returned. When Ickes asked if the treatment had worked, the patient nodded nervously. Ickes then asked him to say something in his new voice. The patient answered in a rich, deep, baritone, demonstrating that the treatment had indeed been a complete success. But then the patient surprised Ickes by reverting back to his falsetto voice and announcing that although he was grateful for the doctor's help, he planned to stick with his old voice.

Ickes reminded the man that during his last visit he had revealed that he had dreamed for two decades of speaking with a deep voice. Now that his dream was within reach, how could he give it up? The patient smiled ruefully, and then, reverting to his falsetto voice, squeaked, "It's not me." Apparently, once this man incorporated the falsetto voice into his self-definition, he couldn't let it go.[18]

Although a falsetto voice is hardly advantageous for men in our society, it is not intrinsically undesirable. John Penman has reported a case study suggesting that people can even become attached to a quality that is on its face highly undesirable—pain.[19] Penman, a neurologist at St. Andrew's Hospital in London, was doing a follow-up study of a group of 275 patients who were victims of tic douloureux, an acutely painful disorder affecting the facial nerves. Earlier, while casting about for a way to deaden his patients' severe pain, he had tried injecting the trigeminal sensory root (a facial nerve) with alcohol. He was delighted to discover that the effects of the injections were dramatic, with 90 percent of the patients experiencing complete relief. Of those patients, a significant number enjoyed complete recoveries and were able to return to full and satisfying lives.

Originally, Penman had intended to collect only neurological data during the follow-up, because he assumed that the patients' emotional reactions "could consist only of gladness at the loss of pain."[20] He was astonished to discover, however, that instead of feeling relieved and joyous, nearly a quarter of his patients seemed disoriented and dissatisfied, some even insisting that life was every bit as intolerable as it had been before. Their complaints included such statements as "I am always ready to cry," "I always seem to be tired," "I don't seem to feel like myself," "I suppose the injection took a lot out of me." Some, recognizing the irony of the situation, were apologetic: "I know I oughtn't to feel like this; there's no real reason for it; please don't think I'm ungrateful."[21]

Noting that all the dissatisfied patients had suffered from chronic pain for at least six months, Penman concluded that for these patients the intense pain had rapidly become incorporated into their self-definitions. When it suddenly disappeared, they felt that they had lost an important part of themselves. The result was a sense of incompleteness and incoherence. Reflecting on his findings, he noted that "when a patient loses a pain and cries 'Oh . . . the difference to me!' his cry may be one of grief."[22]

Together, these case studies suggest that once people have incorporated a characteristic into their self-definition, they will have difficulty relinquishing that characteristic, *even if it brings them intense psychological or physical pain.* The key seems to be that firmly held self-views provide people with a sense of personal coherence that they value even more than they value positive changes. Perhaps this is as it should be. After all, our self-views lie at the center of our psychological universe, providing the context for all of our knowledge. Should our self-views flounder, we would no longer have a secure basis for understanding and responding to the world. To doubt firmly held beliefs about the self is thus to question the very roots of our knowledge system and strip us of our basic means of knowing the world. Psychologist Gardner Murphy likened self-views to a map or chart:

> *The self-picture has all the strength of other perceptual stereotypes and in addition serves as the chart by which the individual navigates. If it is lost, he can make only impulsive runs in fair weather: The ship drifts helplessly whenever storms arise.*[23]

Here, then, is why stable self-views are so important—and why people with low self-esteem will remain mired in self-traps rather than give up them up. Without stable self-views, we would still be able to distinguish superficially favorable evaluations from superficially unfavorable ones, but we would have no reliable way to determine if the evaluations we encountered could be taken at face value. Deprived of the chart by which we navigate, we would lack a reliable set of beliefs and assumptions on which to base our actions.

Some of the most compelling testimonies to the importance of stable self-views come from case studies of people who, quite literally, do not know themselves. One particularly poignant case involved a man who drowned his self-views in alcohol.

The Man Who Erased Himself

Imagine waking up one morning with no idea who you are. The first thing you might notice is that nothing has any particular meaning or significance. You would not recognize the decorations on your bedroom wall, your bedclothes, or even the person sleeping beside you. As you lay there trying to make sense of it all, you would realize that you had no idea what to do next. Lacking a sense of self, you would have no plans, no goals, and, worst of all, no basis on which to fashion such plans and goals. You would be lost in an existential no-man's-land, paralyzed by utter confusion.[24]

Tragically, this scenario is not as farfetched as it might seem. Oliver Sacks has related a case study of a man he calls William Thompson. Chronic alcohol abuse led Thompson to develop Korsakov's syndrome, a brain disease marked by profound memory loss. The memory loss was so severe that Thompson had essentially "erased himself." Able to remember only scattered fragments from his past, he constantly confused fantasy and reality. Whenever this self-less man encountered other people, he launched into a whirlwind of activity designed to determine his own identity. Frantically, he would develop hypotheses about who he was and then test these hypotheses with whomever happened to be present ("I am a grocer and you are my customer, right? Well now, what'll it be—Nova or Virginia? But wait; why are you wearing that white coat? You must be Hymie, the Kosher butcher next door. Yes, that's it. But why are there no bloodstains on your coat?"). Sadly, he could never remember the results of the latest test for more than a few seconds. With characteristic eloquence, Sacks concludes that Thompson was

> *continually creating a world and self, to replace what was continually being forgotten and lost . . . such a patient must literally make himself (and his world) up every moment. . . . The world keeps disappearing, losing meaning, vanishing—and he must seek meaning [by] throwing bridges of meaning over abysses of meaninglessness.*[25]

Desperately seeking an elusive self, Thompson was cast adrift in a world devoid of meaning. But he wasn't the only victim of his amorphous sense of self. Because the staff members and other patients couldn't rely on him to be the same person from one minute to the next, it was impossible to have a meaningful relationship with him. Thompson was oblivious to this, of course, and relentlessly pursued his lost sense of self. The other residents found his activities disquieting if not outright terrifying: "He never stops. He's like a man in a race, a man trying to catch something which always eludes him."[26] His lack of a self thus made Thompson as much of a mystery to others as he was to himself.

By showing what happens when someone lacks self-views, William Thompson illustrates the function of stable self-views in fostering continuity and coherence both intrapersonally (in people's thoughts) and interpersonally (in their relationships). This sense of coherence is so important to psychic and social life that people will go to astonishing lengths to retain it. As we have seen, people with negative self-views may avoid relationships in which they are valued and supported and gravitate toward relationships in which they are exploited or abused. Thus, the desire for inner coherence may foster an allegiance to self-views so powerful that it offsets the desire for praise.

The Pursuit of Praise

There can be no doubt that people have a deep-rooted and extremely powerful desire for favorable evaluations. This desire emerges very early in life, as noted by the U.S. president John Adams at the close of the eighteenth century: "A desire to be observed, considered, esteemed, praised, beloved, and admired by his fellows is one of the earliest as well as the keenest dispositions discovered in the heart of man."[27]

By the time people reach adulthood, they have assembled a veritable army of strategies designed to make them feel that they are loved and valued.[28] Because the denial of reality is pivotal to some of these strategies, they are in a sense illicit. Freud called such illicit strategies defense mechanisms because he believed that they defend the psyche against neurotic anxiety. Later writers pointed out that a desire to enhance or maintain feelings of self-worth could also give rise to these strategies.[29] The process of *rationalization,* for example, involves attempts to interpret one's behavior in a flattering light. Similarly, *compensation* can be understood as efforts to offset perceived shortcomings in one domain (for example, intellectual matters) by intensifying efforts to excel in an independent domain (for example, social activities). *Projection* involves attempts to see one's own failings in other people. Presumably, each of these defense mechanisms maximizes the perception that one has many admirable and worthwhile qualities.

Among people with negative self-views, a desire for praise competes with a desire for self-confirmation. Sidney Shrauger at the State University of New York at Buffalo was among the first to discuss the conflicted responses of people with negative self-views to social feedback. Based on an extensive review of the research literature, he concluded that although people with negative self-views regard favorable evaluations of themselves as inaccurate and untrustworthy, they feel best when they receive such favorable evaluations.[30]

Although early studies confirmed Shrauger's conclusions, recent work has qualified them in two important ways. First, if you prevent people with negative self-views from thinking very deeply before they respond, their desire for praise will take over, and they will say that favorable evaluations are highly accurate. Likewise, in these circumstances they will choose to interact with favorable evaluators over unfavorable ones. When, for example, people with negative self-views chose an evaluator quickly or while they simultaneously tried to remember a phone number, they tended to select the favorable evaluator.[31] Perhaps this phenomenon is what inspired the seventeenth-century Jesuit priest Baltasar Gracian to quip, "Truth always lags last, limping along on the arm of Time."[32]

The second important qualifier to Shrauger's conclusions is that people with negative self-views react very differently to small bits of praise than to hefty chunks of it. Although people with negative self-views are delighted after receiving small doses of praise, when it becomes excessive, they grow anxious.[33] Such findings make sense, for although people with negative self views may be accustomed to hearing occasional words of praise, they are *not* accustomed to having people challenge their basic sense of self by going on and on about how wonderful they are.

Even people with positive self-views will shy away from praise when they feel it is wildly excessive. As noted earlier, in the marital bliss study, people with positive self-views committed themselves to spouses who thought well of them but withdrew from spouses who evaluated them extremely favorably.[34] What distinguishes people with negative self-views is that they become circumspect and anxious with evaluations that are only moderately positive. For such persons, self-traps seem to lurk everywhere.

People's uneasiness with excessive praise becomes easier to understand when one considers that it may deprive them of the sense that their world is predictable and controllable. Consistent with the arguments advanced earlier in this chapter, Martin Seligman and his colleagues at the University of Pennsylvania have shown that when people (or even animals) discover that they cannot predict or control what is about to happen to them, they become confused, demoralized, and distressed.[35] Other research has suggested that lack of control may also take a toll on the body, compromising immune system functioning and diminishing people's ability to cope with stressful living conditions.[36]

Jonathon Brown and his colleagues at Southern Methodist University have taken this reasoning one step further by proposing that unexpectedly favorable evaluations might even threaten people's health. They had teenage girls and college men complete questionnaire measures of self-views, health, and recent life events (for example, moving to a new state, getting married, or taking a new job). Among people in the study with high self-esteem, the more positive events they experienced, the better their health. In contrast, for people with low self-esteem, the more positive events they experienced, the *worse* their health.[37]

Yet people with low self-esteem *want* favorable evaluations at some level; they do report feeling happier after receiving small amounts of praise.[38] Such evidence has led some researchers to wonder whether the desire for coherence offers the best explanation of the paradoxical behaviors of people with negative self-views. Consider, for example, the tendency for people with negative self-views to gravitate toward and remain in relationships in which they are exploited or otherwise abused. Although a desire for coherence *may* underlie such behaviors, other interpretations are at least superficially plausible and are worth considering.

Why People Seek Self-Confirmation

The key finding in the marital bliss study described in Chapter 2 was that people with negative self-views were more committed to spouses who evaluated them unfavorably than to spouses who evaluated them favorably. Although this finding certainly fits with the idea that people with negative self-views prefer unfavorable evaluations, a very different interpretation is possible. Perhaps spouses in this study initially developed a certain level of commitment for reasons having nothing to do with a desire for self-verification and only *later* developed positive or negative evaluations of each other. If so, then the results of the study would merely suggest that people who are committed to each other eventually come to evaluate each other in a manner that confirms their self-views.

The best way to test this idea would be to take spouses back in time and see if they would pick a self-verifying mate or a nonverifying one. Although this is obviously impossible, you could *simulate* this test by bringing a fresh group of people into the psychological laboratory and having them select an interaction partner. If you found that people with negative self-views chose partners who thought poorly of them, then you could be more confident that a desire for coherence underlay the responses of participants in the marital bliss study. Brian Giesler, Bob Josephs, and I tested this idea in what I will refer to as the "Mr. Nice versus Mr. Nasty" study.

We invited men and women from the community and from the university to participate in our study (as it turned out, the adults from the community and the college students responded similarly). Some people had positive self-views (that is, they had high self-esteem and were not depressed); others had negative self-views (some merely had low self-esteem; others both had low self-esteem and were diagnosed as suffering from clinical depression).[39] Shortly after participants arrived, we told them that two evaluators had formed an impression of them based on their responses to a personality test that they had completed earlier. We then showed them some comments that the evaluators (who were actually fictitious) had ostensibly written about them. One evaluator (whom I will call Mr. Nice) was favorably impressed with the participant, noting that he or she seemed self-confident, well-adjusted, and happy. The other evaluator (whom I will call Mr. Nasty) was distinctly unimpressed, commenting that the participant was unhappy, unconfident, and uncomfortable and anxious around people.[40]

We expected that those with positive self-views would prefer to interact with Mr. Nice in a further interaction and that those with negative self-views would prefer Mr. Nasty. This is precisely what happened: most participants with positive self-views (75 percent) chose Mr. Nice, and most of those with negative self-views (73 percent) chose Mr. Nasty. Also, just as people with positive self-views indicated that Mr. Nice had the most accurate impression of them, those with negative self-views asserted that Mr. Nasty's impressions of them were most accurate.[41]

The results of this study show that people with negative self-views do indeed choose unfavorable evaluators over favorable ones. On the surface, these findings might seem to clinch the argument that people with negative views of themselves seek self-verification in their relationships. Yet these findings do not settle the argument. Why not? Because it may be a mistake to take the choices of people with negative self-views at face value. Conceivably, what appears to be a quest for coherence may actually reflect a desire for praise and adulation that, ironically, goes awry.[42]

The Ironic Perspective on Self-Verification

The self-verification theory that I have proposed assumes that people with negative self-views are deeply ambivalent about the evaluations they receive. Although they instinctively want favorable evaluations, once they have thought about it, they realize that such evaluations clash with their firmly held beliefs about themselves. They are caught between their desire for positive evaluations and their desire for self-confirmation.

The ironic perspective on self-verification holds that the idea that people are trapped between two competing motives is unnecessarily complicated. Those who adopt the ironic perspective argue that a single motive—the desire for positive evaluations—can explain all the reactions of people with negative self-views. The key assumption of the ironic perspective is that behaviors that seem to reflect a desire for self-confirmation are really efforts to gain praise in a roundabout way.

The ironic perspective is not as farfetched as it might seem. Edward Jones at Princeton University and Steven Berglas at Harvard Medical School have already discussed one such ironic process—"self-handicapping." Self-handicapping involves setting up obstacles to successful performance, such as going on a bender the night before a big exam or an important presentation at the office. Presumably, such behaviors allow people who are unsure of themselves to preserve some semblance of self-esteem no matter what happens. If they fail, they can blame it on the drinking spree; if they succeed, they can gloat that their talent shines through even when they stack the deck against themselves.[43]

Evidence of self-handicapping helps legitimize the notion that people sometimes use circuitous routes in their efforts to feel good about themselves. Such evidence supports the possibility that the behaviors some researchers have attributed to self-verification strivings are really ironic attempts to attain positive evaluations. Thus, the argument goes, people with negative self-views may gravitate toward partners who think poorly of them in the hope of winning favorable evaluations at some point down the road. But can this or related ironic processes truly explain why people choose self-verifying relationship partners?

The Think-Aloud Study and the Marital Bliss Study Revisited

The most direct way to find out what is on someone's mind is to ask him or her. This was the logic that inspired the "think-aloud" study.[44] The procedure paralleled that used in the Mr. Nice versus Mr. Nasty study, except that we asked people to think out loud into a tape recorder as they chose an evaluator to interact with.[45]As in the earlier study, most people with positive self-views (72 percent) chose the favorable evaluator, and most people with negative self-views (78 percent) chose the unfavorable evaluator.[46]

The self-verifiers—both those with negative self-views who chose unfavorable evaluators and those with positive self-views who chose favorable evaluators—preferred partners who made them feel that they knew themselves. Consistent with self-verification theory, the overriding concern seemed to be the fit between the evaluation and what they knew to be true of themselves:

"Yeah, I think that's pretty close to the way I am."

"[The unfavorable evaluator] better reflects my own view of myself, from experience."

"That's just a very good way to talk about me. Well, I mean, after examining all of this I think [the unfavorable evaluator] pretty much has me pegged."

"I think [the unfavorable evaluator] is a better choice because . . . he sums up basically how I feel."

"I don't like the conflicting opinion of what I actually think."

Some self-verifiers also mentioned a concern with the perceptiveness of the evaluator ("I think I'll choose [the unfavorable evaluator] because they were more insightful"). The people who mentioned being concerned with the perceptiveness of the evaluator were not the same ones who were concerned with the coherence of the evaluations they received, however. There is a subtle but important distinction between these two concerns, similar to the difference between a man who buys a car because it is flashy and another who buys it because it makes *him* feel young. People who mentioned perceptiveness focused on qualities of the *evaluator*, such as being "on the ball" or "smart." In contrast, people who emphasized coherence stressed a concern with feeling that they knew themselves. Responses in the marital bliss study lent further support to this distinction between desiring a partner who was perceptive and desiring self-confirmation. In that study, commitment to relationships was independent of estimates of the perceptiveness of spouses but *was* closely related to people's conviction that their spouses' appraisals "made them feel that they really knew themselves" rather than "confused them."

Also consistent with self-verification theory, self-verifiers voiced a concern with getting along with the evaluators during the forthcoming interaction. Participants wanted their interactions to unfold in a predictable, orderly manner:

"[The unfavorable evaluator] seems like a person I could sort of really get along with."

"If I choose [the unfavorable evaluator] it seems to me that he'll be more prepared for my anxiety about being around people I don't know. Seeing as he knows what he's dealing with we might get along better."

"Since [the unfavorable evaluator] seems to know my position and how I feel sometimes, maybe I'll be able to get along with him."

"Seeing as he knows what he's dealing with we might get along better . . . so I think I'll have an easier time getting along with [the unfavorable evaluator]."

These results support the assumptions underlying self-verification theory by showing that people were concerned both with how well the evaluations fit their self-views and with getting along with the evaluator in the forthcoming interaction. Our findings also provided support for an ironic explanation—a desire for a perceptive partner who might be beneficial to them in some way (for example, by increasing the participant's level of self-insight). Nevertheless, evidence that the desire for perceptiveness was independent of self-verification concerns indicates that both sets of concerns contributed to people's choice of evaluators.

There are other ironic reasons that people with negative self-views might choose unfavorable partners, but research does not support them. Here are a few of the most commonly proposed ones.

Self-improvement. People with negative self-views could have chosen interaction partners who thought poorly of them because they believed that such partners would give them critical feedback that would help them improve themselves later. Self-verifiers in the think-aloud study never mentioned such a concern, however. The results of the marital bliss study also argue against this interpretation: when asked if they thought their spouse would provide them with information that would enable them to improve themselves, people with negative self-views were decidedly pessimistic, thus suggesting that it was not the hope of improving themselves that led them to remain in self-verifying relationships.

Perceived similarity. Considerable evidence indicates that people who have similar values and beliefs like one another more than they like those who have dissimilar values and beliefs. For example, people typically prefer associates who share their political beliefs, tastes in music, and the like.[47] If people believe that those who judge them in ways that confirm their self-views also have similar values and beliefs, then they might find self-verifying partners appealing because they suspect that such partners will agree with them on topics and issues related to these attitudes. When we examined the reasons that self-verifiers gave for choosing their partners in the think-aloud study, however, we found that they scarcely mentioned the partners' attitudes. Nor did the marital bliss study provide any evidence that people committed themselves to self-verifying partners in an effort to align themselves with mates who had attitudes similar to their own.

Winning converts. Could it be that people with negative self-views picked unfavorable evaluators because they hoped to persuade exceptionally harsh critics to see what they secretly believed was their true worthiness? Because converting an enemy into a friend is no mean feat, doing so ought to be especially gratifying. A handful of participants in the think-aloud study did indeed allude to a desire to win over a partner ("I kind of think that [the unfavorable evaluator] is . . . the kind of guy or girl I'd like to meet and I would like to show them that I'm really not that uncomfortable [around people]"). Yet it wasn't the people with negative self-views who mentioned this concern—those who mentioned a desire to win a convert had positive self-views. People with negative self-views apparently had little confidence that they could turn an enemy into a friend.

The marital bliss study provided even more compelling evidence against the winning-converts idea. If people with negative self-views wished to convert a spouse who was initially critical, they should be most interested in partners whose evaluations of them seemed likely to grow *more* favorable over the course of the relationship. On the contrary, people with negative self-views displayed a slight tendency to commit themselves more to spouses whose evaluations they expected to become increasingly negative over time.

This evidence that only people with positive self-views were out to win converts points to a mistake that people often make when attempting to understand the responses of those with negative self-views. They ask *themselves* why *they* would behave as people with negative self-views do ("Hmmm . . . Now let's see, why would *I* choose a partner who thinks badly of *me?*"). The problem with this strategy is that most people in our society have predominantly positive self-views.[48] So when people ask *themselves* why they might choose a rejecting partner, they will usually get the answer of someone with positive self-views. As the results of the think-aloud study show, on those relatively rare occasions when people with positive self-views choose rejecting interaction partners, they do so for reasons very different from those of people with negative self-views.

Although the think-aloud study failed to support several key variations of the ironic perspective, there is yet another possibility. Hoping to have it both ways, people with negative self-views may have desired spouses who recognized their shortcomings but accepted them anyway. Such spouses would be highly desirable because they would simultaneously satisfy people's desire for acceptance and for self-verifying evaluations. Although we could not tell if this is what people really wanted, we do know that it was *not* what people in the marital bliss study got. Spouses who rated their partners negatively on the SAQ attributes were less likely to accept them as "good persons." This means that when people with negative self-views embraced spouses who evaluated them negatively in a *specific* sense (that is, on the SAQ attributes), they were also embracing spouses who regarded them unfavorably in a *general* sense.

In short, the think-aloud and marital bliss studies provide little support for various ironic explanations of self-verification strivings. In some respects, the think-aloud study is the more convincing of the two, because it reveals that people with negative self-views actually choose unfavorable evaluators over favorable ones. Yet the think-aloud study does not necessarily indicate that people with negative self-views are truly *drawn* to unfavorable evaluators; instead, their primary concern may have been to *avoid* favorable evaluators and their only way of doing so was by choosing the unfavorable evaluators. Although distinguishing these two explanations may seem like splitting hairs, if people were merely avoiding favorable evaluators, an ironic interpretation of their choices becomes plausible. If people with negative self-views in the Mr. Nice versus Mr. Nasty study chose the unfavorable evaluator over the favorable one because they feared that the favorable evaluator might soon "find them out" and reject them, they might have decided to play it safe by choosing the unfavorable evaluator (who expected so little that not even a total buffoon could be disappointing). If so, then their choice of interaction partners could reflect a desire for positive rather than self-confirming evaluations.

We tested this possibility by allowing people to choose between interacting with an evaluator and being in a different experiment. People with positive self-views chose to interact with the favorable evaluator over participating in another experiment, and they chose being in a different experiment over interacting with an unfavorable evaluator. In contrast, people with negative self-views chose to interact with the unfavorable evaluator over participating in another experiment and chose being in a different experiment over interacting with a favorable evaluator.[49] Thus, people with negative self-views not only jumped at the opportunity to interact with someone who thought poorly of them, they actually preferred being in a different experiment to interacting with someone who thought well of them. People with negative self-views seem to be truly drawn to self-verifying interaction partners rather than to be simply avoiding nonverifying ones.

Do Some People Deserve Low Self-Esteem?

If people with negative self-views are drawn to unfavorable evaluations, perhaps there is something truly adaptive about their decision to remain in the self-traps in which they find themselves. Is it possible that people with negative self-views seek unfavorable evaluations because they actually are deficient in some way? Perhaps they seal their own fate because they know that, "objectively," they deserve no better.

One immediate problem with arguing that people with negative self-views should seek unfavorable feedback because they are somehow unworthy or deficient is the lack of consensus about what makes anyone "unworthy." For example, how could you prove that people with low self-esteem *deserve* to think of themselves as "worthless?"

One possibility is that people with low self-esteem are saddled with flaws involving qualities that are so uniformly valued by our society that they cannot downplay the importance of these qualities. For example, perhaps people with low self-esteem are so dull-witted, uncoordinated, or unattractive that everyone recognizes them as deficient and worthless. Although this could explain why some people have low self-esteem, it is unlikely that it can explain why many or even most of them do. We all know people who are breathtakingly brilliant, fantastically athletic, or stunningly attractive but who nevertheless have deep-seated misgivings about themselves. Furthermore, numerous studies show that qualities such as school achievement, IQ, and various other skills and abilities are at best weakly related to self-esteem.[50] Although perceptions of physical attractiveness do seem to influence self-esteem (especially that of females), this is true only for those who attach high levels of importance to attractiveness and are preoccupied with their appearance. Similarly, some qualities that seem to be universally valued may actually undermine people's sense of self-worth. Research suggests, for example, that high intelligence is associated with a lower incidence of depression among boys but with an *increased* incidence of depression among girls.[51]

The weak link between self-esteem and most "objective" qualities is surely due, at least in part, to the inherent slipperiness of deciding what gives someone the right to high self-esteem. Yet the same problem arises even when it comes to defining such seemingly concrete qualities as social competence or athletic ability. Both of these qualities can be defined in many different ways. For example, you could base opinions of your social skills on your ability to give a speech, to show empathy for a troubled friend, or to convince a potential buyer to purchase an automobile.[52] Similarly, athletic ability could be defined in terms of timing, coordination, strength, endurance, or, in the case of football, the ability to knock large, menacing men to the ground. This lack of a single "correct" definition applies to many qualities on which people base their self-esteem, such as physical attractiveness, generosity, or even intelligence. Intelligence can be seen as a fixed quality that someone either has or lacks, but it can also be viewed as a malleable attribute that can be acquired through effort. Which conceptualization people adopt is important. Psychologist Carol Dweck found that when students of similar abilities encountered setbacks, those who viewed intelligence as a fixed quality tended to become discouraged and to give up. In contrast, those who saw intelligence as dynamic and improvable remained persistent and upbeat in the face of setbacks—a formula for success and feelings of mastery.[53]

Paradoxically, although there is no legitimacy to the argument that people with low self-esteem *deserve* to think of themselves as worthless, they insist that there is. In fact, a hallmark of people who suffer from low self-esteem and depression is their tendency to punish themselves by emphasizing their weaknesses and downplaying their strengths. Precisely the opposite bias is apparent among people with high self-esteem. William James offered this account of how he maintained high self-esteem:

> I am often confronted by the necessity of standing by one
> of my empirical selves and relinquishing the rest. Not that
> I would not, if I could, be both handsome and fat and
> well-dressed, and a great athlete, and make a million
> a year, be a wit, a bon-vivant, and lady-killer, as well
> as a philosopher; a philanthropist, statesman, warrior,
> and African explorer, as well as a "tone-poet" and saint.
> But the thing is simply impossible. . . . So the seeker of
> his truest, strongest, deepest self must review this list
> carefully, and pick out the one on which to stake his
> salvation. . . . I, who for the time have staked my all on
> being a psychologist, am mortified if others know much
> more psychology than I. But I am contented to wallow in
> the grossest ignorance of Greek. My deficiencies there
> give me no sense of personal humiliation at all. Had I
> "pretensions" to be a linguist, it would have been just the
> reverse.[54]

Numerous studies have documented James's assertion that people who choose to "stake their salvation" on their areas of excellence have high self-esteem whereas those who fail to do so have low self-esteem.[55] This and related evidence has led some researchers to contend that self-serving weighting schemes are beneficial. For example, one researcher suggests that "to feel good about ourselves we may have to judge ourselves more kindly than we are judged. Self-enhancing processing and biased self-encoding may be both a requirement for positive affect and the price for achieving it."[56] Others have extended this argument by arguing that positive illusions about the self promote physical and psychological health. In her recent book *Positive Illusions*, UCLA psychologist Shelley Taylor argues that people who look at life through rose-colored glasses and develop overly favorable views of themselves and their futures live longer, healthier, and happier lives.[57] In contrast, she suggests that perfectly accurate self-views are maladaptive. As discussed in Chapter 1, the self-esteem movement has taken such conclusions to heart. The California task force, dozens of self-help books, and many educators have touted the benefits of positive thinking and self-enhancement while decrying the motivation-sapping qualities of realism.

Yet despite the flurry of testimonials for positive illusions, there are good reasons to hesitate before jumping on the bandwagon. Some of the best reasons were presented earlier in this chapter. Although people seem to enjoy small amounts of undue praise, once the magnitude of the praise becomes too great, they become anxious and distraught. Similarly, although people with high self-esteem thrive on positive life events, people with low self-esteem may actually become sick in the wake of too much good news.

Finally, other researchers have recently challenged some key aspects of the empirical edifice on which advocates of positive illusions have based their arguments.[58] One especially important aspect of this edifice is the suggestion that depressed people are miserable because their self-views are relatively accurate: they see accurately just how wretched they truly are (the "depressive realism" hypothesis). Recent work has undermined this hypothesis, however. For example, Cornell researchers David Dunning and Amber Story had mildly depressed and nondepressed undergraduate students make predictions about their outcomes during the forthcoming semester (for example, getting an A in a favorite course, beginning a major relationship, experiencing a terrible hangover). When students' predictions were compared with their actual outcomes, the predictions of students who had been depressed tended to be no more accurate than those of the nondepressed students.[59] Clearly, if the self-views of depressed people are no more accurate than those of nondepressed people, excessive accuracy cannot be the source of their difficulties.

Advocates of positive illusions counter this evidence by pointing out that normal, healthy people do entertain positive illusions about themselves. Yet this does not guarantee that some people are healthy *because* they entertain positive illusions;

thousands of other factors could be responsible for their good health. On the contrary, over the years countless psychotherapists have emphasized that a major goal of therapy is for patients to recognize and accept themselves for who they really are.[60] Furthermore, until quite recently, leading figures in psychology have stressed the benefits of accurate self-insight. Consider the conclusions of Harvard's Gordon Allport:

> *An impartial and objective attitude toward oneself is held to be a primary virtue, basic to the development of all others. There is but a weak case for chronic self-deception with its crippling self-justifications and rationalizations that prevent adaptation and growth. And so it may be said that if any trait of personality is intrinsically desirable, it is the disposition and ability to see oneself in perspective.[61]*

In short, although a spate of reports published during the 1970s and 1980s seemed to indicate that unrealistically positive self-views were beneficial, more recent analyses have returned to the earlier position that emphasized the importance of the accuracy of self-knowledge. In fact, even some of the most vocal advocates of positive illusions have recently softened their position by suggesting that illusions will be beneficial only if they are quite modest.[62] Perhaps so. What is clear, however, is that when positive illusions get out of hand, reality will ensure that the self-esteem gains they engender are fleeting.

The most emotionally dangerous world, then, is the one in which things are not as they appear to be. This places people with negative self-views in a psychological trap marked by a longing for praise and a simultaneous desire to preserve their self-views. Caught in this internal conflict, people with negative self-views cannot rejoice when they receive substantial praise. Instead, they feel compelled to remain mired in self-traps that feed their negative self-views.

The real tragedy here is that there is no good reason for people with low self-esteem to get caught in self-traps. Such people do not seem to be unusually untalented, unattractive, or otherwise flawed; there is no obvious objective reason that they should consign themselves to lives of unhappiness. So we might ask: If people with negative self-views are not inherently defective, where does their low self-esteem come from in the first place? And once people form negative self-views, what causes these views to remain stable and under what conditions do they change?

4 GHOSTS FROM THE NURSERY

Ann experienced chronic rejection and hostility from her mother [who] called her a "nasty bitch." By preschool Ann vacillated between long bouts of explosive anger and periods of desperate isolation. Nonetheless, one female teacher developed a special fondness for this physically attractive and bright child and stayed emotionally available to her, despite her anger. Late in the term Ann reported a dream to this favorite teacher, in which the teacher had, in a fit of rage, thrown her against a wall. The child obviously was shaken by the dream. The teacher, with arm around her, said, "Oh, Ann, I would never do that." Astonishingly, Ann asked her, "Why?" "Because I like you very much, Ann." Ann then responded, "Why do you like me?" making it clear that this was a perplexing state of affairs, requiring explanation, not a matter of course.[1]

When researchers from the University of Minnesota encountered Ann, they quickly recognized that the four-year-old already had serious doubts about her self-worth. There also seemed to be no mistaking the culprit: her mother. Surely, anyone who would call her child a "nasty bitch" in front of a member of the preschool staff was capable of much worse behind closed doors. Tragically, Ann seemed to have taken such treatment to heart; she had decided that she *deserved* the abusive treatment she received.

Although this account of Ann's plight may be intuitively appealing, it is overly simple. Crucial details about the life circumstances of Ann and her mother have been omitted. When added, such details often belie the stereotype of a malevolent mother who chooses to make her child's life miserable. University of Minnesota psychologist Alan Sroufe, a researcher who has carefully scrutinized dozens of such relationships, has concluded:

I personally haven't seen a mother who doesn't care about her baby. I personally haven't seen a mother that I would want to blame for the outcome. The poor single mothers in our study all want the best for their kids. They maybe can't do it. They may be so beaten down by their histories and their circumstances that they're doing a terrible job, but I have never seen one that didn't want to do it right.[2]

One reason the mothers in Sroufe's study had difficulty was that most fathers were absent, thus depriving mothers of critical emotional and financial support. If one is in the business of assigning blame, much of it should be placed on the fathers who abandoned their children. More generally, there is no evidence that there are "evil" mothers who have discordant relationships with every child they raise. As pressures on mothers wax and wane, they may respond very differently to particular children, and some relationships may suffer whereas others do not. The same mother may have an antagonistic relationship with one child but a mutually satisfying relationship with another.[3]

An equally misguided notion is that there are "evil" children who invariably elicit negative reactions from others. To be sure, some children are born with qualities that are likely to try the patience of the most tolerant of caregivers (for example, high activity levels, irritability, or certain mental or physical disabilities).[4] Although such children run a higher than usual risk of developing strained relationships with their caregivers, this outcome is by no means inevitable. The all-important "chemistry" that initially may develop between two people can be altered even when one of them is a "difficult" child.[5]

The bad news is that if nothing is done to rescue difficult relationships, the children involved can suffer from feelings of rejection, low self-esteem, and related psychological difficulties. In short, relationships between caregivers and children may serve as self-traps that sap children's sense of self-worth and undermine their ability to cope.

Although there is general agreement that some styles of child-rearing are more likely to create self-traps than others, there is considerable controversy about how to interpret this fact. One issue is that because women historically have been responsible for the bulk of caregiving, past research on the effects of caregiving strategies has focused on mothers rather than fathers. This bias has had the unfortunate effect of providing ammunition for those who are poised to blame mothers for any problems their children might encounter. This is obviously unfair and misleading; some fathers clearly have a negative impact on their children, if only through their lack of involvement in caregiving. Recent research has shown that fathers do indeed have an important influence on their children, although they seem to have different effects than mothers do in certain areas, such as gender role development.[6]

Controversy also rages over several scientific issues, such as the extent to which patterns of thought and behavior laid down during childhood persist into later life. University of Pennsylvania psychologist Martin Seligman has recently taken the extreme position that the impact of childhood traumas on adult personality is "barely detectable."[7] Considerable evidence challenges such contentions, however. Psychologist Everett Waters and his colleagues, for example, have recently reported that up to 80 percent of people in their study who had difficult relationships with their parents as infants had psychological difficulties two decades later when they were in their twenties.[8]

The actual extent of continuity from childhood to adulthood undoubtedly lies between the trivial amounts perceived by Seligman and the high levels reported by Waters. What, then, are the particular patterns of caregiving and characteristics of early life that affect later psychological adjustment and self-esteem? And if the roots of self-esteem can be traced to infancy, what are the mechanisms that stabilize it over the life span, and what are the conditions under which it will change?

Attachment Theory and Children's Self-Esteem

While examining the life histories of juvenile delinquents in the early 1940s, the English physician John Bowlby noticed that a large number of them had experienced extended separations from their caregivers as infants.[9] This discovery suggested that children's early experiences with caregivers might influence their subsequent development in profound, previously unrecognized ways. In the decades that followed, Bowlby wove together ideas from evolutionary theory, psychoanalysis, and psychology into a formulation he called attachment theory. The theory spawned several decades of research on the effects of various parenting strategies on children's well-being and self-esteem.

Bowlby began with the assumption that as long as child and caregiver remain fairly close emotionally and physically, the child can explore the world and still count on the caregiver to keep him or her out of harm's way. An emotional bond between children and caregivers should thus increase the chance that children will survive to the age of reproduction, at which point they will have their own children and perpetuate the species. Simply put, Bowlby believed that the attachment bond is biologically adaptive.[10]

Although humans may be predisposed to form the attachment bond, the relationships that develop between caregivers and babies are rarely a matter of love at first sight. In fact, it often takes a full three months before caregivers report having strong positive feelings toward their infants.[11] Infants also develop complex feelings about their caregivers, because a strong desire to explore the environment competes with the desire to seek the caregiver's warm embrace. Bowlby believed that the child resolves this conflict by using the caregiver as a "secure base." Just as the members of an army battalion rely on a center of operations while scouting an area, children rely on their caregivers as a base while they explore their surroundings. Should they become frightened, fatigued, or sick, they beat a hasty retreat back to their caregivers.

As children mature, their caregivers continue to occupy a central position in their psychological universes. Most important for our purposes, caregivers have a pervasive impact on children's self-views. Bowlby explained:

An unwanted child is likely not only to feel unwanted by his parents but to believe that he is essentially unwantable, namely unwanted by anyone. Conversely, a much-loved child may grow up to be not only confident

of his parents' affection but confident that everyone else
will find him lovable too. Though logically indefensible,
these crude overgeneralizations are none the less the rule.
Once adopted, moreover, . . . they are apt hence forward
never to be seriously questioned.[12]

Psychologist Mary Ainsworth translated Bowlby's ideas into
a procedure for distinguishing babies who have worked out a
comfortable, secure relationship with their mothers from those
who have not. The essence of the procedure was to observe 18-
month-old children and their mothers in a room with toys scattered around the floor. The sessions began with the mother
sitting down while the child was permitted to play on the floor.
Later, a stranger entered the room, followed shortly thereafter by
the mother's departure and then by the mother's return.

Children seem to respond in one of three ways in this situation, as exemplified by the responses of Kevin, Mike, and
Daniel. Kevin, whose mother was both positive and sensitive to
his needs, played comfortably with the toys as long as his
mother was present. Although he cried when she left, he was
pleased when she returned and quickly calmed down. Kevin
had a *secure* relationship with his mother. Mike, whose mother
was cool and distant, seemed largely indifferent to her throughout the procedure, and although he seemed somewhat upset
when she left, he avoided her when she returned. Mike had
an *avoidant* relationship with his mother. Daniel, whose
mother was positive toward him but inconsistent in her responses, clung to her throughout the session, became almost
hysterical when she left, and was inconsolable upon her return.
Daniel had an *ambivalent* relationship with his mother.
Extensive research using this paradigm indicates that about
65 percent of middle-class American children have secure
attachment relationships, 23 percent have avoidant relationships, and 12 percent have ambivalent relationships.[13]

Which of these three types of attachment relationships
children establish with their mothers is related to their later
self-esteem and a host of other outcomes. Some of the most
compelling research in this area was conducted by Sroufe
and his colleagues. The first phase of their Minnesota
study showed that 18-month-old babies whose mothers were
positive toward them and sensitive to their needs developed
into two- and three-year-olds who were especially enthusiastic,

persistent, confident, and happy. Later, when these securely attached babies reached preschool, they struck their teachers as
having higher self-esteem and as being more curious, more
forceful in pursuing goals, and more self-directed than their
peers. Teachers also rated them as being assertive but not aggressive toward other children, as having lots of friends, and
as showing leadership potential.

The effect of early attachment experience was still apparent
when the children were 10 or 11 years old, although it was
weaker. Counselors at the children's summer camp rated pre-
teens who had enjoyed harmonious relationships with caregivers as infants exceptionally high in independence, social
competence, self-esteem, and self-confidence. These same children set higher goals for themselves and were more purposeful
and persistent in striving to achieve those goals.[14] Jude Cassidy
at Pennsylvania State University has also confirmed that children in relationships characterized by positivity and sensitivity
had higher self-esteem than those in relationships that lacked
these qualities.[15]

Unfortunately, the early experiences of children who had
endured discordant relationships with their caregivers also
carried over into later life. If children sensed that their caregivers were cold and negative, they appeared to write them
off. Children in such avoidant relationships had difficulty
developing close friendships with peers. In addition, their teachers complained that they were troublesome, noncompliant, and
self-deprecating.

Much like the adults with negative self-views described
earlier, children in avoidant relationships often contribute
to the conditions that foster their own unhappiness, which in
turn reinforces their lack of self-esteem. A preschooler named
Jason is a case in point. Sroufe noted that when children
in Jason's day-care center danced to recorded music, they
often found their invitations to dance refused. Typically,
they took such rejection in stride and asked someone else.
Not Jason. He responded by becoming crestfallen and with-
drawing to a corner. Here he sulked in solitude, quietly gathering additional confirmation for his belief that everyone
disliked him.[16]

Jason's relationship history—his primary caregiver was
cold and rejecting toward him—represents only one of the

two major pathways to low self-esteem and the difficulties associated with it. Curiously, a caregiver who is positive but inconsistently so (the ambivalent relationship described above) can be as damaging to a child's self-views as a uniformly rejecting one. The reason is that children want their caregivers to be *sensitive to their needs* as well as positive. Psychologist Diana Baumrind has emphasized that sensitivity involves providing children with structure: respecting children's wishes yet letting them know how they are expected to behave.[17] The desire for sensitivity is closely related to the desire for self-verification— by definition, self-verifying evaluations are sensitive to people's conceptions of who they are. Sensitivity is a somewhat broader construct, however, because it can entail being responsive to qualities other than self-views (such as goals, needs, and emotions).

Children whose caregivers are insensitive to them tend to conclude that the caregivers cannot be relied upon to be there when needed. So convinced, they feel that their world is unpredictable and uncontrollable and that their feelings and actions are inconsequential: no matter what they do, their caregivers seem not to notice. The result may be low self-esteem coupled with ambivalence toward the on-again, off-again caregivers who made them feel this way.

Children have such a strong desire for sensitivity from their parents that they may sometimes deliberately elicit a rebuke in a last-ditch attempt to establish that there is *something* they can do to get their caregiver to notice them.[18] Such instances have led the psychoanalyst Daniel Stern to comment: "Up to a point, it is better to respond badly than to be non-responsive. . . . Contingency [i.e., responsiveness] itself . . . is a potent and all-pervasive element at the very heart of relatedness." So potent, in fact, that the child of an abrasive and punitive mother may sometimes be more self-reliant and capable of mastering basic skills than the child of a non-responsive mother.[19]

Psychoanalyst Heinz Kohut shared Stern's belief in the importance of responsiveness. He remarked: "An ambiance of responsiveness is as essential for psychological health as a plentiful supply of oxygen is essential for physical health."[20] For Kohut, responsiveness required caregivers to identify children's qualities and treat them appropriately. Whether the qualities are negative or positive is unimportant; the important thing is for caregivers to treat children in ways that are sensitive to children's actual characteristics.

Being sensitive does not require responding to every nuance of a child's behavior, however. In fact, careful analyses of interactions between children and their caregivers in the home have revealed that relationships in which caregivers are hypervigilant are not as healthy as those in which caregivers are *moderately* attentive to children.[21] Children respond to the total pattern of caregiving rather than to the specifics of isolated interactions. Letting a child cry too long or being brusque once in a while will not lead to psychopathology; it is only when these behaviors are sustained over an extended period that difficulties arise. This is what D. W. Winnicott had in mind when he coined the term *good-enough mother;* he sought to convey the importance of being warm and sensitive to children *most* of the time.[22]

Ironically, some of the worst lapses in sensitivity occur among caregivers and teachers who are struggling to be sensitive to children's esteem needs. William Damon, critic of the self-esteem movement in schools, laments the practice of telling students that they are the greatest in every way. Unfortunately, he notes, many children are adversely affected by such messages:

> *Some develop an exaggerated, though empty and ultimately fragile, sense of their own powers. Some dissociate their feelings of self-worth from any conduct that they are personally responsible for. . . . Other children develop a skepticism about such statements and become increasingly inured to positive feedback of any kind. In time, this can generalize into a distrust of adult communications and a gnawing sense of self-doubt.[23]*

In a similar way, parents may unwittingly deflate their children's self-esteem by implicitly or explicitly denying their limitations. The uncoordinated boy who incessantly hears his father applaud his athletic ability, for example, may eventually recognize that his father is really praising not him but the boy he *wishes* his son would have become. Therapist Paul Wachtel is careful to distinguish such false praise from genuine expressions of love and support:

> It is one thing for a parent to give a positive
> interpretation to the child's characteristics if they are
> more or less accurately perceived and reflected. Then the
> child learns to regard himself in a positive and optimistic
> fashion and the foundation for feelings of well-being is
> laid. But when the parent's perceptions are actually
> disjunctive with the child's evolving sense of his own
> reality, then what he experiences is that who he thought
> he was is simply not good enough. He senses in a dim
> way that the parents need him to be someone he is not,
> and whatever real attributes he has will be experienced as
> insufficient and unimportant. Rather than building on a
> solid core of his actual experiences and attributes, he
> begins to chase a will-of-the-wisp and to experience
> self-alienation and a sense of falseness or hollowness.[24]

Whatever form insensitivity takes, it prompts children to believe that they cannot rely on their caregivers (or teachers) to offer them understanding and help when needed. At the same time, the favorable evaluations they receive typically cause them to cling to the hope of eventually eliciting approval on a regular basis. This hope may keep them engaged in that relationship—and, perhaps, other similar relationships—over a lifetime.

Not surprisingly, then, children of insensitive caregivers later develop qualities that are just as troubling as those of children in relationships characterized by little positive feedback. For example, when children reared by insensitive caregivers enter school, their teachers complain that they strive to control the teacher's behavior by being noncompliant and unruly.[25] Nevertheless, because such children also display emotional immaturity and vulnerability, their teachers respond to their misbehaviors by coddling rather than scolding them.

Unfortunately, the same feelings of neediness and vulnerability that lead such children to win the sympathy of their teachers may be detrimental to their relationships with peers. Sroufe has found, for example, that children who have little sense of their own worthiness (that is, those who have low self-esteem or who are uncertain of their self-worth) gravitate toward peers who are critical of them. In one such relationship, Judy led the play and Lauren crawled around after her,

following her like a puppy, begging for her attention,
taunting and teasing her, yet doing it in a sweet and
innocent voice. . . . As Lauren moves closer in, Judy
moves away, and in one instance whispers (3 times),
"Go over there and play." Lauren didn't give up but
continued to try to capture Judy's attention.[26]

Grown-up versions of Lauren abound. A case in point is Kristin, who moved from one exploitive relationship to another. After she had described several such relationships to her therapist, he asked why she didn't avoid such men. She found them challenging, she said, just as Lauren seemed to find Judy challenging.[27] And, just as Judy eventually tired of Lauren's clinginess, so too did Kristin's lovers tire of her desperate attempts to hold onto them.

The suggestion that children's relationships with their caregivers carry over to their adult relationships may seem like a huge leap. After all, why should a relationship that children form with a parent influence the relationships that they form as adults?

Seligman's assertion that the early experiences of children have a negligible effect on adult personality is relevant here. His comment was partly a reaction to those who blame their misfortunes on their parents, thereby abdicating responsibility for remedying their own dysfunctional behaviors. Although early experiences may place people on a particular life path, they don't guarantee that they will ultimately arrive at any particular destination. For example, although victims of abuse are six times more likely to abuse their own children than nonvictims, the vast majority of those who are abused—up to 70 percent—do not abuse their children.[28] Because no outcome is inevitable, our pasts do not absolve us of responsibility for our actions. In this respect, there's truth in Seligman's assertion.

Yet as the research described above makes clear, it is simply untrue that early experiences have a negligible impact on later life adaptation and that "kids can recover from anything." Children who have troubled relationships with their caregivers *are* more likely to suffer from low self-esteem and related problems for years afterward, and these later difficulties are not simply due to garbled genes or turbulent temperaments. Although children are resilient, they will recover only when their life situations are conducive to recovery.*

"Development consists in the closing of doors, . . . in the progressive restriction of possible fates," historian of science Joseph Needham has noted.[29] For this reason, it is crucial to identify the processes that underlie this progressive restriction of fates or, more specifically, the factors that determine the persistence and change of self-views. Only then can we see how children's early attachments affect the relationships they form as adults.

Why Established Self-Views Persist

Many processes may insulate people against evaluations that would cause them to change their views of themselves. Often these processes are woven deeply into the fabric of everyday social interaction. Recall Tommy, the little boy I met at the camp for underprivileged children. Tommy had a baffling affinity for "Crazy Louis," the bully who skulked around the camp with a chip on his shoulder. By choosing to interact with Louis, Tommy entered a self-trap in which he was sure to receive a steady supply of self-confirming negative feedback.

As it turned out, Tommy's penchant for seeking out Louis was just one of several manifestations of his negative self-view. Some of Tommy's most important self-verifying behaviors were scarcely noticeable to someone who wasn't looking for them. For one thing, Tommy had a knack for bringing out the worst in Louis. It was not that Tommy routinely approached Louis and asked: "Hey, you wanna slug somebody? How about me?" Tommy often invited mistreatment in far subtler ways, such as his body language. Most of the time, Tommy slunk around with slumped shoulders and downcast eyes, the human equivalent of a badly beaten dog. Through his demeanor, Tommy told bullies like Louis that he expected to be victimized and would refrain from retaliating if attacked.

---

*The "kids can recover from anything" assumption may also diminish concern about the *immediate* effects of a traumatic childhood. The fact that you can escape from a self-trap doesn't mean that you didn't suffer while you were in it. Nor does it change the fact that you missed out on what could have been a happy and gratifying period of your life.

More remarkable, perhaps, was Tommy's capacity to evoke the ire of the more easygoing and amiable children at the camp. Again, it wasn't that Tommy came right out and begged for abuse. Rather, convinced that he was unlikable, he blundered through most of his social interactions in an impatient and awkward manner that turned everyone off.

In short, not only did Tommy seek relationship partners who thought badly of him, he also systematically soured the opinions of new people he met, either by failing to cultivate harmonious relationships with them or by actively offending them. In this way, he unwittingly but continually reconstructed a social reality that was much harsher than it might have been, a reality in which everyone offered him ample support for his negative self-views. Tommy had thus succeeded in creating what sociologists have referred to as an opportunity structure for his self-views.

Self-Verifying Opportunity Structures

Biologists and ecologists have long noticed that every living organism inhabits a "niche" that routinely satisfies its needs.[30] An opportunity structure is the social-psychological equivalent of the ecological niche. Just as an ecological niche enables a species to satisfy its biological needs, a self-verifying "opportunity structure" helps us to satisfy our psychological need for self-confirmation. In this respect, the concept of an opportunity structure resembles what Robert Bellah and his colleagues have called a *lifestyle enclave*. They use this term to refer to the microsocial environments wherein people insulate themselves to a degree from the remainder of society and are likely to receive validation for their values and goals. Lifestyle enclaves vary in complexity, ranging from a marriage partner to a community or cultural group, such as the "youth culture" that emerged during the 1960s.[31]

Earlier, I described research indicating that we are motivated to enter into self-confirming opportunity structures. For example, in the Mr. Nice versus Mr. Nasty study, people with positive self-views preferred interaction partners who thought well of them, and those with negative self-views preferred partners who thought poorly of them. Other research suggests that when we choose an occupation, we strive to find one in which we are likely to receive confirmation for our self-views.[32]

Once we construct such opportunity structures, we work to preserve them by systematically excluding anyone who might challenge the identities that the opportunity structures are designed to nourish. Consider, for example, the employer who strives to preserve his perceptions of his own dominance by hiring nothing but yes-men and yes-women. We may even avoid family members who somehow threaten our perceptions of who we are. For example, a despondent mother once wrote to me lamenting that her daughter had shut the mother out of her life. The problem had emerged when the daughter had begun seeing a young man who had changed her in ways that the mother disapproved of. Now there seemed to be nothing the mother could do to reach her daughter:

> *My beautiful 19-year-old daughter Cynthia has gotten mixed up with the "Wrong kind of guy." She was not raised with the morals she has developed since living with this guy. Everybody that loves her has tried to talk to her and tell her there is more to life than the way she is living. She is now drawing food stamps and living way beneath her dreams. . . . Her older brother has tried to talk to her and failed each time. He has even offered to go to live with them and get her a job away from Jeff but she has refused. Jeff beats her and tells her she is worth nothing and can do no better. She believes him. She has given up everything for this guy. Her family, friends, job and her home. She has left Jeff 3 times over his beatings, but always goes back when he begged and promised not to let it happen again.*
>
> *We have always been close and done everything together and always been open about everything, until Jeff. I have never approved of him but I accepted him for her sake, until the beatings started, then I read him the riot act. And butted in! This went over like a lead balloon, and now the two of them won't speak to me or any of the other family members. I'm at my wits end.*

One day, Jeff finally went too far with the beatings, and Cynthia left him. Soon thereafter, she renewed her ties with her family. After months of trying to penetrate the opportunity structure that Cynthia had created around herself, her mother was relieved to have her daughter back again. At last report,

Cynthia had found a new, compassionate partner who had proposed marriage.

This example illustrates how opportunity structures can insulate people against information that they wish to avoid. Every time family members sought to dislodge Cynthia from her life-threatening situation, she responded by retreating further into her opportunity structure.

Of course, we cannot always exclude people from our opportunity structures. Nevertheless, when we do encounter "intruders" who attempt to discredit our self-views, we may eradicate the threat they pose by actively bringing them to see us as we see ourselves. One way we may do this is by displaying "identity cues"—overt signs and symbols of who we are. By assuming the posture of a beaten dog, for example, Tommy silently told others that he probably would not retaliate if mistreated.[33] Similarly, the clothes we wear may suggest that we are liberal or conservative, wealthy or destitute, easygoing or meticulous, prudish or promiscuous. And through the skillful use of cosmetics and wigs, we can project dramatically different identities to onlookers before we even open our mouths. Consider the wide array of contrivances some of the wealthy use to convince others that they are youthful: liposuction for the belly, implants for the breasts, and a plethora of potions for restoring hair to balding pates. Even those who are squeamish about surgery or weary of wigs are not lost, for they can obtain fast cars, lavish homes, and impressive titles to convey a certain impression to others.[34] Like footprints on a dusty road, these identity cues may beckon our interaction partners down the well-trodden paths that lead to our own self-verification.

When we actually begin to interact with others, we may behave in ways that elicit self-confirming responses. For example, University of Michigan psychologist James Coyne and his colleagues have shown that depressed people possess a set of well-honed strategies for bringing their interaction partners to see them as they see themselves—negatively. In fact, Coyne's team discovered that a brief phone conversation was all it took for depressed college students to bring unsuspecting strangers to dislike them. One way that depressed people turn off others is by inviting criticism (for example, "I know you will think I am dumb for saying this, but . . .") and by constantly asking for reassurance (for example, "I guess I am just hopeless, you think?"). In addition, depressed people may fail to nurture their relationships by smiling, making eye contact, and acting upbeat and friendly. Such failures to behave in socially appropriate ways may alienate partners as much as actively inviting criticism does.[35]

We seem particularly likely to elicit self-verifying reactions from others when we encounter a threat to an important self-view. For example, imagine a physicist who learns that a colleague has dismissed him as a lightweight, a macho man who overhears someone refer to him as "that Milquetoast," or a Don Juan who overhears a former lover recommend his lovemaking as a cure for insomnia. Recipients of such challenges may take immediate steps to neutralize the challenge to their self-views by bringing others to see them as they see themselves.

Craig Hill and I captured such compensatory activities in a laboratory experiment in which college women played a game (Mastermind) with the experimenter's accomplice. There was a break in the game, and the experimenter asked the student and the accomplice to decide who should be the leader for the rest of the game. This was a cue for the accomplice to challenge the student's conceptions of her dominance. If the student conceived of herself as dominant, the accomplice challenged this conception by commenting, "Well, you really don't seem to be the dominant type. Like a little bit ago you seemed a little hesitant making decisions during the practice session. You're probably happiest when someone else takes charge, don't you think?" If the student conceived of herself as submissive, the accomplice suggested that she was dominant (for example, "Well, you really seem like a forceful person").

When the accomplice contradicted their self-views, students vehemently resisted the evaluation. Thus, those who perceived themselves as dominant became all the more dominant ("What? How can you say that? Whatever gave you the idea that I am some kind of pushover?"). In contrast, those who felt that they had been erroneously labeled dominant became all the more submissive.[36]

Such active attempts to ward off challenges to self-views also stabilized the student's self-views, presumably because being able to resist challenges to their self-views reassured them that their self-views were correct. As a result, when compared with a group of students who were *not* permitted to resist challenges to their self-views, those who did have such an opportunity displayed very little change in their self-views.

Actively fending off attacks to self-views has another advantage: it diminishes the likelihood that the challenger will repeat the attack. People can be confident that as long as they remain in the idiosyncratic social environment they have created for themselves, they will receive a steady supply of nourishment for their self-views. So it was with Tommy. As long as he remained in his self-confirming opportunity structure, chances were good that the children he encountered would already have been "trained" to treat him in a manner that confirmed his negative self-views.[37]

Seeing Self-Confirmation Where It Is Not

No matter what the self-view happens to be, however, the opportunity structures people create to support them are rarely if ever completely self-confirming. The relationship between Tommy and Jim (the sports counselor at the camp) is a case in point. Jim recognized Tommy's gifts of timing and coordination and often devoted his free time to giving Tommy tips on the basketball court. Ignoring Tommy's interpersonal quirks, Jim used these occasions to give the boy some well-deserved praise and encouragement. Yet Jim's support did little to change Tommy's self-views because it couldn't penetrate the psychological wall that Tommy had constructed around himself. Tommy perceived the comments he received as self-verifying even when they were not.

Several distinct processes make up the psychological walls that people like Tommy build around themselves. One such mechanism is selective attention. In one study, Stephen Read and I told participants that they would be looking over some evaluations that another student had made of them. After telling them that the other student probably liked them or probably disliked them, we timed how long people who saw themselves as likable or unlikable spent examining the other student's remarks. Students who thought of themselves as likable spent longer looking at the remarks of evaluators who ostensibly liked them, and those who thought of themselves as unlikable spent longer looking at the remarks of evaluators who ostensibly disliked them.[38]

People also tend to remember best those judgments that support their self-views. In one study, researchers had people listen to comments that someone else purportedly made about them. Although some comments were relatively favorable and others were relatively unfavorable, all were so vague that they could apply to almost anyone. When the participants were later asked to remember as many comments as they could, they tended to remember the statements that confirmed their self-views.[39]

When people encounter self-discrepant evaluations that are impossible to overlook or forget, they may twist such evaluations so that they fit with their self-views. For example, people assert that comments confirming their self-views reveal a great deal about their true personalities, whereas they chalk up judgments that challenge their self-views to idiosyncratic features of the evaluator.[40] Similarly, just as people with high self-esteem stress the importance of their strengths over their weaknesses, people with low self-esteem tend to emphasize their weaknesses over their strengths.[41]

Children display a similar tendency to interpret information so that it fits their conceptions of themselves. Kenneth Dodge and his colleagues have shown that highly aggressive elementary school boys (as identified by clinicians) perceive hostility in others' actions that outside observers view as neutral. What's more, these aggressive boys react to such imagined slights by becoming hostile. When their playmates finally retaliate, they respond with a grim satisfaction, as in the case of one aggressive boy who answered a provocation by exclaiming: "You're a fat domino! Yeah, I knew you'd do that."[42] Together with systematic biases in attention and memory, such selective interpretations may create the illusion of a social environment that offers far more support for people's self-views than the objective evidence warrants.[43]

When we process information in a biased manner, we merely create the *perception* of a self-confirming reality. When we construct opportunity structures, on the other hand, we literally create self-confirming social realities. The available evidence offers no way to determine which of these processes is more responsible for the stability of self-views, although the extent to which each process comes into play almost certainly differs from person to person. What is clear, however, is that these two processes together often make our self-views stubbornly resistant to change.[44]

Scarred for Life?

Consider the vast range of experiences that most of us have from birth until we leave home, take a job, and begin families of our own. Because of the processes outlined above, most of these experiences will support our self-views or, at least, *seem* to support them. Yet no one can expect to avoid completely events that contradict their self-views. One reason for this is that people can never exert complete control over the events in their lives. In addition, at some level people may not *want* confirmation for their self-views. For example, no matter how negative people's self-views, their desire for unfavorable feedback will be balanced by a desire for favorable feedback. For these and related reasons, children who endure unhappy experiences may not be scarred for life.

Consider Ann, the young girl discussed at the beginning of this chapter. The fact that Ann got off on the wrong foot with her mother does not mean that she was necessarily destined for a life of unhappiness and low self-esteem. Relationships between caregivers and infants can improve dramatically if something is done to alter the chemistry of the relationship. A recent study by Dutch psychologist Dymphna van den Boom suggests that improving the chemistry of relationships may be surprisingly easy. Van den Boom based her research on the assumption that mothers of children with "irritable" temperaments (as identified soon after birth) would be likely to form unhealthy relationships with them. She noted, for example, that "irritable" babies smile rarely and cry frequently. When mothers recognize this, they may react in precisely the wrong way. Sometimes they decide that it is best to ignore the child for fear of aggravating an already bad situation. In other instances, they respond by interfering excessively.

Recognizing that both of these reactions might sabotage the mother-infant relationship, van den Boom intervened when the infants were six months old. Over a period of a few weeks, she spent six hours with mothers giving them tips on how to soothe their babies. Her goal was to convince them that they needed to be attentive, yet still give the baby some breathing room. For example, to prevent mothers from overstimulating their children, van den Boom told them that if the baby looked away, they should also look away rather than reposition themselves so that they were once again face-to-face with the baby (a common reaction among mothers eager to engage their babies). When the baby looked back at the mother, interaction could resume. This strategy ensured that mothers continued to interact with their babies, yet it allowed infants who were feeling overwhelmed time to compose themselves.

This very modest intervention was amazingly effective. At nine months of age, the children of mothers who received van den Boom's tips were more sociable, cried less, and explored their surroundings in more sophisticated ways than did children of mothers who received no guidance. Furthermore, mothers who received the tips had developed more positive and responsive relationships with their children than mothers in the no-guidance group.[45]

Clearly, when a caregiver and a child fail to hit it off, there *are* ways to keep the relationship from going off track and to rescue it once it has faltered. And even if children form irreparably discordant relationships with one or more primary caregivers, this by no means seals their fate. One reason is that maturational changes may transform children's identities. For example, children who develop into skilled athletes as adolescents may elicit highly favorable reactions from their peers and from adults, resulting in substantial increases in feelings of self-esteem.[46]

Even if people's identities do not change markedly as they mature, new partners may react more favorably to them than their old ones. Studies of the victims of childhood abuse suggest that relationships with new partners can deliver substantial benefits. Victims of abuse are less likely to abuse their own children if, as children, they develop a good relationship with a supportive adult; if they undergo psychotherapy at any point in their lives; or if, as adults, they establish a nonabusive, emotionally satisfying relationship with a lover. Although early misfortunes may set in motion a chain of events that lead to further misfortune, that chain can be broken.[47]

Apparent recoveries are not always complete, however. University of North Carolina psychologist Leonard Cottrell reported a fascinating case study of a man named Otto. Otto's early childhood went reasonably well. He had a good relationship with his younger sister and a fair one with his mother. But his relationship with his father, a strict disciplinarian, was contentious. When Otto reached adolescence and began to assert himself, his father became progressively more punitive until, by the time Otto was 15 years old, he was beating the boy with broomsticks, choking him, and putting pepper in his eyes. Finally, Otto's parents appealed to the juvenile court for advice about how to deal with their "rebellious" son. The court recommended that Otto move in with his uncle.

Otto adapted well to life with his easygoing uncle. Although he had difficulty finding a steady job at first (whenever a superior reprimanded him, he immediately quit), he eventually took a job with his uncle. He later married, had a son, and seemed to have enjoyed a full recovery from his turbulent adolescence. Yet vestiges of Otto's unhappy relationship with his father remained. For one thing, Otto never learned how to deal effectively with dogmatic authority figures; he merely managed to steer clear of them. In addition, when Otto became a father himself he began to punish his son with an enthusiasm that rivaled his father's punishment of him. At one point, Otto's wife sought professional help because she feared that Otto might seriously injure the boy.

Otto's experiences highlight two important principles about the effects of early experiences on later development. First, although primary caregivers undoubtedly play an important role in children's developmental histories, other people come increasingly to share this role. People establish many relationships during their lives—with fathers and mothers, siblings, playmates, grandparents, teachers, relatives, lovers, and others. Each of these relationships may counterbalance or even override the effects of the other ones.

Second, Otto's case history shows that continuity from childhood to adulthood may be most pronounced when adults are assessed in a context similar to the pertinent earlier relationship. Otto learned early in life that he could establish satisfying relationships with women (his sister and mother) and that he could have such relationships with nonauthoritarian men (his uncle). He also learned that he should expect trouble in unequal power relationships with men. Later in life, these relatively specific self-views were activated when he encountered people who resembled these figures from his past.

One key to understanding the development of self-views, then, is to recognize that life involves a diverse range of experiences and that people's self-views become every bit as differentiated and compartmentalized as the experiences that gave rise to them. Also, it is not simply a matter of children learning about relationships in an abstract sense. Otto did not learn merely that some types of relationships are good (brother-sister) and some bad (father-son), because he observed counterexamples of each type (for instance, his uncle was a warm and supportive father to his male cousins). Rather, Otto came to believe (at least implicitly) that *he* could not maintain a warm and caring father-son relationship but that *he* could maintain harmonious relationships with women.

This suggests a subtle but important shift in our understanding of the legacy of early experiences. Perhaps the most important consequence of early attachment relationships is not that they consign people to a life of high or low self-esteem but that they constrain the ways that people pursue self-esteem later in life. Otto learned that if he was going to feel good about himself, he should steer clear of domineering men and instead seek out women or nonauthoritarian men. Thus, the significance of negative early experiences may be less in permanently depriving people of high self-esteem than in teaching them what they should do if they hope to compensate for threats to their feelings of self-worth.[48]

Compensation: The Search for Pathways to Self-Worth

No matter how harsh our experiences have been or how negative our beliefs about ourselves have grown, we seem to maintain an irrepressible desire for positive evaluations. We may translate this desire for positive evaluations into active efforts to bolster our self-esteem; we may compensate for blows to our sense of self-worth by trying again.

Alfred Adler, a student of Sigmund Freud's, was among the first to discuss compensation processes in his treatment of what he believed to be inborn "inferiority complexes."[49] Although some of Adler's ideas were decidedly odd (he believed that inferiority complexes grow out of defects in bodily organs, especially the bladder and kidneys), he seems to have hit upon a basic truth that theorists have continued to develop and elaborate to this day. Psychologists Tory Higgins and Hazel Markus, for example, have independently championed the notion that we strive to become the people we ideally would like to be or feel we ought to be.[50]

Whether or not Adlei was correct in asserting that compensatory strivings are inborn, there can be no doubt that the rudiments of such strivings emerge very early in life. Psychologist Katherine Nelson described how a two-and-a-half-year-old named Emily compensated in the wake of a perceived slight. As part of her research on the bedtime conversations of young children, Nelson had hidden a tape recorder in Emily's room. One night, her mother cheerfully announced that it was time to sleep by saying, "Goodnight, little dumpling." After she left, Emily (now alone and unaware that the room was bugged) indignantly replied, "Well, I'm not a little dumm. You are little ' dummy. . . . Me not."[51]

Whereas Emily responded to her mother's remark in an eminently healthy manner, the compensatory reactions of children in unhappy relationships may be less healthy. The precise compensation strategy that children adopt seems to be determined at least partially by their experiences in their attachment relationships. A film shot by psychologists Nancy Hazen and Kay Cutler illustrates this point. The film focuses on two boys I described earlier, Mike and Daniel. Mike, who at 18 months was in an avoidant relationship (that is, a relationship in which the caregiver is cold and aloof) with his mother, is three years old in the film. As the film begins, Mike is sitting on the floor with building blocks arrayed in front of him and his mother behind him. When the experimenter encourages him to try the blocks, Mike immediately sets to work, concentrating intently on the task. When it becomes clear that he is making little headway, his mother tries to intervene. Without looking at her or uttering a word, Mike emphatically motions her away. Eventually, he completes the task but displays no emotion or recognition of his mother's perfunctory "Good job." Instead, he joylessly sets about working on the next set of blocks, all the while remaining strangely silent, almost solemn.

Mike's emotional isolation is especially evident when contrasted with the behavior of Daniel, who was in an ambivalent attachment relationship (that is, his mother was inconsistently positive to him) at 18 months. When Daniel begins playing with the blocks, he makes no effort to shut his mother out of his activities. Instead, he carefully monitors every move she makes. Chattering incessantly, he repeatedly attempts to lure her into the building-block task by looking over at her and stopping whenever he becomes the least bit frustrated. She responds to these overtures by nagging him to continue ("Do it for mommy, pleeeease?"), to which he responds by begging, in a whiny voice: "Why don't you do it. I can't. Pleeeease. You do it." If she fails to respond, he sometimes throws a block across the room. Given a choice between working on the blocks and working on his mother, Daniel clearly prefers to work on his mother.[52]

This evidence of a link between attachment relationships at 18 months of age and compensatory strategies a year and a half later argues for a subtle but important reframing of the conventional interpretation of the legacy of such relationships. Perhaps the most important consequence of attachment relationships is not that they shape our self-esteem as we move into adulthood but that they channel the ways we *seek* self-esteem.

Researchers have found, for example, that children in avoidant relationships may give up hope of establishing emotionally satisfying relationships. Rather than abandon their quest for self-worth, however, such children redirect their positivity strivings from personal relationships into nonsocial activities, such as honing a skill or practicing some activity. Thus, they become "thing" persons who systematically seek self-worth through individual achievement and task competence. These children may well develop into adults who display excessive self-reliance and an obsessive but joyless commitment to work.

A very different scenario may unfold for children in ambivalent relationships. If such children conclude that relationships *can* be gratifying but people must be coaxed into responding in the desired manner, they may become "people" persons who organize their lives around courting favor. If extreme enough, such single-minded devotion to relationships could stymie efforts to develop personal competencies.

Whether people learn particular strategies for attaining self-worth from their attachment relationships, from their later experiences, or from some combination of the two, the strategies they develop are generally designed to maximize one of two distinct components of self-esteem. Those who pour themselves into their work focus on beefing up the competence component of their self-esteem, whereas those who strive to win the devotion of others focus on the lovability component. As discussed in Chapter 2, many self-esteem researchers believe that these two components of self-esteem are the fundamental categories that encapsulate all forms of self-worth. And self-esteem researchers are not the first to adopt such a classification—the themes of competence and love are central to most influential theories of psychological well-being.[53] This distinction also appears to have been on Sigmund Freud's mind when a reporter asked him to define psychological health. His answer, "lieben und arbeiten," "love and work," parallels the distinction I am making here. Because this distinction between the lovability and competence components of self-esteem plays an important role in aspects of adult life described in the remainder of the book, I will elaborate on it briefly here.

Competence and Love

Charles Cooley, a sociologist writing at the turn of the century, believed that the rudiments of perceived competence develop very early in life. By *perceived competence* he meant the sense of being efficacious, of being able to set goals and achieve them:

> *The first definite thoughts that a child associates with self-feeling are probably those of his earliest endeavors to control visible objects— his limbs, his playthings, his bottle, and the like. Then he attempts to control the actions of the persons about him, and so his circle of power and self-feeling widens without interruption to the most complex of mature ambitions.[54]*

As children mature, they begin to define their sense of competence in terms of their emerging verbal, physical, and social abilities. On a scale Romin Tafarodi and I developed to measure people's perceived competence, those who are high in perceived competence tend to endorse such items as "I perform very well at a number of things" and "I am a capable person." People who score low in perceived competence endorse such items as "I am not very competent" and "I don't succeed at much."[55]

The other component of self-esteem, *perceived lovability*, consists of the feeling of being intrinsically lovable or likable. Perceived lovability grows out of a conviction that other people admire and accept us and will not unexpectedly abandon us. Whereas primary caregivers presumably play a central role in nourishing people's feelings of perceived lovability in the first months and years of life, close friends and romantic partners tend to take over this role later in life. People who are high in perceived lovability tend to endorse such items as "I like myself" and "I'm secure in my sense of self-worth." Their counterparts who are low in perceived lovability endorse such items as "I do not have enough respect for myself" and "It is often unpleasant for me to think about myself."

People who have chronic deficits in perceived competence or lovability will be especially vulnerable to feelings of depression and anxiety. Consider Mike, who poured himself into the building-block task in an effort to bolster his sense of perceived competence, and Daniel, who worked on his mother to buttress his sense of perceived lovability. Each boy set his focus quite narrowly, striving to improve one component of self-esteem while ignoring the other. This narrow focus is risky for the same reason that putting all your eggs in one basket is risky: should something happen to undercut the one component of self-esteem on which you have based your sense of self-worth, there will be nothing else to keep you from slipping into despair.[56]

In addition, those who invest themselves in a single component of self-esteem to the exclusion of the other may never feel truly satisfied with themselves. People often strive to compensate for deficits in one component of self-worth by attempting to bolster the component that is already strong. This strategy can never succeed completely because the two components of self-worth are substantially independent of each other. Just as the person who pursues competence while ignoring love may learn the dance without being able to feel the music, the person who seeks love while ignoring competence may feel the music without learning the dance. As a result, people may end up in perpetual self-traps in which their compensatory efforts only reinforce their sense of futility.

You might think that the compensatory strategies just discussed would appeal most to people with little sense of self-worth to begin with—that is, to those who have low self-esteem. Paradoxically, however, they may be used most often by people with *high* self-esteem.

Why? Consider first why compensatory strivings might be relatively uncommon among people with negative self-views. People with negative self-views are ambivalent about the favorable evaluations they receive, because of the competing influences of positivity strivings and self-verification strivings. The result is that their efforts to acquire positive evaluations through compensatory activity are often muted. In one study, when researchers challenged the perceived self-worth of participants by evaluating them unfavorably, people with low self-esteem made no efforts to restore their sense of self-worth. People with high self-esteem, however, reacted to the same challenge by taking steps to ensure that they were evaluated more positively the next time around.[57] Relative to people with high self-esteem, then, people with low self-esteem are less likely to seize opportunities to increase their feelings of self-worth.

This leads us to a second question: Why should people who already think well of themselves—those with *high* self-esteem—bother to compensate for challenges to their feelings of self-worth? The explanation lies in the nature of self-knowledge. The self-views that make up self-esteem are rarely all positive or all negative. Although people with high self-esteem think well of themselves *in general,* all acknowledge shortcomings for which they may strive to compensate. In addition, even the most positive of their self-views are not static. Rather, self-views are dynamic structures that must be constantly nourished by a steady supply of confirming experiences.

The need for validation of positive self-views is intensified when we mature and move into new roles and new social contexts, because doing so forces us to reorient ourselves to a new set of cultural expectations and social contingencies. When we move from childhood to adolescence, for example, we must learn how to sustain our self-esteem through a new mixture of social, athletic, and intellectual activities. Later, as we move into adulthood, we may shift to launching a successful career, negotiating a marital relationship, and managing a family as sources of a continued sense of self-worth.

To complicate matters even further, as members of particular groups mature, they may encounter devastating challenges to various facets of their self-esteem. Many of these challenges will focus on specific aspects of the competence component of self-esteem. Women may learn that society assumes they are inept in spheres that traditionally have been dominated by men; men may find that society is incredulous about their ability to express their emotions and be warm and nurturant; and minority group members may discover that society is scornful of their capacity to excel in arenas that historically have been the province of the majority group. Other challenges may be aimed at the perceived lovability of members of certain groups: witness the contempt that is directed at gays, lesbians, and members of some racial groups. Finally, even if we are lucky enough to escape being targeted by esteem-sapping social stereotypes, others may respond to our specific actions by challenging our perceived competence and perceived lovability.

The upshot is that even people with high global self-esteem feel at times that some aspect of their self-worth is under scrutiny if not outright attack. An implicit or explicit recognition of this fact compels them to take steps to shore up their sense of self-worth by seeking favorable evaluations. Maintaining a healthy sense of self-worth is thus a continuous process.

Although the motivation to compensate in the wake of challenges to self-esteem seems to be a fairly common one, the forms that such compensatory activities take are different in members of different societies and even in members of distinct subgroups within the same society. In the United States, gender roles may tell us a great deal about how to make ourselves feel worthwhile. Traditionally, men are encouraged to improve their perceived competence through occupational pursuits, while women have been encouraged to devote themselves to their relationships in an effort to improve their perceived lovability. These gender distinctions still appear to be influential. Recently, psychologist Robert Josephs and his colleagues conducted a study in which they challenged the self-views of women and men who had high self-esteem. Whereas women sought to reaffirm their self-worth by emphasizing their capacity for nurturance and responsiveness to the emotional needs of others, men sought to reaffirm their self-worth by emphasizing their ability to think and work independently.[58] Unfortunately, an exclusive focus on either love or work is problematic because both are essential to psychological health.

An overemphasis on either love or work is not the only self-trap people may fall into, for the specific strategies people employ in pursuing perceived lovability and competence may also be flawed. In pursuit of feelings of lovability, people may strive for relationships similar to those celebrated in the romantic ideal. Unfortunately, as I argue in the next chapter, the romantic ideal is based on a misunderstanding of human relationships and the way in which people derive gratification from those relationships. As a result, those who rely on the romantic ideal in structuring their love relationships may mire themselves in self-traps.

An entirely different but no less perplexing set of difficulties stymies the efforts of those who rely on the American Dream to bolster a sense of competence. Our culture encourages us to view work as a means of achieving markers of success (such as status, material goods, and money) rather than as a source of gratification in its own right. As I argue in Chapter 6, our work may thus foster a sense of alienation and emotional estrangement rather than feelings of competence and self-worth, thereby serving as self-traps that may ensnare us.

5 ROMANTIC SELF-TRAPS

Ulrich's quest had ended when he won her, and in the peculiar psychology of courtly love, most of the magic had vanished with the pain.

—Morton Hunt[1]

The only problem was that, having got this man to fall in love with an unauthentic me, I had to keep on not being myself.

—Gloria Steinem[2]

On the face of it, Gloria Steinem and Ulrich von Liechtenstein have little in common. Steinem is a contemporary feminist writer and lecturer who played a key role in establishing *Ms.* magazine.[3] Ulrich was a thirteenth-century knight who owned three castles and abundant land in Styria (present-day Austria). His experiences would not have prepared him for *Ms.*; from what is known of the man, he would probably have turned down a free subscription.

Yet this unlikely pair do have at least two things in common. Each made important contributions to the revolution in women's rights that began several centuries ago. In addition, both were bruised by a major vehicle of that revolution: the conceptions of courtly love that blossomed during the early medieval period. In fact, by contributing to these conceptions of love, Ulrich helped set the stage for the feelings of self-betrayal, inauthenticity, and self-doubt from which Steinem and thousands of other women and men were to suffer seven centuries later.[4]

The legacy of the ideas of courtly love popularized by Ulrich and his compatriots was the model of a beleaguered lover who makes substantial sacrifices for the beloved. Earlier, I discussed one person whose life embodied this model:

Katherine, who tolerated scorn, derision, and even beatings at the hands of the men she loved. Happily, such cases are extreme. Nevertheless, many of the more commonplace sacrifices people make in the name of love are also demeaning and self-deflating. Researchers Carl Hindy, Conrad Schwarz, and Archie Brodsky describe a man named Charlie, who

> *scrubs his girlfriend's kitchen floor and gets up early to take her children to school, as if to say, "How can you not love me after all I do for you." Forever seeking confirmation of her love, he laments, "I send her flowers, I cook her meals, I wash her car. But the more I do, the farther behind I get. I guess I'm losing her respect." Charlie feels driven to have sex as frequently as possible, not for pleasure but for tangible reassurance that he is in contact with his beloved. Haunted by fears of rejection, he alienates her by searching through her letters and photos, anguished at the thought of what he might find. Not coincidentally, he has chosen a woman who withholds the tokens of affection that he craves. "I want to stop doing this to myself," he muses, "but part of me loves the madness I am living."[5]*

Steinem's decision to adopt a false identity to please her lover, Charlie's scrubbing of his girlfriend's kitchen floor, and Katherine's tolerance of abuse may be more alike than they appear. All three involved significant sacrifices made in the name of the relationship: Steinem forfeited her sense of authenticity; Charlie gave up his dignity; and Katherine endangered her life. All were, in their own ways, caught in a self-trap that forced them to either diminish themselves in some manner or lose the person they loved.

The assumptions that lured Katherine, Charlie, and Steinem into self-traps are inherent in the romantic ideal. This ideal tells us that there is only one perfect marriage partner for us and that we will recognize that person through a mixture of instantaneous rapture, anxiety, and uncertainty. When we encounter this person and experience true love, we must do everything in our power to entice him or her to tie the knot, whether or not the person is well suited to us or the marriage is practical. The conviction that we must follow our hearts in matters of love is so powerful that some people try to cling to the beloved long after it is clear that he or she is not interested.

Consider Kate, a woman in her thirties whose former husband had ended their 10-year marriage more than a year previously. Despite her ex-husband's clear message that he wanted nothing to do with her, Kate frequently drove past his lover's house to see if his car was there. "I idealized this man," she said.

> He helped me grow up; he taught me so much. I
> constantly told him how much I loved him, but still it
> wasn't enough. I don't care what he's done—all the
> affairs he's had. If he called me up tomorrow, I don't
> think I'd even play hard to get. . . . He's the only person
> who understands me totally.[6]

Several years ago, therapist Albert Ellis bemoaned the ruinous effects of the romantic ideal on the lives of his patients.[7] He described a 23-year-old woman who said that she did not want to marry because she felt unworthy of acquiring the ideal man that society had led her to expect. In another instance he cited, a man left his wife of 20 years because she failed to live up to his ideal of romantic love. He also described a man who complained that he couldn't enjoy sex with his wife because they had married originally for practical (nonromantic) reasons. Such cases led Denis de Rougement to conclude:

> The myth [of romantic love] operates whenever passion is
> dreamed of as an ideal instead of being feared like a
> dangerous fever; whenever its irresistible character is
> welcomed, invoked, or imagined as a magnificent and
> desirable disaster instead of simply a disaster.[8]

And:

> Romance is by its very nature incompatible with marriage
> even if the one has led to the other, for it is the very
> essence of romance to thrive on obstacles, delays,
> separations, and dreams, whereas it is the basic function
> of marriage daily to reduce and obliterate these obstacles,
> for marriage succeeds only in constant physical proximity
> to the monotonous present. . . . The logical and normal
> outcome of marriage founded on romance is divorce, for
> marriage kills romance; if romance reappears it will kill
> the marriage by its incompatibility.[9]

Why has romantic love, long revered in our society as a powerful means of achieving a sense of self-worth, become a source of devastation and misery for so many people? The answer lies in understanding the origins of our ideas about romance. These ideas were inspired by the adulterous affairs of members of the nobility during the medieval period—affairs that served a much different function from that of modern-day marital relationships. The disjunction between these two types of relationships is a primary reason that our modern romantic ideal has led so many contemporary Americans into self-traps.

From Courtly Love to the Romantic Ideal

For most of the period from the fall of the Roman Empire in the fifth century to the birth of Ulrich von Liechtenstein in the early thirteenth century, the noblemen of Europe thought of women as part of their estates; they fought over them, they captured them, and they presented them to one another as gifts. Husbands expected wives to be deferent, to provide sexual services, and to run the house like clockwork. If wives failed to perform these duties, their husbands were expected to discipline them. Some restrictions applied. In Wales, for instance, it was illegal for husbands to beat their wives with sticks that exceeded the length of their arms or the thickness of their middle fingers.

Husbands also expected wives to remain faithful, yet to look the other way if the husband should dally. In the eleventh century, King Cnut decreed that an adulterer should pay a modest fine, whereas an adulteress should lose all her possessions plus her nose and ears.[10] The Church not only condemned sexual relations outside of marriage, it also expressed reservations about sex within marriage. Intercourse between spouses, theologians declared, was for procreation rather than enjoyment; one cautioned that "a man should not love his wife with passion, but with judgment. In fact, he who loves his wife too ardently is no more than an adulterer."[11]

To help married people keep their passion in check, clergymen thoughtfully devised an elaborate set of sexual ground rules. There was much discussion about the days on which "the act" could be performed. Many clergymen recommended abstinence during the seasons of fasting and on holidays. Others suggested that sex be avoided on Thursdays to commemorate the arrest of Jesus, on Fridays to honor his death, and on Sundays in remembrance of the Resurrection. Fearful of offending the Blessed Virgin, some theologians tossed in Saturday as a day of abstinence, while still others recommended that Monday also be set aside to commemorate the deceased.

Such denunciations of sexual intimacy left Christian men and women in a quandary. Convinced that their desire for passion was degrading and shameful even in the context of marriage, they were left with no legitimate way to express it. Then courtly love entered the picture.

The Arabs brought the concept of courtly love with them when they conquered Spain in the middle of the eleventh century. The essential idea was that serving a woman was the most ennobling thing a man could do. Although some forms of service were superior to others, the underlying principle was always the same: no pain, no gain. This premise gave rise to several curious beliefs. For instance, because it was the struggles and frustrations that the knight endured in serving his beloved that purified and ennobled him, the more exasperating, pointless, and fruitless the quest, the better. Another belief was that a man who endured a lady's rejection was morally superior to one who did not. The romantic ideal thus elevated feelings of worthlessness and dejection into moral triumphs.

For reasons that are difficult to fathom today, the noblemen in neighboring France were charmed by the concept of courtly love and hastened to spread the word to the rest of Europe.[12] From his autobiography, we learn that Ulrich von Liechtenstein was one of many noblemen who took the idea of courtly love to heart. Inflamed with passion, he dedicated himself to an exhausting 15 years of arduous courtship of a noblewoman who repeatedly rewarded his sacrifices with rebukes. When at last the princess "granted her love" to Ulrich (probably nothing more than a kiss), Ulrich promptly left her and went on to discover another lady, court her, win her, lose interest in her, discover yet another perfect woman, and so on. Ulrich, it appears, was more interested in the process of winning ladies than he was in having relationships with them.[13]

If Ulrich saw love relationships as being fundamentally different from enduring relationships, accounts from this period suggest that he was not alone. Marriages were feudal business transactions that parents arranged to cement political alliances, exchange land, and produce heirs. Love was reserved for the ideal woman, a woman above all the tedious details of maintaining crops, cattle, and castles. Lovers had no expectation of marrying the beloved, and both partners often maintained marriages while conducting affairs on the side (as did Ulrich and the princesses he pursued). Countess Marie of Champagne articulated this division between love and marriage in a judgment issued in 1174:

> *Love cannot extend its rights over two married persons. For indeed, lovers grant one another all things, mutually and freely, without being impelled by any motive of necessity, whereas husband and wife are held by their duty to submit their wills to each other and to refuse each other nothing.*[14]

To its credit, courtly love raised the social status of women among the nobility. Because it was agreed that knights were no fools, the fact that they made sacrifices for women suggested that women must be worth the trouble. Although men still granted women little political power, they increasingly became convinced that they should behave reverently and humbly in the presence of women and perform tasks to please them.[15]

The Dawning of Modern Romantic Love

The conceptions of courtly love that flourished in the twelfth century underwent dramatic changes in the centuries that followed. One of the most significant shifts occurred in the middle of the eighteenth century, when it became fashionable for men to fall in love with marriageable maidens. By the mid-1700s, engaged persons were likely to spend several months exchanging conversation, gifts, and poetry. Influential writers such as Samuel Richardson began to clamor that love was *needed* for marriage. Richardson held that the adulterous liaisons of the aristocracy were immoral and that the loveless relationships of the bourgeoisie were emotionally shallow. These arguments gradually won support in the middle as well as the upper classes. Eventually, European society came to accept the notion that love should form the basis of marriage.[16]

In many respects, linking love, sex, and marriage seemed like an ideal solution to a centuries-old problem. Now all three activities were legitimized and, it appeared, all were the better for it. The institution of marriage seemed to profit the most. Rather than being simply a business transaction arranged by the extended family, marriage came to be seen as a matter of mutual choice and self-expression.

Early residents of the United States were particularly warm to the concept of free-choice marriages. One reason for this was practical. In Europe, arranged marriages allowed families to pass down land holdings from one generation to the next. With America's abundance of unclaimed land, keeping a particular parcel of land in the family was of less concern. In addition, the staunchly individualistic Americans were less beholden to the traditions that they had left behind in Europe. For these and related reasons, free-choice marriages caught on like wildfire in America.[17]

Even though the early Americans championed freely chosen marriages, their version of love differed markedly from the original courtly ideal. In contemplating a potential spouse, they focused on such traits as purity, selflessness, and Christian devotion. They also placed considerable weight on purely pragmatic concerns: women looked for good providers, and men wanted wives who would maintain a suitable household. Although physical beauty was desirable, it was accorded far less significance than it had been given in the courtly ideal.[18]

Even as late as the beginning of the twentieth century, romantic love seemed to play a modest role in the choice of wives and husbands. A survey conducted in 1903 revealed that young women were most interested in their potential husband's strength of character (42 percent). Business ability came in second (25 percent), followed by respect for females (18 percent), and finally by love (17 percent). Men were also pragmatic, with 74 percent of their votes going to "domestic tendency," considerably more than the 45 percent garnered by love.[19]

Although both men and women were highly pragmatic, men voted for love almost three times as often as women. This finding could mean that turn-of-the-century men were more "romantic" than women, but it is more likely that men simply felt freer to act on their feelings of love because they had greater control over their own destinies. In the early 1900s, most women were completely dependent on men financially. Because marrying someone for love presupposes the satisfaction of basic needs such as economic security, women probably felt less free to marry for love.

If financial dependence made American women early in the century reluctant to marry primarily for love, the economic gains of women over the past several decades should have vanquished much of this reluctance. Some evidence suggests that this is indeed the case. Over the past 30 years, researchers have asked college students the following question: "If a boy (girl) had all the other qualities you desire, would you marry this person if you were not in love with him (her)?" In 1967, 65 percent of men and only 24 percent of women responded no to this item. By 1976, these percentages had jumped to 86 percent for men and 80 percent for women. In 1986, both genders had leveled off at 85 percent.[20]

These findings support the idea that the emancipation of modern women from financial dependence has made them feel more free to marry for love. Of course, other factors could help to account for the increased popularity of love, such as more time spent reading romantic novels and watching movies and television shows that feature the romantic ideal. For whatever reasons, the belief that love is a prerequisite for marriage now seems to be nearly universal, at least among the educated youth of our culture.

Researchers have also found evidence that contemporary Americans endorse some of the more extreme aspects of the romantic ideal, such as "love at first sight." James Averill and Phyllis Booth-Royd recruited a group of men and women in Amherst, Massachusetts, ranging in age from 18 to 54 years old. All said that they had been in love at least once. Although there were a few married persons in the sample, most were single college students and professionals.

People began by reading a newspaper article that exemplified the romantic ideal:

On Monday, Cpt. Floyd Johnson, 23, and the then Ellen Skinner, 19, total strangers, boarded a train at San

> *Francisco and sat down across the aisle from each other.
> Johnson didn't cross the aisle until Wednesday, but his
> [future] bride said, "I'd already made up my mind to say
> yes if he asked me to marry him." "We did most of the
> talking with our eyes," Johnson explained. Thursday the
> couple got off the train in Omaha with plans to be
> married. Because they would need to have the consent of
> the bride's parents if they were married in Nebraska, they
> crossed the river to Council Bluffs, Iowa, where they were
> married Friday.*

After people read the paragraph, the researchers reminded them of similar romantic love stories, such as Romeo and Juliet. Then they asked the subjects to indicate how similar their most intense love experiences were to this romantic ideal. Forty percent of the participants reported that they had had similar experiences.[21]

Of course, we will never know if the 40 percent figure accurately reflects the actual number of people who based important life decisions on love at first sight. We do know, however, that participants in psychological research are wary of admitting to anything that might make them appear silly or naive. To the extent that they believe endorsement of the romantic ideal might foster this perception, 40 percent may represent an underestimate of the number who actually experience "love at first sight."

The Romantic Ideal and Low Self-Esteem

If elements of courtly love have seeped into the modern romantic ideal, it is important to consider the likely impact of that ideal on the harmony of relationships and the associated self-esteem of romantic partners. In the classic case of love at first sight, the lover experiences infatuation—a sudden, unexpected, and violent longing for the beloved. Infatuation is an age-old phenomenon that has been observed in countless societies throughout history.[22] In the modern version of the romantic ideal, however, infatuation is often believed to provide the basis for *enduring* relationships.

The value that American society places on enduring relationships, coupled with the belief that being an object of infatuation is the ticket to such relationships, has caused people to do everything possible to lead others to become infatuated with them. The result has been a preoccupation with superficial qualities that are believed to be alluring, such as clothing, material goods, and physical attractiveness. For some people, attaining these superficial qualities becomes an end in itself. Unfortunately, attempting to derive one's self-worth from purely physical qualities tends to undermine self-esteem. For example, Susan Harter at the University of Denver reports that adolescent girls who base their self-esteem on their appearance subsequently suffer losses of self-esteem.[23] An emphasis on infatuation may thus foster superficial values that, in turn, diminish self-esteem.

Another potential problem with the romantic ideal is the emphasis on winning romantic partners as a way to improve self-worth. This leads people to conclude that more desirable partners will foster greater self-improvement than less desirable ones. Viewed as a means to self-betterment, romantic partners became a resource to be protected like wealth or property. The romantic ideal thus justifies efforts to monopolize the attention of lovers, even elevating feelings of exclusivity to much-admired signs of true love. Consider the commentary of one of Jane Austen's characters in *Pride and Prejudice:*

> *Pray, how violent was Mr. Bingley's love?*
> *I never saw a more promising inclination. He was growing quite inattentive to other people, and wholly engrossed by her. Every time they met, it was more decided and remarkable. At his own ball he offended two or three young ladies, by not asking them to dance, and I spoke with him twice myself, without receiving an answer. Could there be finer symptoms? Is not general incivility the very essence of love?*[24]

Even if feelings of exclusivity do not interfere with people's other relationships, viewing lovers as possessions that one must work to retain transforms a sharing relationship into a competence-related skill. When this happens, people can no longer derive feelings of self-worth from being loved and accepted simply for who they are; indeed, the fact that they feel compelled to make frantic efforts to retain their partners suggests that their partners' feelings are conditional. They may thus feel that they are not loved *for their own sake* but only because their actions have elicited the reactions they desire. In the process of winning their partners, they may come to feel controlled and manipulated rather than competent and efficacious. In such instances, romantic relationships may become a source of less rather than more self-esteem.

Unfortunately, people with negative self-views are particularly susceptible to feelings of exclusivity. On scales designed to measure such feelings, people with negative self-views tend to endorse such comments as "I cannot relax if I suspect that my lover is with someone else" and "If my lover ignores me for a while, I sometimes do stupid things to get his/her attention back."[25]

When feelings of exclusivity are combined with the feelings of powerlessness often associated with negative self-views, the result may be catastrophic. Studies of the factors that cause men to abuse their wives are instructive here. John Gottman and his colleagues at the University of Washington discovered that among couples who have a history of domestic violence, men who felt that they had less decision-making power in the relationship than their wives were the most physically abusive. Apparently, the attempts by these men to dominate their wives physically reflected an effort to compensate for their feelings of powerlessness.[26] In these and related instances, feelings of exclusivity may not themselves lower people's self-esteem, but they may cause them to behave in ways that lower the self-respect and self-esteem of their partners.

Love at First Sight, Whirlwind Courtships, and the Authenticity Problem

Another problem with basing lasting commitments on love at first sight is that typically the feelings of intense sexual arousal that fuel the state of infatuation soon fade, depriving people of their primary reason for being in the relationship. Researchers have discovered that, regardless of species (for example, rats, rams, monkeys), the frequency of coitus peaks soon after the beginning of sexual relationships and then drops off fairly quickly. This waning of interest cannot be explained by general fatigue, because introducing a new partner causes the rate of coitus to jump back to its earlier high level.[27]

The closest analogs of these studies done with humans have focused on mate swapping and the effects of length of relationship on sexual interest between spouses. These studies support the notion that sexual novelty inspires passion. Similarly, married men who suffer from impotence with their spouses often recover remarkably rapidly when they encounter new women in sexually provocative situations.[28]

In short, our biological makeup may cause us to become less excited by our sexual partners as we grow accustomed to them. To be sure, steps can be taken to spice up long-term sexual relationships (for example, novel positions, varied techniques, emphasizing the sharing and intimacy aspects of sexual activity). Although such strategies may rekindle sexual interest to a degree, it is probably unrealistic to believe that a partner of several years will arouse the same sexual feelings as a new partner. This is not a serious problem unless sexual attraction is the primary basis of the marriage; if it is, however, marriage partners may end up feeling disappointed and cheated.

Entering a long-term relationship based on love at first sight may also be a problem because in focusing on the superficial qualities of their partners, people tend to ignore everything else. This is unfortunate because "everything else" offers some of the best predictors of later satisfaction. For example, research on close relationships has shown that when people are matched on such dimensions as occupation, age, religion, ethnicity, and education, they are more likely to enjoy long-term happiness in relationships.[29] This makes sense, because similarity is inherently pleasing. In addition, because similar others are particularly likely to know and understand us, our relationships with them are more likely to be smooth and harmonious.

All these factors suggest that relationships based on love at first sight should rarely pan out. Ted Huston and his colleagues at the University of Texas have gathered support for this idea in their research on couples who had "whirlwind courtships"—courtships that led to marriage after a few weeks or months. Such relationships were the *least* likely to be characterized by marital satisfaction later on.[30] Similarly, other researchers have found that people who claim to be intensely "in love" early in the relationship run an exceptionally high risk of breaking up later.[31] If the incompatibility typically present in relationships based on love at first sight leads to marital dissatisfaction, breakup, or both, feelings of failure and low self-esteem will surely follow.

Ulrich, Steinem, and the Problem of Authenticity

Given the potential for whirlwind courtships to lead to disharmony and low self-esteem, it is reassuring that most courtships go on for months and sometimes even years. Yet the deleterious effects of the romantic ideal may extend even to *long-term* courtships. One problem is that the romantic ideal discourages people from really getting to know each other. The rallying cry of the romantic ideal, "All's fair in love and war," encourages lovers to conceive of their relationships as "conquests" in which the "prize" is the affection of the beloved. Thus, they place a premium on presenting a "self" that seems most likely to win the romantic partner; presenting oneself accurately may actually get in the way.

Ulrich's willingness to transform his identity in the name of love was astonishing. When, after 13 years of service, he summoned the courage to ask his princess to reward his service by declaring her love for him, she scolded him for having misled her into thinking that he had lost a finger while fighting for her. Distraught, the noble knight handed his knife to a friend, who dutifully hacked off the offending digit. After mounting it inside a green velvet case, Ulrich sent it to the princess with a poem recounting the incident.

The romantic ideal encourages contemporary lovers to follow in Ulrich's footsteps by adopting whatever identity they feel is needed to win over their partners. As we have seen, however, such fraudulence may ultimately be self-deflating. Attempts to win partners through incentives such as money, gifts, or sexual favors may also backfire. Raising the possibility that the partner's affections have been "bought" may make it impossible to determine if these affections say anything about the lover's feelings toward one. As a result, winning the partner not only will fail to increase self-esteem but may actually diminish it.

Despite this drawback, the romantic ideal helps people rationalize the use of fraudulent and extrinsic strategies to win lovers. Because love is fated and uncontrollable, the argument goes, lovers cannot choose their actions freely and thus cannot be held responsible for what they do. Even if passion compels them to behave in ways that would otherwise be immoral or duplicitous, lovers can reassure themselves that the most important thing is keeping the relationship alive. So convinced, they may present themselves as the people they *expect* or *hope* to be rather than as they really are. Although this is the interpersonal equivalent of writing a bad check, those who are caught up in the romantic ideal can brush it off as a white lie. We even teach our children, through stories, movies, and television, that it is *only natural* for lovers to deceive each other.

Disney's award-winning film *Aladdin* offers an instructive example of how our cultural productions encourage us to recognize that true love may require an occasional lie. As the movie begins, our hero and heroine are disconsolate. Aladdin, a petty thief, is hungry and homeless. Jasmine, a beautiful princess, is lonely and bored. Both are in dire need of a magical rescue. Cupid intervenes and, against all odds, the pair meet and fall in love. Then comes the snag. As a commoner, Aladdin cannot marry a princess. Undaunted, he enlists the aid of a local genie and passes himself off as a prince. At first, Jasmine resists the advances of "Prince" Aladdin because she is still in love with the original, economy model Aladdin. When she finally warms to "Prince" Aladdin, the "real" Aladdin realizes that he is caught in a trap of his own making. If the Princess discovers his masquerade, he loses her. If she does not, he will be forever compelled to pretend to be someone he is not.

Aladdin's problem, of course, is that he has betrayed himself. By taking on a false self to win Jasmine's heart, he implicitly acknowledges that his "real" self is not good enough. Now, as "victory" draws near, he is consumed with feelings of unworthiness and dejection.[32] Then his worst fear is realized: his true identity is revealed. All seems lost until, at the last moment, fate intervenes. A certain villainous character is done in and Jasmine's father, the Sultan, takes pity on the young lovers, pronouncing that Jasmine can marry a commoner after all. As the movie ends, Aladdin and Jasmine are reunited and ride a magic carpet into the night.

Reality sometimes mirrors fiction, at least up to a point. Within weeks of the release of *Aladdin*, Gloria Steinem's *Revolution from Within* hit the bookstores. In her book, Steinem confides that she once got a man to fall in love with her by pretending to be someone else. And, like Aladdin, she soon became the victim of her own subterfuge. Having won her lover, she felt trapped in an identity that clashed with some of her basic values. In Steinem's case, alas, there was no magical rescue, for genies know better than to frequent the streets of New York. Unable to get over the feeling that she was faking it, Steinem broke off the relationship.

How many people find themselves trapped like Aladdin and Steinem? No one knows. We do know, however, that the tendency to look upon courtship relationships as extended qualifying exams lays the groundwork for this type of self-trap. To win a wife, for example, a man is supposed to put his best foot forward. How faithfully his "best foot" reflects his own "true self" is unimportant; the crucial thing is that he "passes the exam." Much the same is true for women. For the American in love, winning isn't the most important thing, it is the only thing. Yet, as Elizabeth Rapaport notes, this philosophy has its costs:

> *The lover . . . must present himself in the guise in*
> *which she would see her beloved. This leads to a false*
> *presentation of the self and the chronic fear of exposure*
> *and loss of love. Along the way the lover loses himself*
> *and necessarily the opportunity to gain love for this*
> *lost self.*[33]

As Rapaport's comment implies, pretending to be someone else will make most well-socialized people feel anxious and uncertain. The romantic ideal anticipates such feelings and helps lovers interpret them. These feelings are understood as *signs of love* rather than as indications that something is amiss. In fact, the romantic ideal encourages lovers to believe, as many contemporary Americans do, that suffering and unhappiness are important measures of true love. As a result, the specter of rejection may feed the emotions that are perceived as love. University of Minnesota psychologist Ellen Berscheid notes: "We see people experiencing the most intense positive emotion in association with persons whom they indicate [are] neither 'kind' nor 'industrious' but rather thoroughly unreliable scoundrels."[34] One author even suggested that people should be careful not to quiet their partner's apprehensions because to do so might "diminish the tension that fuels the passion."[35]

Such commentaries suggest that people with negative self-views would be more inclined to worry about their love lives than would people with positive self-views, because their feelings of worthlessness would contribute to fear of rejection, especially if they are attempting to pass themselves off as prized commodities. Recent research by psychologists Clyde and Susan Hendrick supports this idea. For example, people with low self-esteem are prone to obsess about their love affairs and to characterize their relationships as "unpredictable" and "uncontrollable." They also tend to agree with such statements as "Sometimes I get so excited about being in love that I can't go to sleep" and "When my love affairs break up, I get so depressed that I have even thought of suicide."[36]

By encouraging people to be inauthentic, the romantic ideal may engender feelings of worry, concern, and uneasiness among those who are dating, especially if they possess low self-esteem. Although such feelings may subside somewhat after marriage, a different but no less troubling set of emotions may replace them.

The Marriage Shift

As we have seen, half-truths and lies perpetrated during courtship may come to haunt people later on. This may be particularly true when courtship culminates in marriage or other long-term relationships. Once the dating game is over, mutual trust tends to replace apprehension, and spouses recognize that they can "let it all hang out" without nearly so much risk of forfeiting the relationship. Also, as relationships mature, people's goals (such as maintaining a household, raising children, launching and managing careers) become increasingly intertwined. United in pursuing these goals, spouses realize that their partners must recognize their weaknesses as well as their strengths.[37] Criticism takes on a completely different meaning. No longer a sign that the relationship is in trouble, it is valued as a source of self-insight. At long last, "the flamboyant anticipations of betrothal give way to the sober satisfactions of marriage [and] we lapse back into our ordinary selves."[38]

In the new climate of a marital relationship, people with negative self-views may become increasingly uncomfortable with evaluations that they perceive as overly favorable. Imagine a man who receives what he construes to be undeserved praise from his wife. Although such praise may make him feel optimistic and happy at first, the positive glow will recede if he concludes that his wife could not possibly believe what she said and that, underneath, she secretly wishes that he were better than he really is. And if he is convinced that she does believe what she says, he may decide that she is a fool. In either case, overly favorable evaluations from someone who knows one well may foster a sense of uneasiness, inauthenticity, and distrust of the person who delivered them.

Marriage may thus produce a shift in the kind of evaluations that people want from their partners. During the courtship period, people with negative self-views may enjoy favorable evaluations because their partners don't know them very well and thus pose no threat to the integrity of their self-views. Once they move into a more committed phase, however, they recognize that the partner ought to know them and begin to prefer negative evaluations; they may even put up with abuse.

The marital bliss study described in Chapter 2 documents the evaluation preferences of married persons. In that study, married couples rated themselves and their spouses and then completed a measure of the intimacy of the relationship.[39] As noted earlier, married people "self-verified": those with positive self-views were most intimate with spouses who evaluated them favorably, and those with negative self-views were most intimate with spouses who evaluated them unfavorably. People who were still dating responded quite differently, however. Whether they had positive or negative self-views, the dating partners who reported being most intimate were those whose partners evaluated them favorably. Thus, people who were dating displayed no overriding concern with the fit between their self-views and the evaluations of their partners. Apparently, long-term relationships, as exemplified by marriage, erode people's tolerance for overly favorable evaluations. Although this apparent shift has little impact on the evaluations preferred by people with positive self-views (because positive evaluations are also self-verifying), people with negative self-views move from preferring favorable evaluations to preferring unfavorable ones.[40]

The romantic ideal thus further complicates the efforts of people with negative self-views to strike a balance between their desire for self-verification and their desire for positivity. By encouraging people with negative self-views to prefer favorable evaluations from dating partners, the romantic ideal causes them to embrace partners who will later foster feelings of inauthenticity. Yet people with negative self-views rarely succeed in establishing dating relationships with partners who adore them. In one of the studies discussed in Chapter 2, for example, the dating partners of people with negative self-views maintained relatively negative impressions of them and helped insulate their negative self-views against favorable feedback. Similarly, in the marriage shift study, the partners of people with negative self-views were unfavorable toward them whether they were dating or married.

Why doesn't the romantic ideal cause the majority of people with negative self-views to end up in relationships with the adoring dating partners whom it urges them to seek? Some may discover that their desire for self-verification makes them think twice about their inclination to embrace a favorable partner, thus dissuading them from choosing such a partner. Others may seek favorable partners but find that such persons become disappointed and either develop negative evaluations of them or leave the relationship entirely.

In any case, the marriage shift seems to do more to alter how people with negative self-views *feel* about their partners' evaluations than it does to alter the *actual reactions* such people elicit from their partners. In this way, it will surely contribute to the ambivalence they experience, which may explain why conflict decreases as engaged couples approach marriage and then increases in the months following it.[41]

If the marriage shift is a common phenomenon, why is there so little awareness of it? One reason is that most people have positive self-views, and people with positive self-views do not experience much of a shift at all—they want to be evaluated favorably both before and after marriage. Even people with negative self-views may be unaware of their shifting preferences, however. The shift from preferring positivity to preferring self-verification probably occurs very gradually during the months immediately before and after the marriage ceremony (although the ceremony may serve as a powerful catalyst for the change). As a result, the shift is hardly perceptible. The sociologists Charles Berger and Michael Kellner put it this way:

> The protagonists of the marriage drama do not set out deliberately to re-create their world. Each continues to live in a world that is taken for granted—and keeps its taken-for-granted character even as it is metamorphosed. The new world that the married partners, Prometheus-like, have called into being is perceived by them as the normal world in which they have lived before . . . The dramatic change that has occurred remains, in bulk, unapprehended and unarticulated.[42]

Yet if the marriage shift were the only adverse consequence of the romantic ideal, those relationships that survived it might very well be a source of happiness and high self-esteem. Unfortunately, the romantic ideal ushered in changes that extend well beyond the marriage shift to the very nature of our society. Most important, the custom of expressing our romantic inclinations through free-choice marriages (as opposed to arranged marriages) gave individualism a boost and thus helped to redefine the relationship between the individual and society. More and more, individuals refrained from looking to society for guidance about proper behavior and instead chose actions that suited their own needs and desires. Rather than the individual cultivating society, society now cultivated the individual. As individualism became an increasingly potent force in the American ideology, it made people vulnerable to a newly emerging set of self-traps involving the pursuit of competence.

6 ESTEEM AND THE PURSUIT OF COMPETENCE

Before I quit teaching to stay home with my first baby, I thought that the hardest part of leaving my job would be losing the money. I was wrong . . . the real problem with not earning a paycheck, I found, was keeping up with my self-esteem. If I'm not earning a salary, what am I worth. We live in a world in which Donald Trump gets instant groveling, not because he's a nice guy, not because he's bringing up happy, well-adjusted kids, but because he makes a lot of money. So where does that leave us stay-at-home moms, who work 24 hours a day but don't put money in the bank to prove it? . . . [When] I was filling out a form and came to the box marked "occupation" . . . I understood that the question was really asking how I earned my money, not how I spent my time.[1]

We Americans accord enormous significance to the occupations we pursue. Together with income, material assets, and social status, occupations represent a key marker of competence in the eyes of many people. Unfortunately, because there are relatively few high-status occupations and limited amounts of income and wealth, the great significance we attach to these indicators of competence may be damaging to the self-esteem of those who lack the desire or opportunity to attain them—the have-nots. The mother just quoted, for example, complained that when strangers learned she was staying at home to raise her child, they "spoke to me as if I were not quite bright; I must be staying at home because I had nothing 'better' to return to."[2] Such reactions thrust recipients into self-traps: they at once resent being patronized and are frustrated that they cannot remedy the situation without thwarting other important goals, such as spending time with their young children.

Ironically, those who do obtain the markers of success and status that we take as signs of competence may fall into a different self-trap. The problem is that material goods, wealth, and status are not *inherently* gratifying and may even erode our sense of competence. To truly sustain our sense of self-worth, we need a system of relationships with people who nourish our feelings of competence through their approval. Unfortunately, recent changes in the United States, especially the increase of individualism and the growing fragmentation of the family and community, have weakened the relationships we have traditionally relied upon for self-verification.[3] These changes may thrust us into self-traps in which we not only are alienated from our hard-earned status and material goods but also are estranged from the people we expected would delight in our accomplishments. Feeling deflated and alone, we may attempt to compensate by redoubling our efforts to acquire material goods, which will merely intensify our feelings of futility and low self-esteem.

Consuming Passions

Until the late 1800s, Americans associated the accumulation of material goods with greed, waste, and a lack of self-discipline. This perception began to change when business leaders and others recognized that consumption's bad reputation might be standing between them and higher profits:

> By the late nineteenth century, political economists realized that the ethic of hard work and self-restraint that had helped to industrialize America had serious drawbacks now that most industries had the capacity for mass production. If everyone deferred gratification, who would buy the new products? Between 1870 and 1900, the volume of advertising multiplied more than tenfold. Giant department stores were built to showcase new consumer items for urban residents, while rural residents were exposed to the delights and temptations of mail-order catalogs. The word consumption increasingly lost its earlier connotations of destroying, wasting, or using up, and came instead to refer in a positive way to the satisfying of human needs and desires.[4]

By the 1920s, increased consumption had become an integral part of the American Dream. Some even suggested that consumption was an expression of patriotism. For instance, a Muncie, Indiana, newspaper stated, "The American citizen's first importance to his country is no longer that of citizen but that of consumer."[5] The consumption craze grew rapidly until it began to spill into all aspects of American life. Advertisers played on the self-esteem needs of consumers to instruct them in the art of becoming worthwhile human beings:

> By the 1920's advertisers had come to recognize a public demand for broad guidance . . . about taste, social correctness, and psychological satisfaction. . . .
> Advertising men had now become broader social therapists who offered . . . balms for the discontents of modernity.[6]

Consumers were, in effect, promised that they could become the self-confident, satisfied people depicted in the advertisements by doing whatever the models did—wearing the same clothes, smoking the same cigarettes, or driving the same automobiles. In this world turned upside down, actually developing some skill or expertise seemed less important than merely acquiring the *trappings* of competence.[7] And because buying could alter appearances, it became an increasingly important part of American life.

Today, consumption has become so integral to life in the United States that in some places it has gained the status of an art form. The director of the South Street Seaport museum in New York, for example, defended his decision to involve the museum in commercial development a few years ago by quipping, "The fact is that shopping is the chief cultural activity in the United States."[8]

This "cultural activity" also plays an important role in the quest for self-esteem. Many people believe that acquiring the trappings of an aspired-to self will enable them to elicit reactions that confirm that self. The most convincing acts of consumption are sometimes those whose only conceivable purpose is to elicit self-confirming reactions: purchasing goods that are useless or wasteful. At the end of the nineteenth century, economist Thorstein Veblen named this phenomenon *conspicuous consumption:*

Unproductive consumption of goods is honorable,
primarily as a mark of prowess and a prerequisite of
human dignity; secondarily it becomes substantially
honorable in itself, especially the consumption of the
more desirable goods.[9]

In recent years, the widespread availability of consumer credit has not only fanned the flames of conspicuous consumption but altered its character. Now that people can buy on credit items that they cannot truly afford, they can, at least for a time, take on the appearance of being far more wealthy than they actually are. Propelled by a desire to impress their fellows and, perhaps, themselves, many people have struggled to bolster their self-esteem by consuming themselves into poverty.

What makes such tragedies ironic is that consumption seldom delivers sustained feelings of self-worth. Instead, basing one's sense of competence or lovability on the accumulation of material comforts leads to an extraordinarily fragile sense of self-worth. People who organize their lives around the goal of attaining goods and other extrinsic rewards may soon discover that they no longer enjoy any activity for its own sake. Even actions that were once inherently pleasurable may lose their charm once they become identified as a means of accumulating more goods. Poignant testimony to this possibility comes from former basketball great Bill Russell in his book *Second Wind: The Memoirs of an Opinionated Man:*

I remember that the game lost some of its magical
qualities for me once I thought seriously about
playing for a living. This first happened in 1955,
in my junior year, after USF [University of San
Francisco] won the NCAA national championship.
As a result, all through my senior year at USF I
played with the idea of turning professional, and
things began to change. Whenever I walked on the
court I began to calculate how this particular game
might affect my future. Thoughts of money and
prestige crept into my head. Over the years the
professional game would turn more and more into
a business.[10]

Why might rewards diminish enjoyment in an inherently pleasurable activity? Psychologist Ed Deci at the University of Rochester has argued that rewarding people for performing an activity that they wanted to do anyway changes the meaning of that activity. Once people receive a reward for doing something, they may come to believe that it is the sort of thing they do only because they know they will be rewarded for it. The activity may consequently cease to be a source of feelings of efficacy and self-competence and instead become linked to concerns about being controlled or bribed. Eventually, the activity may begin to engender a sense of alienation.[11]

This reasoning led researchers to wonder whether the use of rewards in schools diminishes children's interest in their schoolwork (just as Russell's large salary seemed to undercut his love for basketball). In one study, Mark Lepper and his colleagues at Stanford University spent two weeks observing how much time fourth- and fifth-grade children spent playing some popular new math games. Then they introduced a reward period during which children received credits toward certificates and trophies for playing the games. Their first finding was unsurprising: although children liked the math games to begin with, when the credits were introduced the games became even more popular.[12]

What happened next *was* surprising, however. When the rewards were cut off, children who had enthusiastically immersed themselves in the math games without rewards suddenly lost interest in them. Presumably, children who played the games for rewards came to see them in a new light. No longer were the games intrinsically motivated activities that they engaged in just for fun; now the games were nothing more than a means of getting rewards. As a result, when the reward disappeared, so too did children's reason for playing the games.[13]

Rewards don't always undermine people's intrinsic interest in activities, however.[14] Psychologist Judy Harackiewicz and her colleagues have shown that rewards may actually increase intrinsic motivation when steps are taken to make recipients feel that the reward indicates they have mastered the task.[15] Nevertheless, when rewards are framed in ways that make people feel controlled or manipulated, they often undercut intrinsic motivation. This phenomenon occurs among both adults and children and over a wide range of activities. Moreover, rewards aren't the only thing that may undercut intrinsic motivation.

Any procedure that makes people feel their behavior is being manipulated in some way—including giving them deadlines, monitoring their behavior, or pressuring them to participate—will sap intrinsic interest. People who work simply to obtain rewards and please others may thus find that their hard-won success provides little personal gratification or feelings of competence and self-esteem.[16] Instead, the more they work, the more they may feel disappointed and frustrated with themselves and alienated from their work.

Worker Alienation and Anomie

If there was ever an environment that seems specifically designed to foster feelings of impotence and helplessness among workers, it was the early industrial workplace:

> *Workers who had been their own masters even though they labored 14 hours or more, were now subjected to penalties which reflected not only their inexperience with the requirements and hazards of factory work but also the employer's anxious endeavor to control their every move. In one spinning factory the doors were locked during working hours; it was prohibited to drink water despite the prevailing heat; and fines were imposed on such misdemeanors as leaving a window open, being dirty, washing oneself, whistling, putting the light out too soon or not soon enough, being found in the wrong place and so on.[17]*

Of course, many of the appalling physical conditions that galvanized social critics during the eighteenth and nineteenth centuries were eventually reformed (although they persist to this day in some regions of the world). Yet even when some of these harsh conditions were eliminated, many workers continued to feel that they were merely doing the bidding of someone who stood in authority over them. Karl Marx believed that this was the root of feelings of alienation among workers:

> *What constitutes the alienation of labor? First, that the work is external to the worker, that it is not part of his nature; and that, consequently, he does not fulfill himself*

in his work but denies himself, has a feeling of misery
rather than well-being, does not develop freely his
mental and physical energies but is physically and
mentally debased. . . . His work is not voluntary but
imposed, forced labor. It is not the satisfaction of a need,
but only the means of satisfying other needs. . . . Finally,
the external character of work for the worker is shown by
the fact that it is not his own work but work for someone
else, that in work he does not belong to himself but to
another person.[18]

Marx and various political philosophers insisted that such conditions reduce workers to automatons who cannot feel truly competent because they cannot control their own fate.[19] The problem was exacerbated by the emergence of "scientific management" during the early years of the twentieth century. Championed by Frederick W. Taylor and others, this management movement sought to maximize worker productivity. Its underlying assumption was that work could be broken down by management into components so simple that even the most ignorant and unmotivated worker couldn't help but master them. Although this movement led to a better understanding of the physiological constraints on performance of routine production tasks, it downplayed the importance of workers' feelings about themselves, their work, and the tasks they were required to perform.[20]

Although Taylorism and the alienation it fosters continue to plague many workers, an entirely different class of esteem-sapping problems has recently been identified. These problems occur when employers require workers to display particular emotions on demand. Sociologist Arlie Hochschild's study at Delta Air Lines offers a case in point. The goal of Delta (and other airlines) is to train flight attendants to make passengers feel appreciated and confident that their flights will be safe and on time. To this end, flight attendants are instructed to suppress their normal emotional reactions and adopt personas that are designed to please and reassure the passengers. For example, one pilot sought to inspire his flight attendants with the following pep talk:

Now girls, I want you to go out there and really smile.
Your smile is your biggest asset. *I want you to go out*
there and use it. Smile. Really smile. *Really* lay it on.[21]

The "girls" learned that all smiles are not created equal; smiles that seemed "painted on" were to be carefully avoided. The flight attendants' trainers exhorted them to actually *feel* happy and calm and to convey these emotions to passengers through their actions. In this respect, Hochschild's flight attendants were not only stripped of the prerogative to express certain emotions, they were deprived of the right to *experience* their own emotional reactions. They were thus compelled to perform emotional labor as well as physical labor. In this area, the demands placed on Delta's flight attendants were more stringent than those that management of the eighteenth- and nineteenth-century sweatshops placed on its factory workers. No matter how wretched the working conditions that prevailed in these earlier times, people were at least free to *feel* tired or bored or hungry or resentful, even if they were not free to express such feelings openly.

One flight attendant related how she once entered a trancelike state while talking to a male passenger: "I wasn't feeling anything. It was like I wasn't actually there. The guy was talking. I could hear him. But all I heard was dead words."[22] Having relinquished control of her emotional apparatus, the worker was now unable to experience her normal emotions. And as she withdrew from the situation psychologically, her emotions no longer "belonged" to her—they had become what Marx termed an "instrument of labor." Furthermore, because she was psychologically removed, the woman could not derive a sense of competence from her work. She might have pride in being a good flight attendant, but it wouldn't be *she* who was enacting the competent behaviors. Her responses could only represent a denial of self and might thus be a source of fraudulence, inauthenticity, and low self-esteem.[23]

The plight of the airline attendants would be easier to ignore if their job requirements were anomalous. They are not. As the economy of the United States becomes increasingly service oriented, more and more employers are demanding that their employees offer up their emotional lives to keep their jobs. After taking a "Vow of Enthusiasm," for example, employees at Mary Kay Cosmetics are instructed in the art of faking emotions. At Disneyland, management carefully indoctrinates workers in the intricacies of smiling and enhancing the self-esteem of visitors. Even workers at some fast-food restaurants find that their paychecks suffer if they fail to display suitably positive emotions.[24]

Rules for emotional displays are not limited to positive emotions. Funeral directors are trained to be somber and reserved; police interrogators and bill collectors learn to exude hostility, chilliness, or pugnacity to suspects or debtors. Still other workers are counseled to display no emotion whatsoever. For example, judges, academic deans, business managers, and other professionals learn to mask their feelings and intentions behind bland, unrevealing personas. Such emotionless demeanors are in keeping with Max Weber's depiction of organizational membership as "life in an iron cage." In such settings, emotional expression is the kiss of death: "Even in the most difficult of circumstances, such as when a promotion doesn't materialize, the professional is supposed to behave appropriately. Never show hurt, never grieve in public, and never grow angry."[25]

The dilemma that many of these workers face goes a step beyond the one Bill Russell confronted. When Russell pondered whether he was playing basketball out of love of the game or for money, he was asking himself whether his behavior was an expression of his own desires or the desires of the team owners who paid his salary. In contrast, the flight attendants could not even begin to ask Russell's question because their work required that they suppress or alter their own feelings. Thus their work represented a denial of an important aspect of self. Although deriving a sense of competence from phony and inauthentic behavior is not logically impossible, it at least requires far more elaborate mental work or rationalization than most people are likely to muster. Those who are unable to do so may learn that their inauthentic behavior fosters feelings of alienation and worthlessness rather than competence and high self-esteem.[26]

Even if workers frantically pursuing the American Dream manage to avoid such feelings of fraudulence and low self-esteem, other self-traps may snag them. Those who set their sights on high salaries, luxurious houses, or fancy cars, for example, may be chagrined to learn that the "glow" produced by the fruits of their labors is surprisingly short-lived. This disappointment can be explained by adaptation level theory.

The Fleeting Gleam of Success

The psychologist Harry Helson originally developed adaptation level theory to explain simple illusions that occur when, for example, people manipulate physical objects.[27] If you lift a 10-pound weight and then a 50-pound weight, the 50-pound weight will feel heavier than if you had first lifted a 45-pound weight. Similarly, if you get $18.00 for performing some service and then receive $20.00 for performing it, the $20.00 will seem like less of a payoff than if you had initially received $5.00. In these and many similar instances, we evaluate new experiences relative to earlier ones.

Our capacity to adapt can have far-reaching effects, as shown by a study of lottery winners in Illinois. The winners in this study enjoyed an average take of $500,000, a particularly impressive sum in the late 1970s when the research was conducted. Despite this windfall, a year later the winners were no happier than a comparable group of nonwinners. Winning the lottery eroded the winners' capacity to enjoy the simple pleasures of life. Compared to less fortunate players, winners reported deriving *less* pleasure from such everyday events as talking with a friend, watching television, hearing a funny joke, reading a magazine, or even receiving a compliment. Apparently, winning the lottery caused people to set their standards for happiness so high that the ordinary pleasures of life simply couldn't measure up any more.[28]

Our tendency to adapt quickly to a certain level of affluence may also explain our seemingly insatiable thirst for ever more elaborate and numerous material goods. By virtually any index of wealth, Americans are much better off today than we were, say, in the 1950s. We have, on average, far more "things" than we used to. Since the 1950s, for example, we have enjoyed a 484 percent rise in the number of homes with air conditioners, a 134 percent increase in freezers, a 356 percent increase in clothes dryers, and an astonishing 743 percent increase in homes with dishwashers.[29] This extraordinary growth, however, has led to the expectation that we will continue to acquire new things at the same rate. Adaptation level theory suggests that we judge our current prosperity relative to what we have become accustomed to.

The problem is that our economy is no longer growing. During the past two decades, 60 percent of the work force has suffered *losses* in their standard of living.[30] In addition, corporate America has discovered that it can increase its profit margins by hiring foreign workers overseas who work for lower wages than domestic workers. The result has been massive layoffs of workers in the United States.

The recent financial losses suffered by many Americans are problematic for several reasons. For one thing, reductions in our supply of material goods, wealth, and secure jobs mean that we have fewer markers of competence to use in eliciting esteem-sustaining reactions from others. In addition, for many people, these losses signal that the economy may be tightening even more in the future, which would result in further losses not only in markers of competence but perhaps even in basic services such as health care.

To compensate for such feelings, many people now seem to be attempting to shore up their self-esteem and financial security by intensifying their efforts to accumulate money. In 1970, only 34 percent of college freshman in the United States declared that "being very well off financially" was an important life goal. In 1991, that number had risen to 75 percent.[31] And Americans are doing more than paying lip service to their dream of getting rich. Briefer vacations and longer working hours combined to produce an increase of 30 working days per year from 1967 to 1987.[32] Although women were responsible for more of this increase in working hours than men, both genders showed an increase. If these trends continue, projections are that by the year 2000 Americans will be spending as much time working as their grandparents did in the 1920s— and considerably *more* time than the peasantry did during the early Middle Ages. The projections suggest that by 2010, the average person will work even more—60 hours a week, 50 weeks a year—the same rate that prevailed in Charles Dickens's England.[33]

Even if the struggle to improve our financial status by increasing our work hours does not leave us feeling controlled, the positive feelings accompanying the new material possessions acquired with our increased income will vanish rapidly. The pursuit of more becomes a Sisyphean task that is unsatisfying at best and alienating and deflating at worst. Some observers have even blamed the explosion of sleep and anxiety disorders and other stress-related illnesses on the increasingly frenetic pace of American life. In Japan, the only major industrial country whose workers spend more time on the job than American workers do, overworking has become a serious health problem.[34]

With such concerns in mind, psychologist Richard Ryan and his colleagues sought to identify the emotional and spiritual costs associated with pursuing the American Dream of status, wealth, and material possessions. They surveyed students from the University of Rochester and adults from the city of Rochester, New York. Among both groups, those who were most concerned with financial success and fame were more likely to suffer from depression, anxiety, conduct disorders, and an inability to function effectively in social situations. For some residents of Rochester, keeping their "eyes on the prize" led to disaster.[35]

The work of Ryan and his colleagues suggests that even if overworked people remain healthy, they will be relatively ineffective in social situations. Their relationships may suffer accordingly. In addition, spending more time working almost inevitably means spending less time with friends, spouses, lovers, and children. For instance, between 1960 and 1986, the time parents spent with their children dropped 10 hours per week for whites and 12 hours per week for African Americans.[36] If parents are stressed or distracted during the time they do manage to squeeze in with their children, they not only risk damaging children's self-views but also may foster guilt and resentment in themselves when they feel stretched well beyond their limits.

A highly individualized quest for material goods, wealth, and status may thus plunge people into self-traps in which their quest for markers of competence comes between them and their friends, lovers, and family members. These are, of course, the very persons on whom they must rely for confirmation of their feelings of competence and self-worth.

The Price of Individualism

Although individualism is, as anthropologist Clifford Geertz put it, a "rather peculiar idea within the context of the world's cultures,"[37] it remains a central component of Western thought. Historically, individualism has brought significant benefits to society. By emphasizing the specific services people could perform rather than the position of their relatives in the community, individualism has given the poor more opportunity to improve their status than they have had for much of human history. Individualism's recognition that each person has unique value and worth has also led to principles such as civil liberties. And individualism provided the motivational impetus that fueled the success of capitalism by fostering the replacement of communal relationships with contractual arrangements based on personal gain.[38]

Because individualism encourages each of us to believe that we must establish our competence and self-worth on our own, however, we come to feel that we can enlist the help of others only at the cost of sabotaging our chances of emerging as the "most competent person"—the one who gets credit for the work. Richard Sennett and Jonathan Cobb comment on this dilemma:

> *If ability is a demonstration about you . . . then the more you have to act together with other people, the less chance you have to be rewarded for emerging from the mass—which is the social definition of ability itself. While labor grows every day more interdependent, the dream of independent action remains strong because it seems the only way to show that you accomplish things.*[39]

By pitting people against one another, individualism's concept of competence encourages people to be suspicious and distrustful of their peers. Playwright Tennessee Williams, for example, referred to his success as a "kind of death" because it caused him to suspect that his friends were merely manipulating him and giving him false praise.[40] Convinced that he could not trust his companions, Williams was left with no one he respected and cared about to validate his accomplishments and nourish his feelings of competence.

Although individualism enables people to feel free to "make it on their own," this freedom has been won at the cost of weakening their links to friends, family, and members of the larger community. Without the sense of belonging to a greater, all-embracing structure, many people have come to associate their newfound freedom with the rootlessness that Janis Joplin lamented. Paradoxically, our sense of individual freedom has made the goal of establishing and maintaining a sense of competence and self-worth far more daunting:

> *Just when he could count on fewer and fewer people for "unconditional acceptance," the individual had to be self-disciplined, competitive, ambitious, able to respond to rapidly changing situations and demands, able to leave home to go to school and follow the opportunities of professional advancement.*[41]

Today, increased individualism has combined with growth in the popularity of televisions, VCRs, and home computers to contribute to the progressive weakening of family and community ties. In a recent essay, political scientist Robert Putnam argued that signs of this transformation have cropped up in virtually every facet of American life. Since 1964, participation in parent-teacher associations has plummeted from 12 million to 7 million. Volunteering help for various community activities is becoming increasingly rare; volunteerism rates have dropped 26 percent for the Boy Scouts and a whopping 61 percent for the Red Cross. We are even bowling alone: although there was a 10 percent *increase* in the number of bowlers from 1980 to 1993, the number of people bowling in organized leagues *decreased* by 40 percent.[42]

Our declining sense of community has altered the moral fabric of society at large. Sociologist Amitai Etzioni writes that when people's sense of "we-ness" gives way to a self-centered quest for personal advancement, society loses a basis for moral behavior.[43] The declining sense of community may also be one reason that people have become increasingly resentful of paying taxes used to benefit the larger society. Despite the fact that Americans enjoy a lower rate of taxation than any major industrial nation save one, voters continue to clamor for further reductions. In one sense, these clamorings are understandable, because the Reagan tax reforms caused 75 percent of taxpayers to owe more taxes than they would have if the 1977 laws had remained in effect, while the wealthiest 5 percent of the population enjoyed a tax cut. The Reagan tax reforms also hurt the general public in many less direct ways.

During the 1980s, federal spending for the general good dropped in several key areas, including law enforcement and government (down 42 percent), education and training (down 40 percent), and the transportation infrastructure (down 32 percent).[44] By supporting Reagan's tax reforms, Americans diminished the quality of life in their cities and communities so that the very rich could stash more money away in their coffers.

Reaganomics hit poor people and minorities the hardest, virtually eliminating public housing, slashing funding for cities, and tightening restrictions on various benefits. Given this, one might have predicted that minorities and their traditional allies on the political left would have banded together in opposition. Sociologist Todd Gitlin notes that this has not happened. On the contrary, the liberal party has disintegrated into a chaos of distinct cultural interest groups, each grasping for confirmation of its own identity and satisfaction of its own self-esteem needs while failing to strive for the common good. As Gitlin puts it, "The squandering of energy on identity politics, the hardening of the boundaries between groups, the insistence that individuals are no more than their labels, is an American tragedy."[45]

Of all the indices of America's deteriorating sense of community, however, the most direct may be the results of national polls designed to probe the perceptions that Americans have of their relationships. In a survey conducted during the 1980s, 70 percent of Americans reported feeling a void in their lives because they had many acquaintances but few close friends. In addition, 41 percent reported that they had fewer close friends than they did in the recent past.[46] And when pollsters asked a nationwide sample of people whether they would be willing to give up their families and never see them again in exchange for $10 million, a surprising 25 percent of the respondents said they would take the money.[47]

The growing sense of estrangement from community may have personally devastating effects as well. Psychologist Robert Karen has even suggested that it is responsible for long-term shifts in the landscape of psychopathology:

Freud's patients tended to know who they were, or at least who they thought they should be, and to feel a natural sense of belonging and of responsibility to both

their families and their social milieu. They suffered from
annoying symptoms—compulsions, hysterical paralyses,
phobias, fetishes—that they hoped to discard, but
otherwise experienced themselves as emotionally intact.
The new analytic patients . . . did not display these
obvious symptoms. They were haunted by feelings of
self-doubt and emptiness, were prone to dislike or hate
themselves, and were unclear about who they were or
should be. During [the last century] many of the
character neuroses—schizoid, narcissistic, borderline, as
well as Winnicott's false self—came to the fore.[48]

Although no one can be sure why we are now seeing more disorders related to self and self-esteem,[49] individualism may well play a role. In collectivist societies, the community takes an active role in regulating the affective states of members. A case in point is the Kaluli, a tribe in New Guinea. Depression is virtually unknown among the Kaluli. This fact seems to be linked to the tendency for community members to rush to the aid of those who have suffered some setback:

If you lose something valuable, such as your pig, you
have a right to recompense. There are rituals (such as
dancing and screaming at the neighbor you think killed
the pig) that are recognized by the society. When you
demand recompense for loss, either the neighbor or the
whole tribe takes note of your condition and usually
recompenses you one way or another. . . . [This] prevents
sadness from becoming depression.[50]

In contrast, highly individualistic societies leave their members to regulate their affective states on their own. Individuals are also responsible for regulating virtually all of their other activities, including those through which they pursue a sense of competence. And if people fail to attain markers of competence such as occupations, material goods, or wealth, observers are likely to conclude that they must have suffered from some inherent defect in their abilities or character.

The Fate of the Poor

A reporter once asked billionaire John D. Rockefeller, "Do you think the poor boy stands much of a chance in the race for success?" Rockefeller's answer conveyed the ebullient optimism that everyone longed to hear:

The poor boy is in a position of impregnable advantage. He is better off than the son of the rich man, for he is prepared to do what the latter will not do, or rarely so; that is, plunge in with his hands and learn a business from the bottom. It is to them, the sons of hardy Americans, that we look to carry into the future the progress of the present. The future, with all of its infinite possibilities, is in their hands . . . Yes, decidedly, the opportunities for the young American boy are greater today than they have ever been before; and no boy, however lowly—the barefoot country boy, the humble newsboy, the child of the tenement—need despair. I see in each of them infinite possibilities. They have but to master the knack of economy, thrift, honesty, and perseverance, and success is theirs.[51]

Although inspiring and emotionally uplifting, there is little evidence that Rockefeller's rhetoric about the prospects of the poor has any basis in fact. Even the Horatio Alger stories, which are so often touted as examples of the phenomenal success that Rockefeller seemed to envision, are not what they are widely believed to be. Alger is associated with the "rags-to-riches" story, in which a person who is cursed with lower class origins manages to ascend to the top through hard work. In reality, the heroes in Alger's books are often boys from the middle class. More important, luck rather than pluck typically propels Alger's characters to fame and fortune. A final myth is that Alger modeled his heroes after himself. Far from it. The son of a minister, Alger enjoyed the best of upbringings, receiving a degree from Harvard and then securing a position in the ministry. His stint as a minister didn't last long; Alger was expelled for allegedly performing "deeds too revolting to relate" with young boys.[52] Although he went on to become a prolific writer, his works hardly won the acclaim that would justify the conclusion that he "rose to the top."

To be sure, poor people sometimes *do* pull themselves up by their bootstraps. Nevertheless, being born poor significantly raises the chances of dying poor, and being a member of certain racial or ethnic groups dramatically increases the likelihood of being a member of the underclass. The existence of the underclass is a convenient arrangement for members of the dominant group, because their own prosperity hinges on the willingness of someone who has little alternative to do the work that is boring, repetitive, fatiguing, and sometimes demeaning. This is the arrangement in the United States, where the task of performing the least paid and most undesirable jobs has fallen on the shoulders of a more or less permanent underclass and a small number of migrant workers.[53]

In a society that is supposed to be egalitarian in opportunity, however, the existence of a permanent underclass is bound to cause tension. Members of the underclass inevitably ask why they always seem to wind up unemployed or working in the worst jobs, if opportunity is ostensibly available to all. Historically, defenders of the dominant group have answered by promoting the view that members of the underclass have inherent deficiencies in character or abilities. This was, for example, the justification that South African whites used to rationalize the apartheid system. This is also the thrust of Richard Herrnstein and Charles Murray's analysis of class and racial differences in IQ, which they present in *The Bell Curve*. In reality, there is no compelling evidence that members of certain racial or ethnic groups suffer from innate deficiencies that justify their consignment to low-paying jobs.[54] On the other hand, there *is* persuasive evidence that decades of oppression can leave a psychological legacy that makes upward mobility particularly difficult. For example, poverty is often linked with parenting strategies that are associated with children's low self-esteem and underachievement.[55] In addition, people from the lower socioeconomic classes are socialized to believe that they must be conformists to secure jobs—an attitude that is hardly conducive to the entrepreneurial spirit that is so important to success in a capitalistic economy.[56]

In the spirit of such findings, social critic Shelby Steele has suggested that years of discrimination have engendered feelings of doubt about their level of competence among African-American members of the underclass:

One of the worst aspects of oppression is that it never ends when the oppressor begins to repent. There is a legacy of doubt in the oppressed that follows long after the cleanest repentance by the oppressor, just as guilt trails the oppressor and makes his redemption incomplete. These themes of doubt and guilt fill in like fresh replacements and work to duplicate the oppression. I think black Americans are today more oppressed by doubt than by racism, and that the second phase of our struggle for freedom must be a confrontation with that doubt. Unexamined, this doubt leads us back into a tunnel of our oppression where we reenact our victimization just as society struggles to end its victimization of us. . . . For us freedom has so long meant the absence of oppression that we have not yet realized it also means the conquering of doubt.[57]

Claude Steele, Shelby Steele's brother and a researcher at Stanford University, has attempted to identify the mechanisms through which self-doubt perpetuates the oppression. He sought to understand why affirmative action programs have done little to eliminate racial disparities in school achievement and dropout rates. He noted, for example, that the dropout rate for black college students is 70 percent, as compared to 47 percent for whites. Of those who graduate, grades are two-thirds of a letter grade higher for whites. Both results occur even when one compares blacks and whites who have *the same level of preparation.*[58]

If such racial differences in academic success are not due to academic preparation (or, presumably, to variables that can influence academic preparation, such as genetic endowment), what does cause them? Claude Steele speculated that because most blacks are socialized to doubt their ability to excel in academic settings, they work to insulate themselves against failure by disidentifying with academic tasks. To test this idea, he and Joshua Aronson examined the factors that influence how equally well qualified whites and blacks perform on aptitude tests. They discovered that blacks performed more poorly than whites when they were subtly reminded of their racial identity prior to taking such tests (by being asked to reveal their race), but that blacks and whites performed equally well when they received no reminder of their racial identity.[59] Steele also demonstrated the existence of a parallel phenomenon among white women. In one study, Steele and Steven Spencer first replicated a common finding: true to social stereotypes suggesting that men are more "mathematical" than women, male Stanford University students outperformed women on the math subsection of an aptitude test but performed no differently on the English subsection of the test. When the experimenter told students before the exam that it was gender-neutral, however, no gender differences emerged on either subsection of the test.[60]

By showing that racial differences in scores on aptitude tests disappear when testing procedures are designed to minimize feelings of self-doubt, Steele's research contradicts the notion that racial differences in achievement are a result of genetic factors. His findings also raise a further issue, however. If significant numbers of people among some groups (such as women, African Americans, and other minorities) disidentify with one or more types of academic pursuit, to what domains do they shift their psychological investment?

Seeking Self-Worth in Worlds of Limited Opportunity

How people go about surmounting roadblocks to their sense of self-worth will depend on the specific impediments they confront, their personal characteristics, and qualities of the groups to which they belong. For example, women who internalize social norms suggesting that they cannot excel in mathematics or science may invest themselves in any of dozens of alternative pursuits, including nonacademic ones.

Those who feel that there is nothing they can do that will be rewarded by the larger society have a more serious problem, especially if they reside in inner-city ghettos. Here, they live in a subculture that labors under an extraordinarily pessimistic vision of future opportunities. Such pessimism is well-founded—over the last few decades, the possibilities for escaping poverty have become increasingly remote. Historian Michael Katz attributes this decrease in opportunities to vast changes in the socioeconomic environment:

> *Deindustrialization and depopulation, not growth, shape the new context. Very few opportunities exist for industrial work. Government jobs, one avenue toward economic security and mobility for African Americans,*

*have shrunk. For the most part, new jobs in the service
sector divide into those which pay well but demand more
education than most minorities acquire and those which
offer part-time, nonunion work that pays badly. The
value of public benefits directed exclusively to poor
people has eroded, many programs have been scaled
back or cut, and the construction of public housing
almost ceased during the 1980's. . . . Poverty now
increasingly exists within a context of hopelessness.*[61]

Recognizing that they are unlikely to cash in on the American Dream through conventional means does nothing to diminish the fervor with which members of the underclass want to share in that dream.[62] In fact, researchers have discovered that people in the lowest socioeconomic classes are particularly likely to set their sights on achieving financial success.[63] When they recognize that large obstacles stand in the way of achieving their goals, however, they may conclude that members of their group have been unfairly disenfranchised by the larger society.[64] The perception that they have been wrongfully cut out of the American Dream may foster a pervasive sense of alienation from, and bitterness toward, the larger society.[65] These feelings, combined with the legacy of self-doubt resulting from years of oppression, may place the poor in a vicious self-trap consisting of resentment against their oppressors but worry that they might not be good enough to succeed if barriers to their success were removed.

Convinced that conventional pathways to the American Dream are closed off and eager to retaliate against those who have closed them off, some may turn to crime. The appeal of this pathway is twofold. First, violating laws becomes a way of striking back at those who have written the laws (that is, the dominant society), and criminals become heroes struggling against the forces of evil. Second, because some crimes (such as dealing drugs and theft) can be profitable, they hold out the possibility of a quick and easy shortcut to the fruits of the American Dream. For the poor, then, crime may represent an understandable—and, in a limited sense, adaptive—strategy for attaining self-esteem.

Sociologist Howard Kaplan and his colleagues have reported research related to this possibility. They followed nearly 2000 low-income junior high school students over time. They discovered that students who did poorly in school attempted to compensate for their resulting negative self-views by decreasing their investment in school and becoming increasingly deviant (for example, by exhibiting antisocial tendencies). Their increased deviance predicted poor school performance later on, which fueled further feelings of rejection, greater disposition to deviance, further failure, and so on.[66]

Other researchers have shown that deviance may actually increase the self-esteem of low-income boys. In a study of tenth-grade adolescent boys, Morris Rosenberg and his colleagues found that the more juvenile delinquency the boys reported engaging in at one point in time, the more their self-esteem had *increased* two years later. This relationship held only for lower class boys; those from the higher socioeconomic classes derived no self-esteem benefits from deviant behavior.[67]

This analysis suggests that if social planners had consciously decided to engineer crime-ridden environments, they could hardly have done better than to construct the inner-city ghetto. And it is not just members of the underclass who suffer from this state of affairs. In increasingly noticeable ways, the dire conditions that have long plagued the poor are diminishing the quality of life enjoyed by the entire society, including the privileged. For example, many of those who can afford to do so have sought refuge in suburbia, venturing into the cities only with trepidation. Fearful that they are unsafe even in the suburbs, some of the wealthy have hunkered down in "enclaves"—entire communities that are encircled by fences and thick walls. Ensconced in these fortresslike communities, the wealthy command battalions of private security guards to protect them, their homes, and their children, which helps to explain why America now employs more private security guards than police officers.[68] The feelings of vulnerability that inspire such living arrangements surely erode people's self-confidence in a fundamental way, for the inability to move about in our environment without experiencing fear fosters a nagging feeling of powerlessness and ineptitude.

Although the social, economic, and psychological forces that have given rise to America's fortress society are complex, the decline of community participation and the accompanying rise of self-centeredness have made important contributions to it. From the time we are young children, we learn that we stand alone, that we each should be masters of our own destiny. As a result, when we see that others are in trouble, we assume that it is their fault; perhaps it is even in their genes. In contrast, less individualistic people (from both the United States and other countries) are more likely to attribute such behavior to the constraining role of social circumstances.[69]

To the extent that the world appears just and opportunities for advancement seem available, when individuals come up short, a ready conclusion is that they deserve their lot. Researchers have shown that the belief in a just world is so widespread that people blame victims of misfortune even when their fate is clearly beyond their control.[70]

The belief in a just world works with individualism to provide the members of the majority with moral justification for working to gratify their own individual desires while ignoring the plight of the less fortunate. In this respect, individualism fails as a social ethic, because rather than binding people together, it thrusts people into competition: men against men; women against women, employee against employee; race against race; and social class against social class. The result is a chaos of competing interests, in which everyone demands the right to pursue competence and self-worth but refuses to support the efforts of others to do the same thing. The impoverished surely suffer the most from this arrangement, because they are trapped between a desire for conventional forms of competence and a conviction that this goal is beyond their grasp. Yet even the well-to-do may discover that the feelings of competence their wealth and status affords them are compromised by feelings of vulnerability growing out of the recognition that they fear for their lives in the "just" world they have helped construct. In this world of multilayered self-traps, it is not only the impoverished who are diminished; it is all of us.

7 RAISING SELF-ESTEEM

> *But first I must tell you*
> *That I should really like to think there's something wrong*
>   *with me—*
> *Because, if there isn't, then there's something wrong,*
> *Or at least, very different from what it seemed to be,*
> *With the world itself—and that's much more frightening!*
> *That would be terrible. So I'd rather believe*
> *There is something wrong with me, that could be put right.*
> *I'd do anything you told me, to get back to normality.*

—T. S. Eliot[1]

The tortured ponderings of Celia, the protagonist in T. S. Eliot's *The Cocktail Party,* capture the instinctive reaction of people with negative self-views to adversity. When something goes awry, they automatically look inside in the expectation of finding something amiss with themselves.

Yet because self-knowledge generally emerges from, and is sustained by, our experiences with others, negative self-views have interpersonal as well as personal components. This means that for people to enjoy improvements in their self-views, changes must occur not only in the way they think about themselves but also in the environments that sustain their self-views. Simply put, to enjoy higher self-esteem, changes must occur on the outside, in the social environment, as well as inside, in people's hearts and minds.

Both aspects of changes in self-concept are brilliantly illustrated in Elia Kazan's novel *The Arrangement.*[2] Eddie Anderson, the protagonist, takes up with a mistress who, after gaining his respect, launches a devastating attack on his self-views. The attack leads him to recognize that he despises the identity he has managed to "choke down" throughout his adult life (he is an advertising man charged with marketing "clean" cigarettes"). This recognition triggers a chain of events that eventually results in a "new Eddie" who rejects his sleazy self of the past. Some of these events occur in Eddie's head; he spends several months in a mental hospital rethinking who he is, who he wants to be, and what he needs to do to become this new person. Equally important, however, are the subsequent changes Eddie makes in his social environment: he demolishes his old social environment by divorcing his wife, quitting his job, and dumping his business associates. He then constructs a completely new environment that includes a different wife, career, friends, and acquaintances. Only after Eddie has "switched worlds" is the process of change complete.

Although Eddie's dramatic transformation was extreme, it is typical of most changes in self-views in that it involved both internal and external processes. In what follows, I discuss some of the most important of the obstacles that must be overcome for self-views to change.

Dodging Disintegration Anxiety

When people who have spent many years thinking of themselves in a particular way attempt a new self-definition, they may experience the feeling of falling apart that Heinz Kohut called disintegration anxiety. As an obstacle to change in self-views, the fear of disintegration should not be underestimated. In fact, many people go to their graves with low self-esteem simply because they were suffused with anxiety every time they imagined a better self.[3] Gloria Steinem has written insightfully about this phenomenon:

> *Change, no matter how much for the better, still feels cold and lonely at first—as if we were out there on the edge of the universe with wind whistling past our ears—because it doesn't feel like home. Old patterns, no matter how negative and painful they may be, have an incredible magnetic power—because they do feel like home.[4]*

This affinity for familiar identities may even cause victims of horrific experiences to cling to identities that are extremely negative. Consider, for example, the ambivalence of this former victim of sexual abuse as she contemplated recovery:

> There were a lot of positive things about those negative aspects of my personality. And I didn't want to give them up. Maybe it wasn't the best way of coping, but at least I was used to it. I felt incredibly vulnerable having to let go in order to make the room to create a new person. In what void would I be thrown if I let go of this stuff? I felt like a raw muscle walking around for a long time.[5]

Such accounts raise a troubling question: How can one discourage people from worrying that their old self is falling apart when, in a sense, it is? One possibility is to recognize that people are usually more complex than they appear on the surface. People with low self-esteem invariably possess positive as well as negative self-views, and, on some level at least, they desire confirmation of these self-views. This raises the possibility of encouraging people to think of change in terms of the awakening of some latent self-views that already exist rather than in terms of the loss of old ones. Trained therapists can be especially effective in convincing people to see changes in self-views in this way, but anyone who is sensitive and motivated can fill the bill.

Oliver Sacks's account of a man named Ray illustrates this point. Ray suffered from a neurological disorder called Tourette's syndrome. When Ray came in for treatment, Sacks noted that he was

> almost incapacitated by multiple tics of extreme violence coming in volleys every few seconds. . . . Since leaving college . . . he had been fired from a dozen jobs—always because of his tics, never for incompetence—was continually in crises of one sort and another . . . and had found his marriage threatened by involuntary cries of "Fuck!" "Shit!", and so on, which would burst from him at times of sexual excitement.[6]

Sacks began treating Ray with Haldol. Unfortunately, the drug impaired Ray's sense of timing so much that he got caught in a revolving door, and Sacks halted the Haldol treatments. Discouraged, Ray began to question whether he even wanted to be free of tics: "'Suppose you *could* take away the tics,' he said. 'What would be left?'"[7]

Recognizing that Ray's problems were in large part psychological, Sacks initiated intensive weekly therapy sessions. During the sessions, he encouraged Ray to consider how freedom from Tourette's would enable him to live out many of his dreams: he would be able to maintain steady employment, he would be socially accepted, and he could enjoy many activities that had always been off limits.[8] Sacks thus enjoined Ray to see that the Haldol would enable him to explore dormant aspects of his personality. After three months of these sessions, Sacks reinitiated the Haldol treatment. This time it worked; Ray was free of tics and suffered no side effects he could not manage. Thereafter, he resumed a steady job, enjoyed a stable marriage, and even became a father.[9]

Researchers have discovered that confirming some self-views can indeed make people more receptive to information that challenges other self-views. Psychologists Stephen Finn and Mary Tonsager, for example, were successful in raising the self-esteem of patients seeking therapy if they provided these patients with a mix of self-confirming and favorable evaluations. Interestingly, this mixture bolstered self-esteem despite the fact that some of the self-confirming evaluations were decidedly negative (for example, patients were told that they were depressed, thought disordered, angry, obsessional).[10] Apparently, such critical but confirming evaluations not only bolster the credibility of the therapist but also create a psychological "secure base" that enables people to accommodate positive evaluations that would otherwise be rejected out of hand.

Of course, enabling people to overcome their fear of change does not ensure that they will sustain new self-views. As long as people see their old, negative self-views as plausible, they will give heavy weight to evaluations that confirm these self-views. Insofar as they pay more attention to self-confirming evaluations, remember them better, and interpret them selectively, people's self-views will remain stubbornly resistant to change.

One way to circumvent these systematic biases is to refrain from trying to change a person's self-views and instead encourage people with low self-esteem to place more weight on their strengths and less on their weaknesses. Some types of psychotherapy are specifically designed to help people restructure the interpretations they give to their presumed deficiencies.

Of the talk therapies, cognitive therapy, cognitive-behavioral therapy, and interpersonal therapies have the strongest track record for reducing the symptoms of people who are depressed.[11]

A major shortcoming of all of these approaches, however, is that there is no evidence that any of them, by themselves, produce long-term improvements in self-esteem.[12] In fact, one of the greatest difficulties in treating depression is the high rate of relapse. When therapists place their patients on anti-depressant drugs to treat depression, they often recommend that the patients remain on the drugs for three years or more. This makes sense, because the longer patients remain on drugs, the more likely it is that the external sources of distress that inspired their depression and low self-esteem will have disappeared.[13] Of the many such sources of distress, the be-havior of the patients' lovers and close friends may be the most significant.

Interpersonal Impediments to Change

Psychologist Julian Hafner has studied the ways in which peo-ple's partners may block improvements in their self-views and related beliefs. Hafner has focused on agoraphobia, a condi-tion that is particularly common among women. Taken from the Greek term meaning "fear of the marketplace," agorapho-bia refers to apprehension triggered by being in public places. Victims of this affliction are deathly afraid of what may hap-pen to them in so many places (restaurants, sports arenas, airports, shopping malls, and so forth) that they sometimes refuse to leave their homes.[14]

Although agoraphobia can be treated successfully, during the early phases of therapy husbands are often reluctant to al-ter their own behaviors and self-views to accommodate the change in their partners. Often, the reasons for the husband's reticence are obvious. Some husbands are threatened because their wives' recoveries allow them to take jobs outside the home and thus strip the man of the exclusive-breadwinner role. In other cases, as their symptoms decrease, wives be-came increasingly interested in sex, which may, in turn, cause further difficulties:

One husband developed premature ejaculation, another became depressed and concurrently impotent, and four became abnormally jealous of their wives, seemingly projecting their denied libidinal problems onto them. Several husbands developed fears of abandonment by wives who had become more assertive and independent; before treatment the husbands' dependency problems had been obscured by the patients' agoraphobia and their consequent dependency on their husbands. Once both partners became aware of the husbands' personal difficulties, the [wives] became able to take more responsibility for their own problems.[15]

If people attempting to overcome low self-esteem encounter resistance from their partners when they strive to elicit more favorable reactions from them, they have several options. Because many partners are simply unaware of the impact they have on each other,[16] sometimes raising their awareness is enough to convince them to change their behaviors. Alternatively, people can seek training in how to get their partners to recognize and meet their needs. Assertiveness training may be especially effective in this regard. Such training is sometimes used as part of interpersonal therapy, a technique that focuses on improving the way that patients relate to others.[17]

This discussion suggests an important corollary of Mark Twain's adage, "A man cannot be comfortable without his own approval."[18] To be comfortable with themselves, people must be concerned not only with gaining *their own* approval but also with winning the approval and support of their interaction partners, including friends, coworkers, lovers, relatives, and so on. People will be able to sustain improvements in their self-views over the long run only if they focus on environmental as well as internal self-traps. This task can be daunting, because people's social environments are often extraordinarily complex and multifaceted. This is one of the many reasons that it is best to avoid forming strong negative self-views in the first place. One important way to understand how to avoid doing so is to examine child-rearing practices closely.

The Importance of Positive and Responsive Caregivers

As John Bowlby put it, no experiences have more far-reaching effects on a child's emerging sense of self than

> *his experiences with his family: for, starting during his first months in his relation with both parents, he builds up working models of how attachment figures are likely to behave towards him in any of a variety of situations, and on those models are based all his expectations, and therefore all his plans, for the rest of his life.*[19]

Bowlby's attachment theory specifies how caregivers can foster a sense of self-worth in children. Specifically, caregivers who are both positive and sensitive to their children will maximize the positivity of the children's self-views. This prescription sometimes seems counterintuitive to caregivers who believe that the best way to foster independence is to give children a minimum of support and encouragement. German child psychologist Klaus Grossmann notes that, paradoxically, attempting to foster independence by being cool and aloof can have precisely the opposite of the effect intended:

> *We fight the notion that crying doesn't matter, that it strengthens the lungs. We fight the notion that independence has to be trained, or that you must punish a child by withdrawal of availability or love. We've explained over and over again that those children who get the most sensitive responsiveness on the part of the mothers are the ones who will be least clinging.*[20]

Parents sometimes counter such exhortations with reactions like these: "You want me to be sensitive and gentle to that little tyrant? He's driving me crazy—he cries all the time and nothing I do makes him stop." Although some children are born with relatively difficult temperaments, the results of van den Boom's research summarized in Chapter 4 challenge the notion that certain types of children inevitably develop into "holy terrors." On the contrary, van den Boom discovered that brief training sessions enabled most mothers to avert the difficulties commonly encountered with temperamentally irritable children.[21] Thus, even though a difficult temperament may launch some children along life trajectories rife with negative feedback, parents who are attuned to their children's idiosyncratic needs can respond in ways that change those trajectories and save such children from low self-esteem.

Of course, not all children are lucky enough to find themselves in the hands of caregivers who are able and willing to meet their individual needs. Tragically, such children may attempt to compensate by developing strategies for enhancing self-esteem that are counterproductive. For example, some children may compensate for their experiences with a harsh caregiver, sibling, or teacher by attempting to convince themselves and others that they are actually better than everyone else. The narcissistic self-views of such children are typically far too positive to sustain easily, and often children end up frantically attempting to evoke praise and reassurance from others. When such reactions are not forthcoming, the children may escalate their attempts by adopting more coercive tactics. These tactics will often backfire; instead of winning the adulation of the people around them, they win scorn and derision. Such reactions will reinforce their self-doubts, prompting them to intensify further their attempts to acquire confirmation for their grandiose but fragile self-views.

As difficult as it may be to break such cycles, the case study of four-year-old Joey suggests that it can be done. The child of a rejecting mother, Joey had developed a knack for alienating people. In fact, his talent was so well-honed that he managed to alienate nearly the entire staff of his preschool in Minneapolis. According to one observer, Joey's

> acts of hostile aggression toward weaker children, his devious behavior, and his blunt, matter-of-fact noncompliance ('No way, Jose!') infuriated the teachers. . . . [Furthermore] his malicious, antisocial behavior, his apparent pleasure at others' distress, and his fearless contesting of wills with the teachers had all the marks of incipient sociopathy. His elaborate deviousness and his swaggering style seemed to confirm that he was beyond reach.[22]

Luckily, one man at the preschool saw in Joey not an incipient sociopath but a needy child, desperate for warmth and affection. He prevailed upon the teachers to be patient with Joey no matter what. All punishment ceased. If Joey's misconduct forced teachers to separate him from the other children, one of the teachers remained with him. Within an astonishingly brief period, Joey began to mellow:

> *Having difficulty confirming his image of himself as bad, and being totally unable to confirm the belief that he was unworthy, Joey had little choice but to change his behavior. He formed a strong attachment to a male teacher and made remarkable progress toward learning how to meet his basic needs for closeness, as well as toward learning the rewards that may be found in relationships.*[23]

Like van den Boom's research with temperamentally difficult children, Joey's story illustrates that many so-called hopeless cases are hopeless only if their caregivers lack the knowledge, resources, and motivation to recognize and respond to their needs. And even if children do develop negative self-views, recent evidence suggests that it may be possible to ward off depression and associated feelings of low self-esteem by teaching them to identify and remedy patterns of thinking and behaving that are known to be associated with depression.[24] Timing may be crucial: Susan Harter at the University of Denver suggests that self-esteem improvements are likely when children are reached while still relatively young and before their self-views become too negative.[25]

Left untreated, low self-esteem may remain low even if people struggle to improve it. One reason that older children and adults may have so much difficulty recovering from low self-esteem is that our cultural beliefs encourage us to emphasize one major component of self-esteem at the expense of the other. Whereas some of us pursue lovability by emphasizing intimate relationships at the expense of work, others pursue competence by emphasizing work at the expense of relationships. Either imbalance leaves us with a vulnerable and incomplete sense of self-esteem. And even if people strive for a balanced sense of self-worth, they may use specific strategies that are self-defeating.

Rethinking Love

To an unprecedented degree, contemporary Americans are convinced that romantic love should serve as the basis for marriage. Anthropologist Ralph Linton has commented:

Most societies are less keen on romance than on congeniality. They train their young people to believe that any well-bred boy or girl, once married, will be able to live together contentedly and will in time develop a real fondness for one another. In most cases this seems to be correct.[26]

Unfortunately, as discussed in Chapter 5, America's love affair with romance has taken a toll on modern marriages. The solution? One possibility is to acknowledge the legitimacy of a form of love that is currently out of vogue. *Companionate love* refers to the deep affection people feel for those whose values, goals, and fates they share. Marked by feelings of warmth, mutual understanding, and concern for the welfare of the partner, it grows naturally out of an ongoing relationship. As such, it is based on recognizing and accepting partners rather than idealizing them and attempting to win them.

Because companionate love is not necessarily accompanied by the intense feelings of passionate love, some people have been tempted to conclude that it is "unemotional" and therefore not "true" love. Psychologist Ellen Berscheid explains that this critique misses an important point: companionate love *is* heavily laden with emotion; it is just that people aren't as aware of their emotional investment and do not consciously recognize it.[27] Consider, for example, the intense distress that people experience when a long-term companionate love relationship ends with the death of one spouse—despite the fact that the partner may not have elicited any *passionate* feelings for years.

Perhaps the most compelling evidence for the viability of companionate love comes from a comparison of the fate of arranged marriages and those based on romantic love. Researchers asked 50 couples in India who had been married for varying periods of time to complete a scale designed to measure their affection for each other. Not surprisingly, newlyweds in romantic love marriages reported more love than those in arranged marriages. In older relationships, however, the reverse was true: those in arranged marriages reported considerably more love than those in romantic marriages.[28]

Although such findings suggest that companionate love may be a better predictor of relationship quality than romantic love, companionate love alone will seldom be enough to sustain most healthy marriages. As Helen Fisher and others have pointed out, sexual attraction and passionate involvements hold enormous appeal for humans of all cultures and epochs.[29] The ideal marriage partner, then, may be a "passionate companion."

People with negative self-views may be particularly apt to benefit from relationships characterized by companionate love. Because passionate companions tend to view each other as partners working together to meet life's challenges rather than as trophies won during the dating game, they will value their partners and recognize them as good people even as they acknowledge their ostensible shortcomings, including low self-esteem. In such warm and accepting environments, the self-views of people with low self-esteem may gradually improve.

Self-Esteem and the Pursuit of Competence

The American Dream impresses upon our children how lucky they are to have been born in America, for here they can pursue boundless wealth, fame, status, and related markers of competence. Many quickly become convinced that the essence of life is a quest for these markers and that the more they acquire, the higher their self-esteem will soar.

Unfortunately, the American Dream may all too often become the American nightmare. One problem is that people who set their sights on the acquisition of markers of competence typically come to see their work as a means to an end rather than a gratifying end in itself. A partial solution to this problem is to increase the possibilities for fulfilling work. Recent experimentation suggests that work can be restructured in ways that improve morale, raise self-esteem, *and* boost or maintain productivity. One such success story is Chaparral Steel, a steel mill in Medlothian, Texas. Since it began operation in 1975, Chaparral has been producing steel at a breakneck pace, setting a new world record in 1982 for tonnage produced in a month by a single electric furnace–continuous casting combination. In 1990, its productivity of

1.5 worker-hours per rolled ton of steel greatly surpassed the U.S average of 5.3 worker-hours, as well as the Japanese and German averages of 5.6 and 5.7 worker-hours, respectively.

A key to Chaparral's success has been its effort to empower workers by making them feel personally responsible for solving problems and allowing them to share in the rewards of increased productivity. Workers responded to this arrangement by developing a feeling of pride and ownership. One operator said, "The more money the company makes, the more money I make. The profit-sharing system creates built-in pride." Another stated that "I feel like this company partly belongs to me. Owning part of the company makes you care. I take better care not to waste anything because I feel like I'm paying for it."[30] Such comments show that work can be a source of fulfillment and self-esteem rather than alienation and a diminished sense of self-worth.

Another effective strategy for increasing worker satisfaction is to organize workers into teams rather than have them compete with one another. Experiments in Scandinavia indicate that banishing one of the sacred cows of the industrial revolution—the assembly line—can make people much happier with their jobs while still maintaining high levels of productivity. One experiment was begun in 1969 at the Saab-Scania engine plant in Sweden. Both management and the trade unions supported the experiment: management wanted to lower the 70 percent annual turnover rate; the unions wanted workers to have more autonomy and control over their work. Together, they hatched a plan to institute a radically different approach to engine assembly. They organized workers into semiautonomous groups, each composed of about 10 workers. In addition, they allowed workers to pace themselves. Finally, they permitted the members of each group to see the assembly process through to completion rather than glimpsing only a small portion of the task. This new arrangement not only allowed workers to retain the high levels of productivity established before the reorganization but also made the work far more satisfying to them.[31]

A separate problem caused by the American Dream is that contemporary Americans are working such long hours that they have little time to cultivate the relationships they count on for self-confirmation. In *The Overworked American,* Juliet Schor suggests some ways to get out of this self-trap. To counter the tendency of employers to goad salaried workers into working excessive hours, she suggests that all firms be required to set some standard schedule of hours for salaried jobs. If workers exceed the number of hours they are contracted to work, they should be paid for them. Of course, workers who are intent upon advancing their careers may forgo vacations and refrain from claiming extra hours in the hope of getting ahead. Although such instances will inevitably occur in today's highly competitive work environments, clearly defined expectations about working hours would at least provide a mechanism for keeping employers honest. And as more people become weary of life on the work-and-spend treadmill, they may hold employers to these limits.

Schor advances other suggestions that are worth considering: reimbursing overtime work with time rather than money; making part-time work more feasible by giving part-time workers benefits prorated by their hours of work; and allowing workers to give up future income for time off. She also applauds efforts to equalize the division of labor within the family. These efforts, she believes, are essential to making the workplace more responsive to the needs of parents, because as men take on more responsibilities at home, they will add their voices to the chorus demanding that employers accommodate the needs of working caregivers.

Many of these solutions could result in a reversal of the current trend toward longer working hours. To those who worry about the ability of the U.S. economy to compete with the economies of Japan, Germany, and other countries, Schor points out that competitiveness in international markets is determined more by productivity than by time spent working and adds that these two variables are not as closely linked as is commonly assumed. On the contrary, shorter work hours can actually increase productivity by making workers feel fresher, more vigorous, and more enthusiastic.[32]

If there is an obvious limitation to Schor's advice, it is that her recommendations speak only to the work arrangements of those who have stable, well-paying jobs. Those who do not must contemplate more basic issues, such as where to find the next meal.

Poverty and Competence

Like all Americans, members of the underclass are socialized to see status, wealth, and material goods as markers of competence. Yet they learn quickly that their chances for these attainments are slim, and they may abandon attempts to succeed.

Of the many recent reactions to this problem, one that has gained considerable popularity assumes that government assistance has backfired by making the poor lazy and complacent. A straightforward solution springs from this conclusion: cut government programs designed to assist the poor. Yet this solution is predicated on the mistaken assumption that government funding has intensified the problems of the poor by removing their motivation to work. Urban historian Michael Katz questions this analysis:

> *President Ronald Reagan once said that America fought a war on poverty and that poverty won. His statement misrepresented history. For one thing, it ignored the very real achievements of the federal government, such as cutting poverty among the elderly by two-thirds, expanding the supply of public housing, improving nutrition, and increasing medical assistance to poor people. For another, it implied the impotence of the federal government and cast doubts on its competence. . . . The federal government remains potentially the most powerful weapon in the anti-poverty arsenal.[33]*

Katz buttresses this conclusion by noting that the programs associated with the War on Poverty and the Great Society during the 1960s and 1970s were, in reality, very successful, reducing poverty among fully employed African Americans from 43 percent to 16 percent. Furthermore, when critics of welfare have succeeded in cutting public assistance programs, the economic and social benefits that they predicted have failed to materialize. For instance, the campaign against general assistance that swept through the country during the 1980s and 1990s increased destitution and suffering but did not save public funds or reduce unemployment.[34]

A concern that the government has made life too easy for the poor has also fueled recent attacks on affirmative action.

Many of the loudest complaints have been voiced by members of the upper class, a group that has enjoyed a long history of favoring its own. Unlike affirmative action programs, however, the forms of favoritism that have benefited the upper class are difficult to document or quantify. For example, those who are charged with the task of hiring new employees may consciously or unconsciously favor people of a similar gender or race because they "feel more comfortable" with similar others. Other forms of favoritism are discreetly hidden from public view. One example is the system of rigging university entrance policies so that children of alumni, or "legacies," are more likely to gain admission. At Yale, for example, legacies are two and a half times more likely to be accepted than other applicants with similar test scores; at Harvard the bias is even greater. One result of this practice is that the test scores of legacies are noticeably lower than the average score of all students admitted.[35] When one considers the combined effect of these programs, together with sources of bias such as the "comfort factor" in hiring decisions just mentioned, complaints about the fairness of affirmative action programs from members of the upper class sound hypocritical.

This is not to say that affirmative action programs are a perfect way to correct current inequities. Whether or not such programs actually *are* unjust, if they are *perceived* as unjust they will contribute to race or class tension. In addition, these programs seem to represent a mixed blessing for their intended beneficiaries. By reinforcing social stereotypes about the alleged shortcomings of minorities and women, affirmative action programs may contribute to the perceived incompetence of members of these groups. This may damage their self-views, encourage them to withdraw effort, and diminish job satisfaction.[36] In response to such problems, some people have advocated reducing the visibility of affirmative action programs, as has been done with special admission polices for legacies. Others have argued for the elimination of affirmative action programs based on race or gender in favor of programs based on monetary status. Although this arrangement might further stigmatize the poor, programs designed to raise people out of poverty can, in principle, allow their beneficiaries to improve their economic status.

Surmounting poverty is important, not only in the obvious ways linked to physical survival, but also in hundreds of subtle ways linked to psychological survival and self-esteem. Psychologist Joelle Sander writes:

Living in poverty strongly adds to many children's feelings of deprivation, disadvantage, degradation; to their need to get out of their homes; to their overall sense of instability. It often exacerbates their fantasies of the perfect family, a family which in their mind cancels out the hardships of their family of origin.[37]

Unfortunately, children may compensate for such feelings of deprivation by seeking to establish meaning and self-worth through early parenthood, well before they are economically or psychologically prepared to do so. This results in degraded home environments in which parents are no better equipped to prepare children to deal with adult responsibilities than *their* parents were, thus perpetuating a cycle.

Although the behavior of caregivers represents an important first step in the development of children, it would be naive to think that the problems of poverty are located exclusively in faulty home environments. Even if caregivers perform their role in an exemplary manner, this by no means guarantees that children will develop into happy, productive adults. In schools, for example, children may encounter teachers who are skeptical of their ability and motivation to learn. Instead of challenging them with difficult problems, such teachers may encourage them to recite hollow affirmations or give them easy problems to "build their self-esteem." In their communities, children may be forced to choose among spending their free time wandering aimlessly around the neighborhood, joining a gang, or remaining in relatively unstimulating home environments.

It doesn't have to be this way. Schools could return to demanding curricula that foster a sense of competence by encouraging children to overcome real challenges. Steps could also be taken at the grass-roots level to remedy some of the problems with decaying inner-city environments. In their study of youth organizations across the United States, Shirley Brice Heath and Milbrey McLaughlin identified some organizations that do provide environments for children that not only are safe and challenging but also provide informal guidance from attentive adults.[38] According to Heath and McLaughlin, YMCAs, community basketball leagues and other athletic associations, boys and girls clubs, and other organizations are the "greatest untold story in America." Most important, these organizations increase the physical survival rates of children who frequent them, by keeping them off the streets where they may fall victim to gang members who often prey upon unaffiliated youth. For some children, these organizations may also provide havens from home environments that are every bit as treacherous as life on the street.

Yet community organizations do much more than merely ensure physical survival. William Damon suggests that by requiring children to conform to strict codes of behavior, the organizations give them a predictable and supportive structure within which to grow and develop.[39]

Despite the effectiveness of community organizations, they are chronically underfunded and are thus limited in their ability to offset the effects of the harsh environments that have emerged throughout contemporary America. Those who have recognized this fact or who have encountered similarly daunting difficulties have searched widely for solutions to their problems. Many have turned to the self-esteem movement. As we saw in Chapter 1, however, the self-esteem movement has failed to deliver on its extravagant promises.

If the Quest for Self-Esteem Is So Elusive, Why Do We Embark on It?

In her wry commentary on the recovery movement (that is, recovery from alcoholism, drug addiction, sex addiction, and so forth), writer Wendy Kaminer lambasted nonexpert advice-givers whose only claim to expertise is having made a shambles of their own lives.[40] While doing so, she was careful to emphasize that she herself was not an expert advice-giver. She was thus dumbfounded when people later asked her for advice about how to heal themselves, as this cast her into precisely the role that she had criticized others for assuming. The experience left her wondering why people search in the most unlikely places for solutions to their problems of living.[41]

A similar criticism could be made of the self-esteem movement, which relies on many of the same techniques as the recovery movement, such as the use of affirmations. Given the lack of scientific evidence showing that such procedures raise self-esteem, you might think that people would quickly give them up. Yet this hasn't happened. Why?

First, some of the strategies used by the leaders of the self-esteem movement may bring short-term relief from depression. For example, in his book *Ten Days to Self-Esteem,* David Burns promotes the techniques of cognitive therapy that are known to be effective in alleviating depression.[42] Although it is by no means established that reading self-help books will alleviate depression, if reading such books does give temporary relief, people might mistake an improvement in mood or outlook for a prelude to long-term gains in self-esteem.[43]

A second, and perhaps more important, reason that people turn to the self-esteem movement for help is that many contemporary Americans are desperate to find remedies for the real social and personal problems that plague them. These problems have reached epidemic proportions at every level of society. For example, personal psychopathology is escalating (rates of depression are 10 times higher today than they were in the days of our grandparents),[44] the divorce rate has reached astonishingly high levels, the unemployment rate is increasing, and the gap between the underclass and the overclass is widening. In the face of these problems, many Americans have become desperate for a solution, *any* solution.[45]

The California task force and other representatives of the self-esteem movement have responded to this heartfelt need by compressing a large number of these daunting difficulties— from drug addiction to welfare dependency to dropping out of high school—into the relatively compact problem of low self-esteem. By proclaiming that solving these complex problems is as easy as asserting that "I am lovable and capable," the self-esteem movement has told us precisely what we wanted to hear. Yet in doing so it overlooks the fact that self-traps are intricately woven into the fabric of people's lives and involve not only qualities of people themselves but also qualities of their relationship partners and the larger society. When the full scope of self-traps is recognized, it becomes obvious that the self-esteem movement has vastly underestimated the subtlety and complexity of the solutions they require. Merely recognizing self-traps for what they are will not, in itself, allow us to avoid or escape them. It is, however, a beginning.

NOTES

Chapter 1: The Holy Grail of Self-Esteem

1. The author of this letter was inspired to write to me by a special segment on medicine that her local news station was running on my research into relationships and low self-esteem. Here and throughout the book, I have changed the names of people I describe to protect their identities.

2. W. Damon (1995). *Greater Expectations: Overcoming the Culture of Indulgence in America's Homes and Schools*. New York: The Free Press. L. Williams (1990). Using self-esteem to fix society's ills. *New York Times* (March 26):C1. A schoolteacher recently told me that the school counselor had advised her not to ask difficult questions of students whom she had diagnosed as having low self-esteem. The teacher was exasperated. How could she find out how much the student knew without asking him or her?

3. For examples, see M. McKay and P. Fanning (1992). *Self-Esteem*. Oakland, Calif.: Harbinger Publications. D. D. Burns (1993). *Ten Days to Self-Esteem*. New York: Quill William Morrow.

4. N. Branden (1994). *Six Pillars of Self-Esteem*. New York: Bantam, 95.

5. Branden (1994). Branden occasionally acknowledges that such claims are extravagant, noting that "self-esteem is not an all-purpose panacea" and that "a well developed sense of self is a necessary condition of our well-being but not a sufficient

condition." See pp. *xv* and 21. This vacillation between thoughtful remarks and extravagant claims characterizes much of the volume.

6. State of California, Assembly Bill No. 3659, Chapter 1065. Approved by the governor, September 23, 1986.

7. B. Krier (1987). The quest for self-esteem. *Los Angeles Times* (June 14) (part IV):11.

8. Damon (1995).

9. J. Adler (1992). Hey I'm terrific! *Newsweek* (Feb. 17):46–51. For a more general indictment of the self-help and recovery program industry, see W. Kaminer (1993). *I'm Dysfunctional, You're Dysfunctional: The Recovery Movement and Other Self-Help Fashions.* New York: Addison-Wesley. There are substantial links between the recovery movement and the self-esteem movement. For example, both movements explicitly or implicitly assume that low self-esteem resulting from early experiences is a major source of difficulty, and both rely heavily on reciting affirmations as a means of improvement. In addition, although the vast majority of programs associated with these movements have little or no scientific evidence to support their effectiveness, they adamantly assert that they do. For example, when I called the central branch of the National Self-Esteem Council in Santa Cruz, California, I asked the woman who answered the phone if she knew of any scientific evidence that supported the efficacy of self-esteem enhancement programs. She replied by asking if I was a member of the National Self-Esteem Council. When I indicated that I was not, she made it clear that our conversation would soon be over if I did not agree to pay the $35 membership fee. Eventually I assented, and she then triumphantly informed me that as soon as she received my $35, she would send me a complete bibliography of studies supporting the efficacy of self-esteem programs. When the document arrived, however, I was disappointed to learn that I had been hoodwinked. It was not that I thought the studies listed were flawed—some of *my own work* was listed in the bibliography—it was that few if any of the studies had anything to do with changing self-esteem, and none presented convincing evidence for the efficacy of programs inspired by the self-esteem movement.

10. A. M. Mecca, N. J. Smelser, and J. Vasconcellos, eds. (1989). *The Social Importance of Self-Esteem.* Berkeley: University of California Press.

11. In fairness, I should note that some self-esteem programs offer more than simple affirmations. For example, the Phoenix Self-Esteem program also includes exercises designed to clarify values, increase self-responsibility, decrease delinquency, and address other problems that they assume to be caused by self-esteem deficits.

12. All indices of self-esteem are inherently relative. The statement that at least a quarter of Americans possess low self-esteem is based on evidence (some of which will be described later in this book) indicating that this proportion of people behave in ways that most people would take as evidence of low self-esteem. Also, although there is evidence that self-esteem plays a role in the onset of depression, the precise role that it plays remains controversial. For a useful discussion, see H. Tennen and G. Affleck (1993). The puzzles of low self-esteem: A clinical perspective. In R. Baumeister, ed. *Self-Esteem: The Puzzle of Low Self-Regard.* New York: Plenum. For studies of the links between self-esteem and depression, see S. Arieti and J. Bemporad (1980). The psychological organization of depression.*American Journal of Psychiatry* 137:1360–1365. A. C. Butler, J. E. Hokanson, and H. A. Flynn. (1994). A comparison of self-esteem lability and low trait self-esteem as vulnerability factors for depression. *Journal of Personality and Social Psychology* 66:166–177. For studies of the relationship between self-esteem and life satisfaction, see E. Diener (1984). Subjective well-being. *Psychological Bulletin* 95:542–575.

13. For evidence that self-esteem is not associated with various specific behaviors, see R. Wylie (1979). *The Self Concept.* Lincoln: University of Nebraska Press. See also Mecca, Smelser, and Vasconcellos (1989). J. Hattie (1992). *Self-Concept.* Hillsdale, N.J.: Erlbaum. H. W. Marsh (1992). The content analysis specificity of relations between academic achievement and academic self-concept. *Journal of Educational Psychology* 84:34–42.

14. I am using the term *self-view* as a catchall to refer to all thoughts and feelings about the self, including those pertaining

to self-esteem and various specific self-concepts such as those associated with intelligence, athletic ability, and so forth. I recognize that useful distinctions can be made between these terms, and will refer to them later in the book.

15. P. D. Kramer (1993). *Listening to Prozac: A Psychiatrist Explores Antidepressant Drugs and the Remaking of the Self.* New York: Viking.

16. E. Wurtzel (1994). *Prozac Nation: Young and Depressed in America.* New York: Houghton Mifflin, 307.

17. Kramer (1993).

Chapter 2: Groucho's Paradox

1. R. F. Baumeister (1982). A self-presentational view of social phenomena. *Psychological Bulletin* 91:3–26. E. E. Jones (1964). *Ingratiation.* New York: Appleton-Century-Crofts. E. E. Jones and T. S. Pittman (1982). Toward a general theory of strategic self-presentation. In J. Suls, ed. *Psychological Perspectives on the Self.* Hillsdale, N.J.: Erlbaum. B. R. Schlenker (1980). *Impression Management.* Belmont, Calif.: Wadsworth. S. E. Taylor and J. D. Brown (1988). Illusion and well being: Some social psychological contributions to a theory of mental health. *Psychological Bulletin* 103:193–210. A. Tesser (1988). Toward a self-evaluation maintenance model of social behavior. In N. L. Berkowitz, ed. *Advances in Experimental Social Psychology.* Vol. 21. New York: Academic.

2. A. Marx (1954). *Life with Groucho.* New York: Simon & Schuster.

3. The term *masochism* was coined by Richard von Krafft-Ebing after Leopold von Sacher-Masoch, a nineteenth-century Austrian novelist whose male characters were humiliated by beautiful women. The term was limited to the enjoyment of pain and humiliation in the context of sexual contact. Freud later expanded the definition of masochism to include nonsexual behaviors by which people placed themselves in situations that fostered their own unhappiness. In keeping with most contemporary usages of the term, here I am using it in the broader sense rather than the specifically sexual one introduced by

Krafft-Ebing. For discussions, see R. F. Baumeister (1989). *Masochism and the Self.* Hillsdale, N.J.: Erlbaum. S. Freud (1961). The economic problem in masochism. In J. Strachey, ed. *The Standard Edition of the Complete Works of Sigmund Freud.* Vol. 19. London: Hogarth Press and the Institute of Psycho-Analysis. R. V. Krafft-Ebing (1950). *Psychopathia Sexualis: A Medico-Forensic Study.* New York: Pioneer Publications (original work published 1901).

4. See R. A. Berk, S. Berk, D. R. Loseke, and D. Rauma (1983). Mutual combat and other family violence myths. In D. Finkelhor, R. J. Gelles, G. T. Hotaling, and M. A. Straus, eds. *The Dark Side of Families: Current Family Violence Research.* Newbury Park, Calif.: Sage. R. J. Gelles (1974). *The Violent Home.* Beverly Hills, Calif.: Sage. D. G. Saunders (1988). Other "truths" about domestic violence: A reply to McNeely and Robinson-Simpson. *Social Work* 33:179–183. S. K. Steinmetz (1977). *The Cycle of Violence: Assertive, Aggressive, and Abusive Family Interaction.* New York: Praeger. M. A. Straus and R. J. Gelles (1986). Societal change and change in family violence from 1975 to 1985 as revealed by two national surveys. *Journal of Marriage and the Family* 45:465–479.

5. O. H. Mowrer (1950). *Learning Theory and Personality Dynamics.* New York: Arnold Press, 486.

6. T. A. Widiger (1988). Treating self-defeating personality disorder. *Hospital and Community Psychiatry* 39:819–821. Widiger suggests that people who display such symptoms suffer from a "self-defeating personality disorder," a diagnostic category that the American Psychological Association introduced several years ago and discarded a short time later. The diagnostic category proved controversial for several reasons, but to me the most compelling was that it was ripe for misuse. For example, an abusive man might use the fact that his wife was diagnosed as having the disorder as a legal defense. A related concern was sex bias in the diagnosis of the disorder. See T. Widiger and R. L. Spitzer (1991). Sex bias in the diagnosis of personality disorder: Conceptual and methodological issues. *Clinical Psychology Review* 11:1–22. Other researchers have suggested that the diagnostic category overlaps too much with other categories, limiting its usefulness. See A. E. Skodol,

J. M. Oldham, P. E. Gallaher, and S. Bezirganian (1994). Validity of self-defeating personality disorder. *American Journal of Psychiatry* 151:560–567.

7. Although this is happy news for people with positive self-views, it means that researchers interested in isolating the unique effects of positivity strivings from those of self-verification strivings cannot learn much from studying such people. On the one hand, if people with positive self-views seek favorable evaluations (as they ordinarily do), both their positivity strivings and self-verification strivings could have been at work. If such people were to seek unfavorable evaluations, however, neither their desire for positivity nor their desire for self-verification could have been responsible.

8. R. Scott (1991). Invited address presented at the annual meeting of Social Psychologists in Texas (SPIT). For related accounts, see O. Sacks (1993). To see or not to see. *The New Yorker* (May):59–73. A. Valvo (1971). *Sight Restoration after Long-Term Blindness: The Problems and Behavior Patterns of Visual Rehabilitation.* New York: American Foundation for the Blind.

9. For a description of the perceptual and psychological difficulties of such patients, see Valvo (1971).

10. J. H. Griffin (1977). *Black Like Me.* 2nd ed. Boston: Houghton Mifflin, 12. A similar reaction to a drastic change in skin color and, by extension, racial identity, was noted by R. Firstman. When a disease called vitiligo caused the skin of a 41-year-old African American woman to turn white, she reported experiencing severe psychological trauma. See R. C. Firstman. Black, white: Woman just wants to be whole. Appeared in the June 12, 1981, *Daily Camera.*

11. C. H. Cooley (1902). *Human Nature and the Social Order.* New York: G. Scribner's Sons. G. H. Mead (1934). *Mind, Self and Society.* Chicago: University of Chicago Press. See also J. Baldwin (1897). *Social and Ethical Interpretations in Mental Development.* New York: Macmillan.

12. See M. Rosenberg (1973). Which significant others? *American Behavioral Scientist* 16:829–860. Note that this formulation can accommodate the influence of genetic factors on

self-knowledge in that such genetically determined traits as physical appearance and temperament may influence the reactions of others, which, in turn, influence our self-views.

13. D. A. Cole (1991). Change in self-perceived competence as a function of peer and teacher evaluation. *Developmental Psychology* 27:682–688. R. B. Felson (1981). Self and reflected appraisal among football players. *Social Psychology Quarterly* 44:116–126. R. B. Felson (1985). Reflected appraisal and the development of self. *Social Psychology Quarterly* 48:71–78. R. B. Felson (1989). Parents and the reflected appraisal process: A longitudinal analysis. *Journal of Personality and Social Psychology* 56:965–971. D. R. Hoge, E. K. Smit, and S. L. Hanson (1990). School experiences predicting changes in self-esteem of sixth- and seventh-grade students. *Journal of Educational Psychology* 82:117–127.

14. S. E. McNulty and W. B. Swann, Jr. (1994). Identity negotiation in roommate relationships: The self as architect and consequence of social reality. *Journal of Personality and Social Psychology* 67:1012–1023. Parenthetically, we encountered somewhat stronger evidence for the opposite process: students influenced their roommates to see them as they saw themselves.

15. K. J. Hayes and C. H. Nissen (1971). Higher mental functions in a home-raised chimpanzee. In A. M. Schrier and F. Stollnitz, eds. *Behavior of Non-Human Primates.* Vol. 4. New York: Academic.

16. R. B. Giesler, R. A. Josephs, and W. B. Swann, Jr. (In press). Self-verification in clinical depression: The desire for negative evaluation. *Journal of Abnormal Psychology.*

17. In adopting this position, I am departing from the view of psychoanalysts such as Otto Kernberg who equate narcissism with self-love or self-esteem. For additional discussions, see O. Kernberg (1975). *Borderline Conditions and Pathological Narcissism.* New York: Jason Aronson, 317. D. Westen (1990). The relations among narcissism, egocentrism, self-concept, and self-esteem: Experimental, clinical, and theoretical considerations. *Psychoanalysis and Contemporary Thought* 13:183–239. D. Westen (1988). Transference and information processing.

Clinical Psychology Review 8:161–179. O. P. John and R. W. Robins (1994). Accuracy and bias in self-perception: Individual differences in self-enhancement and the role of narcissism. *Journal of Personality and Social Psychology* 66:206–219. R. Raskin, J. Novacek, and R. Hogan (1991). Narcissism, self-esteem, and defensive self-enhancement. *Journal of Personality* 59:19–38.

18. E. Goffman (1959). *The Presentation of Self in Everyday Life.* New York: Anchor Books. S. Stryker and A. Statham (1985). Symbolic interaction and role theory. In G. Lindzey and E. Aronson, eds. *Handbook of Social Psychology.* Vol. 2. Hillsdale, N.J.: Random House. G. J. McCall and J. L. Simmons (1966). *Identities and Interactions: An Examination of Human Associations in Everyday Life.* New York: The Free Press.

19. M. Buber (1951). Distance and relation. *The Hibbert Journal: Quarterly Review of Religion, Theology and Philosophy* 49:105–113. I hasten to add that Buber was referring here to implicit or existential self-views rather than explicit or conscious ones. I believe, however, that both forms of self-knowledge are functionally equivalent in that they guide our strivings for self-verification.

20. K. R. Popper and J. C. Eccles (1977). *The Self and Its Brain.* New York: Springer.

21. S. Freud (1917). *Introductory Lectures on Psychoanalysis.* New York: Norton, 248.

22.To account for Katherine's attraction to abusive men, for example, Freud might have searched for evidence of a formative experience with some significant figure from her childhood, most likely her father. Such a search would be based on the assumption that the early experience produced anxiety that she was now attempting to reduce by reenacting the earlier relationship with lovers who resembled her father. Freud would have believed that if she could be made aware of these unconscious impulses, her anxiety—and the problematic behavior it fueled—would disappear.

23. Another link between Freud's thinking and my own is the parallel between the concepts of positivity strivings versus

self-verification strivings and the pleasure principle versus the reality principle.

24. P. Wachtel (1977). *Psychoanalysis and Behavior Therapy: Toward an Integration.* New York: Basic Books.

25. H. S. Sullivan (1953). *The Interpersonal Theory of Psychiatry.* New York: Norton. See also E. Erikson (1968). *Identity: Youth in Crisis.* New York: Norton. K. Horney (1939). *New Ways in Psychoanalysis.* New York: Norton. D. Westen (1988). D. W. Winnicott (1971). *Playing and Reality.* New York: Basic Books.

26. P. Lecky (1945). *Self-Consistency: A Theory of Personality.* New York: Island Press, 50–51, 66. See also K. Goldstein (1939). *The Organism.* New York: American Book Co.

27. Other theorists echoed this hypothesis over the next few years, but it was not directly tested for two decades. The most pertinent works include J. D. W. Andrews (1991). *The Active Self in Psychotherapy: An Integration of Therapeutic Styles.* Boston: Allyn & Bacon. E. Aronson (1968). A theory of cognitive dissonance: A current perspective. In L. Berkowitz, ed. *Advances in Experimental Social Psychology.* Vol. 4. New York: Academic. S. Epstein (1991). Cognitive experiential self-theory: An integrative theory of personality. In R. Curtis, ed. *The Relational Self: Convergences in Psychoanalysis and Social Psychology.* New York: Guilford. P. F. Secord and C. W. Backman (1965). An interpersonal approach to personality. In B. Maher, ed. *Progress in Experimental Personality Research.* Vol. 2. New York: Academic. W. B. Swann, Jr. (1983). Self-verification: Bringing social reality into harmony with the self. In J. Suls and A. G. Greenwald, eds. *Social Psychological Perspectives on the Self.* Vol. 2. Hillsdale, N.J.: Erlbaum. Also related are R. Rogers (1967). *Coming into Existence: The Struggle to Become an Individual.* Cleveland: World. Mowrer (1950). D. Syngg and A. W. Combs (1949). *Individual Behavior: A New Frame of Reference.* New York: Harper & Bros.

28. E. Aronson and J. M. Carlsmith (1962). Performance expectancy as a determinant of actual performance. *Journal of Abnormal and Social Psychology* 65:178–182. I say that this study tested a "variant" of Lecky's hypothesis because Lecky's theory would have required measuring rather than manipulat-

ing self-views. In any event, Aronson and Carlsmith were apparently unaware that they were actually testing a variation of Lecky's theory. Although their study has the distinction of being the most provocative and widely cited of early efforts along these lines, Deutsch and Solomon published a related study several years earlier that offered somewhat less compelling support for Lecky's hypothesis: M. Deutsch and L. Solomon (1959). Reactions to evaluations by others as influenced by self-evaluations. *Sociometry* 22:93–112. For accounts of the theory that inspired Aronson and Carlsmith's research directly, see L. Festinger (1957). *A Theory of Cognitive Dissonance.* Evanston, Ill.: Row & Peterson.

29. I believe that this lovely phrase ("scientific Valhalla . . .") comes from Paul Wachtel. For summaries of research in the tradition of Lecky's hypothesis, see J. S. Shrauger (1975). Responses to evaluation as a function of initial self-perceptions. *Psychological Bulletin* 82:581–596. Also see W. B. Swann, Jr. (1990). To be adored or to be known: The interplay of self-enhancement and self-verification. In R. M. Sorrentino and E. T. Higgins, eds. *Foundations of Social Behavior.* Vol. 2. New York: Guilford.

30. In the hope of showing that students' negative self-views *caused* their responses, Aronson and Carlsmith (1962) attempted to *create* negative self-views by telling the students that they had done poorly on a test of social perceptiveness. The problem with this approach is that most people think they are quite perceptive, and giving them several failures on a test is not likely to convince them otherwise. Thus, the students lacked a compelling reason to sabotage their own performance. This is why most contemporary researchers measure rather than manipulate self-views.

31. W. B. Swann, Jr., J. G. Hixon, and C. De La Ronde (1992). Embracing the bitter "truth": Negative self-concepts and marital commitment. *Psychological Science* 3:118–121. For a more recent replication of these results, see V. Ritts and J. R. Stein (1995). Verification and commitment in marital relationships: An exploration of self-verification theory in community college students. *Psychological Reports* 76:383–386.

32. This finding is reported in W. B. Swann, Jr., C. De La Ronde, and G. Hixon (1994). Authenticity and positivity strivings in

marriage and courtship. *Journal of Personality and Social Psychology* 66:857–869.

33. J. G. Hixon and W. B. Swann, Jr. (1993). When does introspection bear fruit? Self-reflection, self-insight, and interpersonal choices. *Journal of Personality and Social Psychology* 64:35–43. D. T. Robinson and L. Smith-Lovin (1992). Selective interaction as a strategy for identity maintenance: An affect control model. *Social Psychology Quarterly* 55:12–28. W. B. Swann, Jr., C. De La Ronde, and J. G. Hixon (1994). W. B. Swann, Jr., J. G. Hixon, A. Stein-Seroussi, and D. T. Gilbert (1990). The fleeting gleam of praise: Behavioral reactions to self-relevant feedback. *Journal of Personality and Social Psychology* 59:17–26. W. B. Swann, Jr., B. W. Pelham, and D. S. Krull (1989). Agreeable fancy or disagreeable truth: Reconciling self-enhancement and self-verification. *Journal of Personality and Social Psychology* 57:782–791. W. B. Swann, Jr., B. W. Pelham, and T. Chidester (1988). Change through paradox: Using self-verification to alter beliefs. *Journal of Personality and Social Psychology* 54:268–273. W. B. Swann, Jr., and S. J. Read (1981a). Acquiring self-knowledge: The search for feedback that fits. *Journal of Personality and Social Psychology* 41:1119–1128. W. B. Swann, Jr., and S. J. Read (1981b). Self-verification processes: How we sustain our self-conceptions. *Journal of Experimental Social Psychology* 17:351–372. W. B. Swann, Jr., A. Stein-Seroussi, and B. Giesler (1992). Why people self-verify. *Journal of Personality and Social Psychology* 62:392–401. W. B. Swann, Jr., R. W. Tafarodi, and E. C. Pinel (under review). Seeking criticism in the wake of praise: Compensatory self-verification and anxiety. *Personality and Social Psychology Bulletin.* W. B. Swann, Jr., R. M. Wenzlaff, D. S. Krull, and B. W. Pelham (1992). The allure of negative feedback: Self-verification strivings among depressed persons. *Journal of Abnormal Psychology* 101:293–306. W. B. Swann, Jr., R. M. Wenzlaff, and R. W. Tafarodi (1992). Depression and the search for negative evaluations: More evidence of the role of self-verification strivings. *Journal of Abnormal Psychology* 101:314–317.

34. W. B. Swann, Jr., and S. C. Predmore (1985). Intimates as agents of social support: Sources of consolation or despair? *Journal of Personality and Social Psychology* 49:1609–1617.

35. Most women were office workers and had an average annual income of $15,000; most men were manual workers and had an average annual income of $27,000. See C. E. Buckner and W. B. Swann, Jr. (1995). Physical abuse in close relationships: The dynamic interplay of couple characteristics. Paper presented at the annual meeting of the American Psychological Association, Washington, D.C.

36. W. F. Fry, Jr. (1962). The marital context of the anxiety syndrome. *Family Process* 1:248.

37. R. D. Laing and A. Esterson. (1964). *Sanity, Madness, and the Family.* Vol. 1. London: Tavistock Publications, 135–136.

38. G. H. Mead (1934). Henry Stack Sullivan (1953) has gone even further than Mead by suggesting that self-views are abstractions that lie not only in individuals' minds but in the minds of their interaction partners.

Chapter 3: The Verified Self

1. Also known as Hannibal.

2. C. Neider, ed. (1959). *Autobiography of Mark Twain.* New York: Harper & Row, 84.

3. D. Berlyne (1971). *Psychobiology and Aesthetics.* New York: Appleton-Century Crofts. D. O. Hebb (1949). *The Organization of Behavior.* New York: Wiley. S. R. Maddi (1961). Affective tone during environmental regularity and change. *Journal of Abnormal and Social Psychology* 62:338–345. J. Piaget (1952). *The origins of intelligence in children.* New York: University Press. J. Piaget (1954). *The construction of reality in the child.* New York: Basic Books. W. White (1959). Motivation reconsidered: The concept of competence. *Psychological Review* 66:297–333.

4. Of course, sometimes people indulge their desire for novelty in ways that are potentially disruptive to their perceptions of predictability and control. The classic example is the middle-aged married man who takes up with a woman half his age. Such instances illustrate more than the appeal of novelty, however, because they typically result in extremely painful disruptions for many people, including the wife, the couple's friends and families, and the man himself. Hence,

when a desire for novelty is allowed to intrude into domains that are highly important to people, psychological carnage may result.

5. O. L. Tinkelpaugh (1928). An experimental study of representative factors in monkeys. *Journal of Comparative Psychology* 8:224.

6. This predisposition seems to be due to the presence of neural receptive fields that are excited by specific patterns in the visual environment. R. C. Sluyters, J. Atkinson, M. S. Banks, R. M. Held, K. Hoffman, and C. Shatz (1990). The development of vision and visual perception. In L. Spillman and J. S. Werner, eds. *Visual Perception: The Neurophysiological Foundations*. San Diego: Academic.

7. K. R. Popper (1963). *Conjectures and Refutations*. London: Routledge, 47–48. For a discussion, see V. F. Guidano and G. Liotti (1983). *Cognitive Processes and Emotional Disorders*. New York: Guilford.

8. Lecky (1945), 62–63.

9. Lecky (1945), 53.

10. L. A. Pervin (1963). The need to predict and control under conditions of threat. *Journal of Personality* 31:570–587. L. A. Pervin (1964). Predictive strategies and the need to confirm them: Some notes on pathological types of decisions. *Psychological Reports* 15:99–105.

11. Pervin (1964), 100–101.

12. L. Musante, M. A. Gilbert, and J. Thibaut (1983). The effects of control on perceived fairness of procedures and outcomes. *Journal of Experimental Social Psychology* 19:223–238.

13. R. May (1979). *The Meaning of Anxiety*. New York: Washington Square Press, 192–193.

14. H. Kohut (1984). *How Does Analysis Cure?* Chicago: University of Chicago Press.

15. V. Hugo (1961). *Les Miserables*. C. E. Wilbour, trans. New York: Fawcett, 146–151.

16. Physically, the problem is that they fail to apply enough muscular effort while speaking. The result is that they do not

exhale forcefully enough as they speak, and the vocal folds are brought together weakly. The psychology underlying this phenomenon has not been spelled out. See A. E. Aronson (1990). *Clinical Voice Disorders: An Interdisciplinary Approach.* 3rd ed. New York: Thieme, 333. See also D. R. Boone (1971). *The Voice and Voice Therapy.* Englewood Cliffs, N.J.: Prentice-Hall.

17. Aronson (1990), 333.

18. My thanks to William Ickes, Sr., who related this case to me in a phone conversation. Disintegration anxiety also seems to have played a role in the fate of patients featured in Oliver Sacks's *Awakenings* (later made into a movie starring Robin Williams). After decades of immobility caused by encephalitis, they began to move freely thanks to the drug L-dopa. Unfortunately, their recoveries were short-lived. At least part of the problem seems to have been that the removal of their symptoms left an existential vacuum that sucked them back into the pathologies from which they had escaped.

19. J. Penman (1954). Pain as an old friend. *Lancet* 266: 633–636.

20. Penman (1954), 634.

21. Penman (1954), 634.

22. Penman (1954), 635.

23. G. Murphy (1947). *Personality: A Biosocial Approach to Origins and Structure.* New York: Harper & Bros., 715.

24. For related discussions, see J. Bronowski (1971). *The Identity of Man.* Garden City, N.Y.: American Museum Science Books. P. M. Churchland (1984). *Matter and Consciousness. A Contemporary Introduction to the Philosophy of Mind.* Cambridge, Mass.: MIT Press/Bradford Books. D. Dennett (1978). *Brainstorms.* Montgomery, Vt.: Bradford Books.

25. O. Sacks (1985). *The Man Who Mistook His Wife for a Hat and Other Clinical Tales.* New York: Simon & Schuster, 110–111.

26. Sacks (1985). Sacks has told me that he believes Thompson's state was due to orbito-frontal syndrome as well as Korsakov's. The latter condition may account for Thompson's

special jocosity, which those who suffer only from Korsakov's generally do not display.

The Russian neurologist A. R. Luria told an equally poignant story of a soldier he treated who had suffered a bullet wound to his head during World War II. When the man first awoke, he realized that he had no idea who he was:

> *I'm in kind of a fog all the time like a heavy half sleep.*
> *My memory's a blank. I can't think of a single word. All*
> *that flashes through my mind are some images, hazy*
> *visions suddenly appear and just suddenly disappear,*
> *giving way to fresh images. . . . At first I couldn't even*
> *recognize myself, or what had happened to me, and for*
> *a long time (days on end) didn't even know where I'd*
> *been hit. My head wounds seemed to transform me into*
> *some terrible baby. . . . I felt as though I was lost in*
> *some nightmare world, a vicious circle from which*
> *there was no way out, no possibility of waking. Nothing*
> *I saw made any sense to me.* (From A. R. Luria, 1972.
> *The Man with a Shattered World.* New York: Basic
> Books, 9, 11, 16.)

27. J. Adams (1805). *Discourses on Davila.* Boston: Russell & Cutler, 1.

28. E. Berscheid (1985). Interpersonal attraction. In G. Lindzey and E. Aronson, eds. *Handbook of Social Psychology.* Vol. 2. New York: Random House. Baumeister (1982). Jones (1964). Jones and Pittman (1982). Schlenker (1980).

29. G. Murphy (1947). *Personality.* New York: Harper. G. W. Allport (1955). *Becoming.* New Haven: Yale University. E. R. Hilgard (1949). Human motives and the concept of the self. *American Psychologist* 4:374–382.

30. For Shrauger's original statement, see J. S. Shrauger (1975). Responses to evaluation as a function of initial self-perceptions. *Psychological Bulletin* 82:581–596. For empirical support for his argument, see D. B. McFarlin and J. Blascovich (1981). Effects of self-esteem and performance on future affective preferences and cognitive expectations. *Journal of Personality and Social Psychology* 40:521–531. R. L. Moreland and P. D. Sweeney (1984). Self-expectancies and reaction to evaluations of personal performance. *Journal of Personality*

52:156–176. W. B. Swann, Jr., J. J. Griffin, S. Predmore, and B. Gaines (1987). The cognitive-affective crossfire: When self-consistency confronts self-enhancement. *Journal of Personality and Social Psychology* 52:881–889. For a report of the final study mentioned, see Swann, Wenzlaff, Krull, and Pelham (1992). For a recent extension, see T. E. Joiner and G. I. Metalksy (1995). A perspective test of an integrative interpersonal theory of depression: A naturalistic study of college roommates. *Journal of Personality and Social Psychology* 69:778–788.

31. Swann, Hixon, Stein-Seroussi, and Gilbert (1990). Hixon and Swann (1993).

32. B. Gracian (1930). *The Art of Worldly Wisdom.* J. Jacobs, trans. London: Macmillan (original work published 1647), 146.

33. For studies examining reactions to different amounts of praise, see Swann, Tafarodi, and Pinel. *Personality and Social Psychology Bulletin* (under review). A related finding is that students become anxious when they receive grades that exceed their expectations; see P. Brickman (1972). Rational and nonrational elements in reactions to disconfirmation of performance expectancies. *Journal of Experimental Social Psychology* 8:112–123.

34. Swann, De La Ronde, and Hixon (1994).

35. M. E. P. Seligman (1992). *Helplessness: On Depression, Development, and Death.* New York: W. H. Freeman. In light of the psychological significance of perceptions of predictability and control, it should come as no surprise that specialists in pain regulation focus on both variables. Lamaze programs, for example, attempt to minimize the pain of mothers during childbirth in at least two ways. First, they carefully prepare the mother for the events leading up to delivery, thus increasing the predictability of the events. Second, they encourage mothers to pursue active strategies (such as breathing exercises) that foster a sense of control over the delivery process. Being able to predict an event often makes it *seem* more controllable. For this reason, *perceptions* of predictability are usually even more important than *actual* predictability.

36. A. Bandura, D. Cioffi, C. B. Taylor, and M. E. Brouillard (1988). Perceived self-efficacy in coping with cognitive stres-

sors and opioid activation. *Journal of Personality and Social Psychology* 55:479–488. D. C. Glass and J. E. Singer (1972). *Urban Stress: Experiments on Noise and Social Stressors.* New York: Academic. A. H. McFarlane, G. R. Norman, D. L. Streiner, R. Roy, and D. J. Scott (1980). A longitudinal study of the influence of the psychosocial environment on health status: A preliminary report. *Journal of Health and Social Behavior* 21:124–133. J. W. Pennebaker (1985). Traumatic experience and psychosomatic disease: Exploring the roles of behavioral inhibition, obsession, and confiding. *Canadian Psychology* 26:82–95. J. Rodin (1986). Aging and health: Effects of the sense of control. *Science* 233:1271–1276. J. Rodin and E. Langer (1977). Long-term effect of a control-relevant intervention with the institutionalized aged. *Journal of Personality and Social Psychology* 35:897–902. Seligman (1975). J. Suls and B. Mullen (1981). Life change in psychological distress: The role of perceived control and desirability. *Journal of Applied Social Psychology* 11:379–389. S. E. Taylor (1979). Hospital patient behavior: Reactance, helplessness, or control? *Journal of Social Issues* 35: 156–184.

For a discussion of related research on animals, see R. Sapolsky (1992). Endocrinology alfresco: Psychoendocrine studies of wild baboons. *Recent Progress in Hormone Research* 48:437. R. M. Sapolsky (1994). *Why Zebras Don't Get Ulcers: A Guide to Stress, Stress-Related Diseases, and Coping.* New York: W. H. Freeman.

37. J. D. Brown and K. J. McGill (1989). The cost of good fortune: When positive life events produce negative health consequences. *Journal of Personality and Social Psychology* 55:1103–1110. For an overview, see W. B. Swann, Jr. and J. D. Brown (1990). From self to health: Self-verification and identity disruption. In I. Sarason, B. Sarason, and G. Pierce, eds. *Social Support: An Interactional View.* New York: Wiley.

Brown's provocative findings not only are interesting in their own right, they also may help to explain why researchers have had so much difficulty finding consistent support for the intuitively appealing idea that favorable life events foster physical health. Conceivably, had researchers looked separately at people with negative and positive self-views, they would have discovered that favorable events improve the health of people with positive self-views but *undermine* the health of those with negative self-views, resulting in weak effects overall. For reviews of this literature, see I. G. Sarason and B. R. Sarason (1984). Life changes, moderators of stress, and health. In A. Baum, J. E. Singer, and S. E. Taylor, eds. *Handbook of Psychology and Health: Social Psychological Aspects of Health.* Vol. 4. Hillsdale, N.J.: Erlbaum. J. Suls (1983). Social support, interpersonal relations, and health: Benefits and liabilities. In G. S. Sanders and J. Suls, eds. *Social Psychology of Health and Illness.* Hillsdale, N.J.: Erlbaum. P. A. Thoits (1983). Multiple identities and psychological well-being: A reformulation and test of the social isolation hypothesis. *American Sociological Review* 48:174–187.

38. For example, see Swann, Wenzlaff, Krull, and Pelham (1992).

39. We conducted several studies in this series. A study of people who were clinically diagnosed as suffering from depression can be found in Giesler, Josephs, and Swann. *Journal of Abnormal Psychology* (in press). Several more can be found in Swann, Wenzlaff, Krull, & Pelham (1992) and in Swann, Wenzlaff, and Tafarodi (1992).

40. In all our research involving such evaluations, we tailored the evaluations to the self-views of participants. In this case, we wondered if people would choose partners whose evaluations confirmed their level of self-esteem and depression. For this reason, the feedback focused on social ease, happiness, and feelings of worth.

41. People who merely had low self-esteem chose Mr. Nasty 64 percent of the time; those who suffered from both low self-esteem and depression chose Mr. Nasty 82 percent of the time. This difference was not a result of differences in the positivity of their self-views, because both groups had equally negative self-views. Instead, I think it reflects the fact that people who are depressed tend to focus more on their negative self-views. See J. A. Bargh and M. E. Tota (1988). Context-dependent automatic processing in depression: Accessibility of negative constructs with regard to self but not others. *Journal of Personality and Social Psychology* 54:925–939. Thus, when they were deciding on an evaluator, the clinically depressed

people in our sample were more apt to be thinking negative things about themselves and hence chose an evaluator who would confirm those negative self-views.

42. In its most general form, the ironic perspective assumes that many seemingly self-destructive behaviors are actually positivity strivings run amuck. Karen Horney was one of the first to propose this idea in a somewhat different context. More recently, similar claims have been made by clinicians such as James Coyne and Paul Wachtel and by social psychologists such as Roy Baumeister and Claude Steele. For relevant readings, see R. Baumeister (1989). The optimal margin of illusion. *Journal of Social and Clinical Psychology* 8:176–189. J. C. Coyne (1976). Toward an interactional description of depression. *Psychiatry* 39:28–40. J. C. Coyne, R. C. Kessler, M. Tal, J. Turnbull, C. B. Wortman, and J. F. Greden (1987). Living with a depressed person. *Journal of Consulting and Clinical Psychology* 55:347–352. Horney (1939). C. M. Steele (1988). The psychology of self-affirmation: Sustaining the integrity of the self. In L. Berkowitz, ed. *Advances in Experimental Social Psychology.* Vol. 21. New York: Academic. E. F. Wachtel and P. L. Wachtel (1986). *Family Dynamics in Individual Psychotherapy: A Guide to Clinical Strategies.* New York: Guilford.

43. A. H. Baumgardner and P. E. Levy (1988). Role of self-esteem in perceptions of ability and effort: Illogic or insight? *Personality and Social Psychology Bulletin* 14:429–438. E. E. Jones and S. Berglas (1978). Control of attributions about the self through self-handicapping strategies: The appeal of alcohol and the role of underachievement. *Personality and Social Psychology Bulletin* 2:200–207. F. Rhodewalt and S. K. Hill (1995). Self-handicapping in the classroom: The effects of claimed self-handicaps on responses to academic failure. *Basic and Applied Social Psychology* 16:397–416.

44. Swann, Stein-Seroussi, and Giesler (1992).

45. A secretary then transcribed their statements, and we gave the transcriptions to a team of judges who had been trained to identify various reasons that people might choose an interaction partner. Finally, we averaged the judges' ratings and tallied them. This think-aloud technique, referred to loosely as "introspection," has something of a checkered reputation in

psychology. First introduced by the eminent German psychologist Wilhelm Wundt during the late 1800s, its early advocates billed it as a means of uncovering the mechanisms underlying rudimentary psychological processes such as vision. Unfortunately, this promise was never fulfilled, in part because the mechanisms that underlie perceptual processes occur much too rapidly to be accessed consciously. More recently, researchers have used introspection to illuminate the thought processes involved in solving logical problems and playing chess. Introspection is more useful in studying these processes because they are much slower than perceptual processes (or at least can be slowed down). In addition, researchers have learned to avoid some of the pitfalls associated with early introspective techniques. For example, having learned that people tend to forget the reasons underlying their behaviors quite quickly, contemporary researchers have them report what they are thinking *as they are engaged in the behavior.* For a critique of introspective techniques, see R. E. Nisbett and T. D. Wilson (1977). Telling more than we can know: Verbal reports on mental processes. *Psychological Review* 84:231–259. For a defense of these techniques, see K. A. Ericssen and H. A. Simon (1980). Verbal reports as data. *Psychological Review* 17:215–251.

46. A companion study showed that the act of thinking out loud had no impact on which evaluators people chose.

47. D. Byrne (1971). *The Attraction Paradigm.* New York: Academic.

48. Although most of the support for this assertion comes from studies of college students (for example, Taylor and Brown, 1988), the tendency for people to be biased toward rating themselves favorably also appears in studies of non–college age populations. See M. Rosenberg (1965). *Society and the Adolescent Self-Image.* Princeton, N.J.: Princeton University Press.

49. Swann, Wenzlaff, and Tafarodi (1992).

50. F. D. Alsaker (1989). School achievement, perceived academic competence and global self-esteem. *School Psychology International* 10:147–158. G. Maruyama, R. A. Rubin, and G. G. Kingsbury (1981). Self-esteem and educational achievement: Independent constructs with a common cause? *Journal*

of Personality and Social Psychology 40:962–975. M. M. Mboya (1989). The relative importance of global self-concept and self-concept of academic ability in predicting academic achievement. *Adolescence* 24:39–46.

51. For research on the relationship of physical attractiveness to self-esteem, see S. Harter (1993). Causes and consequences of low self-esteem in children and adolescents. In R. F. Baumeister, ed. *Self-Esteem: The Puzzle of Low Self-Regard.* New York: Plenum, 98. For links between intelligence and depression among boys and girls, see J. H. Block, P. F. Gjerde, and J. H. Block (1991). Personality antecedents of depressive tendencies in 18 year olds: A prospective study. *Journal of Personality and Social Psychology* 60:726–738.

52. Of all the self-views discussed in this book, the only one that researchers have found to be closely related to an "objective" criterion is self-conceived sociability. Nevertheless, even this finding is questionable. Dave Kenny at the University of Connecticut points out that although self-rated sociability is closely related to the ratings of people's friends, roommates, and acquaintances, it is only modestly related to the ratings of objective observers of people's behavior in laboratory settings. Because Kenny believes that the ratings of such objective observers are ultimately the most valid index of any quality, he concludes that there is little support for the idea that people's self-views on the sociability dimension are truly accurate. Whether or not such skepticism proves warranted, at this point there is very little basis for believing otherwise, particularly when it comes to the highly global and subjective self-views that make up measures of self-esteem and depression. For a discussion, see D. A. Kenny (1994). *Interpersonal Perception: A Social Relations Analysis.* New York: Guilford.

53. C. S. Dweck and E. L. Leggett (1988). A social-cognitive approach to motivation and personality. *Psychological Review* 25:109–116. Limitations in viewing intelligence as a fixed quality are also supported by the fact that IQ tests are not good predictors of future performance. Researchers have found that when the IQ scores of young students are used to predict their later life accomplishments, those who score in the outstanding range do only slightly better than those who score in the average range. If researchers want to do a respectable job of fore-

casting success, they must combine scores on aptitude tests with scores on measures of motivation and creativity. For an overview of this work, see J. S. Renzulli (1978). What makes giftedness? Reexamining a definition. In W. B. Barbe and J. S. Renzulli, eds. *Psychology and Education of the Gifted.* New York: Irvington.

Similarly, when the U.S. Army tried to predict the job performance of enlisted personnel in their first tour of duty, they quickly discovered that scores on the aptitude test they were using (the Armed Forces Vocational Aptitude Battery) predicted only a narrow range of performance, such as the ability to operate machinery or knowledge of job requirements. Aptitude test scores had almost no relationship to a wide array of important behaviors related to performance on the job, such as initiative and leadership, ability to get along with colleagues, and even being punctual. See J. P. Campbell, J. J. McHenry, and L. L. Wise. (1990). Modeling job performance in a population of jobs. *Personnel Psychology* 43:313–333.

54. W. James (1890). *The Principles of Psychology.* Vols. 1, 2. New York: Henry Holt.

55. J. Crocker and B. Major (1989). Social stigma and self-esteem: The self-protective properties of stigma. *Psychological Review* 96:608–630. D. Dunning, J. A. Meyerowitz, and A. D. Holzberg (1989). Ambiguity and self-evaluation: The role of idiosyncratic trait definitions in self-serving assessments of ability. *Journal of Personality and Social Psychology* 57:1082–1090. V. Gecas and M. A. Seff (1990). Social class and self-esteem: Psychological centrality, compensation, and the relative effects of work and home. *Social Psychology Quarterly* 53:165–173. Rosenberg (1965). S. Stryker (1980). *Symbolic Interactionism.* Menlo Park, Calif.: Benjamin/Cummings.

56. W. Mischel (1979). On the interface of cognition and personality: Beyond the person-situation debate. *American Psychologist* 34:740–754.

57. S. E. Taylor. (1989). *Positive Illusions: Creative Self-Deception and the Healthy Mind.* New York: Basic Books. Taylor and Brown (1988).

58. C. R. Colvin and J. Block (1994). Do positive illusions foster mental health? An examination of the Taylor and Brown formulation. *Psychological Bulletin* 116:3–20.

59. D. Dunning and A. L. Story (1991). Depression, realism, and the overconfidence effect: Are the sadder wiser when predicting future actions and events? *Journal of Personality and Social Psychology* 61:521–532.

60. E. R. Hilgard (1949). Human motives and the concept of the self. *American Psychologist* 4:374–382.

61. G. W. Allport (1939). *Personality: A Psychological Interpretation.* New York: Holt, 422. See also M. Jahoa (1958). Current concepts of positive mental health. New York: Basic Books.

62. S. E. Taylor and J. D. Brown (1994). Positive illusions and well-being revisited: Separating fact from fiction. *Psychological Bulletin*116:21–27. For an earlier version of this same argument, see R. F. Baumeister (1989). The optimal margin of illusion. *Journal of Social and Clinical Psychology* 8:176–189.

Chapter 4: Ghosts from the Nursery

1. L. A. Sroufe (1989). Relationships, self, and individual adaptation. In A. J. Sameroff and R. N. Emde, eds. *Relationships, Self, and Individual Adaptation in Early Childhood: A Developmental Approach.* New York: Basic Books. I have substituted the name Ann for the initials R. V. that appeared in the original.

2. Quoted in R. Karen (1994). *Becoming Attached.* New York: Warner, 378.

3. M. J. Ward (1988). Attachment of one sibling to another. *Child Development* 69:643–651.

4. See J. R. Reid, G. R. Patterson, and R. Loeber (1982). The abused child: Victim, instigator, or innocent bystander? In D. J. Berstein, ed. *Response Structure and Organization.* Lincoln: University of Nebraska Press. For useful discussions of the role of temperament, see J. Belsky and M. Rovine (1987). Temperament and attachment security in the strange

situation: An empirical rapprochement. *Child Development* 58:787–795. A. Caspi, B. Henry, R. O. McGee, T. E. Moffitt, and P. A. Silva (1995). Temperamental origins of child and adolescent behavior problems: From age three to age fifteen. *Child Development* 66:55–68. H. H. Goldsmith and J. A. Alansky (1987). Maternal and infant temperamental predictors of attachment: A meta-analytic review. *Journal of Consulting and Clinical Psychology* 55:805–816. M. Gunnar, S. Manglesdorf, M. Larson, and L. Hertsgaard (1989). Attachment, temperament, and adrenocortical activity in infancy: A study of psychoendocrine regulation. *Developmental Psychology* 25:355–363. B. E. Vaughn, J. Stevenson-Hinde, E. Waters, A. Kotsaftis, G. B. Lefever, A. Shouldice, M. Trudel, and J. Belsky (1992). Attachment security and temperament in infancy and early childhood: Some conceptual clarifications. *Developmental Psychology* 28:463–473.

5. L. A. Sroufe (1983). Infant caregiver attachment and patterns of adaptation in preschool: The roots of maladaptation and competence. In M. Perlmutter, ed. *The Minnesota Symposium on Child Psychology*. Vol. 16. Hillsdale, N.J.: Erlbaum. N. A. Fox, N. L. Kimmerly, and W. D. Schafer (1991). Attachment to mother/attachment to father: A meta-analysis. *Child Development* 62:210–225.

6. For discussions of the impact of fathers on children, see M. J. Cox, M. T. Owen, V. K. Henderson, and N. A. Margand (1992). Prediction of infant-father and infant-mother attachment. *Developmental Psychology* 28:474–483. M. Main and D. R. Westen (1981). The quality of the toddler's relationship to mother and to father: Related to conflict behavior and the readiness to establish new relationships. *Child Development* 52:932–940. V. Phares and B. E. Compas (1993). Fathers and developmental psychopathology. *Current Directions in Psychological Science* 5:162–165. M. Putallaz, P. R. Costanzo, and T. P. Klein (1993). Parental social experiences and their effects on children's relationships. In S. Duck, ed. *Learning about Relationships: Understanding Relationship Processes Series*. Vol. 2. Newbury Park, Calif.: Sage. K. S. Rosen and F. Rothbaum (1993). Quality of parental caregiving and security of attachment. *Developmental Psychology* 29:358–367. L. M. Youngblade and J. Belsky (1992). Parent-child an-

tecedents of 5-year-olds' close friendships: A longitudinal analysis. *Developmental Psychology* 28:700–713.

7. M. E. P. Seligman (1994). *What You Can Change and What You Can't.* New York: Knopf, 231.

8. E. Waters, J. Trebous, J. Crowell, S. Merrick, and L. Albersheim (1995). From the strange situation to the adult attachment interview: A 20-year longitudinal study of attachment security in infancy and early adulthood. Paper presented in a poster session entitled "Parent-child relationships: A prototype of later love relationships?" at the biennial meeting of the Society for Research in Child Development, Indianapolis, Ind. The finding of Waters et al. is highly controversial, not only because it is so surprising but also because a group of German researchers found much less continuity in a similar study. See P. Zimmerman, E. Fremmer-Bombik, G. Spangler, and K. E. Grossmann (1995). Attachment in adolescence: A longitudinal perspective. Paper presented at the biennial meeting of the Society for Research in Child Development, Indianapolis, Ind.

9. J. Bowlby (1944). Forty-four juvenile thieves: Their characters and home life. *International Journal of Psycho-Analysis* 25:19–52, 107–127. Reprinted in 1946 as a monograph. London: Bailiere, Tindall, & Cox.

10. Attachment theory was developed as an alternative to the psychoanalytic theory of object relations and behaviorism. See J. Bowlby (1969). *Attachment and Loss.* Vol. 1, Attachment. New York: Basic Books. J. Bowlby (1973). *Attachment and Loss.* Vol. 2, Separation. New York: Basic Books. J. Bowlby (1980). *Attachment and Loss.* Vol. 3, Loss sadness and depression. New York: Basic Books. J. Bowlby (1982). *Attachment and Loss.* Vol. 1, Attachment. 2nd ed. London: Hogarth.

11. See K. S. Robson and H. A. Moss (1970). Patterns and determinants of maternal attachment. *Journal of Pediatrics* 77:976–985.

12. Bowlby (1973), pp. 204–205. Some of Bowlby's followers have made a sharp distinction between people's self-views and their "models of relationships," with the latter referring to people's beliefs about the qualities of other people (for example, friendly, hostile, trustworthy). Although this is certainly

a valid distinction in principle, I believe that it is potentially misleading because it encourages people to separate self-views from the social transactions from which they spring.

13. M. D. S. Ainsworth, S. M. Bell, and D. J. Stayton (1971). Individual differences in strange situation behavior of one-year-olds. In H. R. Schaffer, ed. *The Origin of Human Social Relations.* London: Academic. M. D. S. Ainsworth, M. C. Blehar, E. Waters, and S. Wall (1978). *Patterns of Attachment: A Psychological Study of the Strange Situation.* Hillsdale, N.J.: Erlbaum.

14. L. A. Sroufe, E. Carlson, and S. Shulman (1993). Individuals in relationships: Development from infancy through adolescence. In D. C. Funder, R. D. Parke, C. Tomlinson-Keasey, and K. Widaman, eds. *Studying Lives through Time: Personality and Development.* Washington, D.C.: American Psychological Association. For related studies, see R. Arend, F. Gove, and L. A. Sroufe (1979). Continuity of individual adaptation from infancy to kindergarten: A predictive study of ego-resiliency and curiosity in preschoolers. *Child Development* 50:950–959. L. Matas, R. Arend, and L. A. Sroufe (1978). Continuity of adaptation in the second year: The relationship between quality of attachment and later competent functioning. *Child Development* 49:547–556. E. Waters, J. Wippman, and L. A. Sroufe (1979). Attachment, positive affect, and competence in the peer group: Two studies in construct validation, *Child Development* 50:821–829. B. Egeland and L. A. Sroufe (1983). Developmental sequelae of maltreatment in infancy. In R. Rizley and D. Cicchetti, eds. *New Developmental Perspectives in Child Maltreatment.* San Francisco: Josey Bass. Sroufe has also reported that although intellectual aptitude was associated with performance, infant attachment relationship was also associated with performance even when researchers controlled for IQ.

15. J. Cassidy (1988). Child-mother attachment and the self in six year-olds. *Child Development* 59:121–134. For a broader discussion of these issues, see J. Cassidy (1990). Theoretical and methodological considerations in the study of attachment and the self in young children. In M. Greenberg, D. Cicchetti, and E. M. Cummings, eds. *Attachment in the Pre-school Years: Theory, Research, and Intervention.* Chicago: University of Chicago Press.

16. Sroufe (1989), 88.

17. D. Baumrind (1967). Child care practices anteceding three patterns of preschool behavior. *Genetic Psychology Monographs* 75:43–88. D. Baumrind (1995). *Child Maltreatment and Optimal Caregiving in Social Contexts.* New York: Garland Press. Bowlby suggests clear and direct links between the three basic attachment classifications and Baumrind's distinctions among different parenting styles; see Bowlby (1973), 350–354.

18. R. G. Wahler and J. E. Dumas (1986). "A chip off the old block": Some interpersonal characteristics of coercive children across generations. In P. Strain, ed. *Children's Social Behavior: Development, Assessment, and Modification.* New York: Academic.

19. D. Stern (1977). *The First Relationship.* Cambridge, Mass.: Harvard University Press, 117.

20. E. S. Wolf (1988). *Treating the Self: Elements of Clinical Self Psychology.* New York: Guildford, 39.

21. J. Belsky, M. Rovine, and D. G. Taylor (1984). The Pennsylvania infant and family development project. III. The origins of individual differences in infant-mother attachment: Maternal and infant contributions. *Child Development* 55:718–728.

22. D. W. Winnicott (1958). *Collected Papers.* New York: Basic Books.

23. W. Damon (1995).

24. P. Wachtel (1982). Vicious circles: The self and the rhetoric of emerging and unfolding. *Contemporary Psychoanalysis* 18:259–273.

25. Sroufe, Carlson, and Shulman (1993). For a succinct review of the effects of styles of caregiver discipline on children, see S. G. O'Leary (1995). Parental discipline mistakes. *Current Directions in Psychological Science* 4:11–13.

26. Sroufe (1989), p. 91. I have added the first names.

27. I thank Dr. Stephen Finn for sharing this case study with me.

28. J. Kaufman and E. Zigler (1989). The intergenerational transmission of child abuse. In D. Cicchetti & V. Carlson, eds.

Child Maltreatment: Theory and Research on the Causes and Consequences of Child Abuse and Neglect. Cambridge, Mass.: Cambridge University Press. Some researchers believe that this number is too conservative and that the actual rate of carryover is much higher. See B. Egeland, D. Jacobvitz, and L. A. Sroufe (1988). Breaking the cycle of abuse. *Child Development* 59:1060–1088.

29. J. Needham (1968). *Order and Life*. Cambridge, Mass.: MIT Press, 244.

30. G. L. Clark (1954). *Elements of Ecology*. New York: Wiley. E. P. Odum (1963). *Ecology*. New York: Holt, Rhinehart & Winston. E. O. Wilson (1974). *Sociobiology: The New Synthesis*. Cambridge, Mass.: Harvard University Press.

31. For a discussion of opportunity structures, see McCall and Simmons (1966). For a discussion of lifestyle enclaves, see R. N. Bellah, R. Madsen, W. M. Sullivan, A. Swidler, and S. M. Tipton (1985). *Habits of the Heart: Individualism and Commitment in American Life*. New York: Harper & Row.

32. A. K. Korman (1966). Self-esteem variable in vocational choice. *Journal of Applied Psychology* 50:479–486. A. K. Korman (1967). Self-esteem as a moderator of the relationship between self-perceived abilities and vocational choice. *Journal of Applied Psychology* 52:484–490. A. K. Korman (1969). Self-esteem as a moderator in vocational choice: Replications and extensions. *Journal of Applied Psychology* 53:188–192. For an overview of the links between self-concepts and occupational choices, see J. Brockner (1988). *Self-Esteem at Work: Research, Theory, and Practice*. New York: Lexington Books.

33. Some readers may object to including relatively "automatic" processes such as physical appearance in a discussion of active attempts to self-verify. They could point out, for example, that Tommy didn't consciously slump his shoulders as a way to elicit negative reactions. This objection has some merit, because genetically programmed characteristics and other constitutional factors may influence the reactions people elicit from others quite independently of their self-views. I include identity cues in this discussion, however, because they are influential contributors to the reactions people receive and sometimes reflect conscious efforts to acquire self-verifying evaluations.

34. For discussions of the effects of overt appearance and behavior on the reactions people receive, see R. W. Belk, (1988). Possessions and the extended self. *Journal of Consumer Research* 15:139–168. J. Douglas, G. A. Feild, and L. Rarpey (1970). A self-image theory. In S. H. Britt, ed. *Consumer Behavior in Theory and Action*. New York: Wiley. E. L. Grubb and H. L. Grathwohl (1970). Consumer self-concept, symbolism, and market behavior: A theoretical approach. In S. H. Britt, ed. *Consumer Behavior in Theory and Action*. New York: Wiley. M. J. Levesque and D. A. Kenny (1993). Accuracy of behavioral predictions at zero acquaintance: A social relations analysis. *Journal of Personality and Social Psychology* 65:1178–1187. R. A. Wicklund and P. M. Gollwitzer (1982). *Symbolic Self-Completion*. Hillsdale, N.J.: Erlbaum. B. R. Schlenker (1980). *Impression Management*. Belmont, Calif.: Wadsworth.

35. S. Strack, and J. C. Coyne (1983). Social confirmation of dysphoria: Shared and private reactions. *Journal of Personality and Social Psychology* 44:798–806. For related discussions, see J. G. Holmes and J. K. Rempel (1989). Trust in close relationships. In C. Hendrick, ed. *Review of Personality and Social Psychology: Close Relationships*. Vol. 10. Newbury Park, Calif.: Sage. Swann, Wenzlaff, Krull, and Pelham (1992).

36. W. B. Swann, Jr., and C. A. Hill (1982). When our identities are mistaken: Reaffirming self-conceptions through social interaction. *Journal of Personality and Social Psychology* 43:59–66.

37. See also J. Boissevain (1974). *Friends of Friends: Networks, Manipulators, and Coalitions*. Oxford: Blackwell. J. Boissevain, J. and J. C. Mitchell (1973). *Network Analysis: Studies in Human Interaction*. The Hague, Netherlands: Mouton. Goffman (1959).

38. Swann and Read (1981b). See study 1.

39. Swann & Read (1981b). See study 3. W. G. Crary (1966). Reactions to incongruent self-experiences. *Journal of Consulting Psychology* 30:246–252. I. Silverman, I. (1964). Self-esteem and differential responsiveness to success and failure. *Journal of Social Psychology* 69:115–119.

40. Swann, Griffin, Predmore, and Gaines (1987).

41. B. W. Pelham and W. B. Swann, Jr. (1989). From self-conceptions to self-worth: On the sources and structure of global

self-esteem. *Journal of Personality and Social Psychology* 57:672–680.

42. K. A. Dodge, G. S. Pettit, C. L. McClaskey, and M. M. Brown (1986). Social competence in children. *Monographs of the Society for Research in Child Development* 51:53.

43. Although many behavioral scientists might agree that choosing a congruent relationship partner or resisting incongruent evaluations should be construed as evidence of a desire for self-verification, they might insist that selective recall of congruent information is produced by an "automatic" or "schematic" processing bias. For this reason, they might argue that such "amotivational" processes are not expressions of a self-verification motive.

Such contentions raise many issues that are beyond the scope of this chapter, including the criteria that should be used to distinguish a motivated behavior from a nonmotivated one. Apparently, some selective attention and recall processes are produced by a tendency for the *anticipation* of self-confirming feedback to energize cognitive activity. In the Swann and Read (1981b) studies, for example, people looked at feedback longer (study 1) and were more inclined to recall it (study 3) when they suspected that it would confirm their self-views. In addition, even if a particular instance of information processing can be attributed to the structure of people's thought processes rather than to the vigor with which they engage those structures, self-verification processes may have been responsible for the formation of those structures in the first place.

44. The puzzle of the ship of Theseus offers a useful metaphor for understanding how self-views remain stable despite the fact that people's lives are composed of a myriad of diverse experiences that may depart radically from their previous ones. The puzzle is meant to illustrate a philosophical question: When has the identity of a given object truly changed? In this puzzle, each time a plank of a ship wears out, it is removed and replaced. Each time this process is repeated, the result is merely the same ship with a new plank, for the replacement of a single plank obviously does not alter the identity of the ship. Even when all the materials that made up the original ship are

eventually removed and replaced, it will still be regarded as the same ship.

The planks of the ship are analogous to the evaluations people receive. Just as these planks must be routinely replaced from a fresh supply of planks, so too must self-views be continuously nourished by self-confirming evaluations. And just as the fresh planks will help keep the ship afloat only if they fit into their assigned spaces, the evaluations people receive will keep their self-views viable only if they fit with relevant existing self-views. Evaluations that are disjunctive with people's existing self-views but considered plausible by them will foster change in their self-views.

Philosopher Robert Nozick continues the story by posing the following question: If it happened that the original planks were stored away as they were replaced and then reassembled, which would be the real ship? His answer can be found in his thoughtful book: R. Nozick (1981). *Philosophical Explanations*. Cambridge, Mass.: Harvard University Press, 33.

45. D. C. Van den Boom (1994). The influence of temperament and mothering on attachment and exploration: An experimental manipulation of sensitive responsiveness among lower-class mothers with irritable infants. *Child Development* 65:1457–1477.

46. E. G. Hall, B. Durborow, and J. L. Progen (1986). Self-esteem of female athletes and nonathletes relative to sex role type and sport type. *Sex Roles* 15:379–390. J. B. Holloway, A. Beuter, and J. L. Duda (1988). Self-efficacy and training for strength in adolescent girls. *Journal of Applied Social Psychology* 18:699–719.

47. Egeland, Jacobvitz, and Sroufe (1988).

48. For a somewhat different but related and intriguing treatment of the links between early experience and later adaptation, see C. Hazan, C. and P. R. Shaver (1990). Love and work: An attachment theoretical perspective. *Journal of Personality and Social Psychology* 59:270–280. M. Main (1990). Parental aversion to infant-initiated contact is correlated with the parent's own rejection during childhood: The effects of experience on signals of security with respect to attachment. In K. E. Barnard and T. B. Brazelton, eds. *Touch: The Foundation*

of Experience. Madison, Conn.: International Universities Press.

49. A. Adler (1917). *Study of Organ Inferiority and Its Psychical Compensation: A Contribution to Clinical Medicine.* S. E. Jelliffe, trans. New York: Nervous and Mental Disease Publishing Co. (original work published 1907). A. Adler (1912). *The Neurotic Constitution: Outlines of a Comparative Individualistic Psychology and Psychotherapy.* B. Glueck and J. E. Lind, trans. New York: Moffat, Yard and Co. (original work published 1912).

50. For discussions of attempts to attain ideal selves, see E. T. Higgins (1987). Self-discrepancy: A theory relating self and affect. *Psychological Review* 94:319–340. H. Markus and P. Nurius (1986). Possible selves. *American Psychologist* 41:954–969. For related discussions of various forms of compensation, see Crocker and Major (1989). M. Rosenberg (1965). M. Rosenberg (1967). Psychological selectivity in self-esteem formation. In C. Sherif and M. Sherif, eds. *Attitude, Ego-Involvement, and Change.* New York: Wiley. C. M. Steele (1988). The psychology of self-affirmation: Sustaining the integrity of the self. In L. Berkowitz, ed. *Advances in Experimental Social Psychology.* Vol. 21. New York: Academic. Stryker (1980).

51. K. Nelson (1993). Developing self-knowledge from autobiographical memory. In T. K. Skrull and R. S. Wyer, eds. *The mental representation of trait and autobiographical knowledge about the self: Advances in Social Cognition.* Vol. 5. Hillside, N.J.: Erlbaum, 115.

52. K. Cutler and N. L. Hazen (1995). Parent-child and child-parent communication: Effects of attachment and gender. Paper presented at the biannual meetings of the Society for Research in Child Development, Indianapolis, Indiana.

53. E. H. Erikson (1963). *Childhood and Society.* 2nd ed. New York: Norton. A. Maslow (1954). *Motivation and Personality.* New York: Harper & Row. C. R. Rogers (1961). *On Becoming a Person.* Boston: Houghton Mifflin.

54. C. H. Cooley (1902). *Human Nature and the Social Order.* New York: G. Scribner's Sons, 145–146. For discussions of the unique qualities of self-liking and self-competence, see

J. C. Diggory (1966). *Self-Evaluation: Concepts and Studies.* New York: Wiley. D. D. Franks and J. Marolla (1976). Efficacious action and social approval as interacting dimensions of self-esteem: A tentative formulation through construct validation. *Sociometry* 39:324–341. V. Gecas (1971). Parental behavior and dimensions of adolescent self-evaluation. *Sociometry* 34:466–482. V. Gecas and M. L. Schwalbe (1983). Beyond the looking-glass self: Social structure and efficacy-based self-esteem. *Social Psychology Quarterly* 46:77–88. S. Harter (1985). Competence as a dimension of self-evaluation: Toward a comprehensive model of self-worth. In R. Leahy, ed. *The Development of the Self.* New York: Academic. S. Harter (1990). Causes, correlates, and the functional role of global self-worth: A lifespan perspective. In R. J. Sternberg and J. Kolligian, Jr., eds. *Competence Considered.* New Haven, Conn.: Yale University Press. R. W. Tafarodi and W. B. Swann, Jr. (1995). Self-liking and self-competence as dimensions of global self-esteem: Initial validation of a measure. *Journal of Personality Assessment* 65:322–342.

55. These items are taken from a self-esteem scale developed by Romin Tafarodi and William B. Swann. See Tafarodi and Swann (1995).

56. For related discussions, see P. W. Linville (1987). Self-complexity as a cognitive buffer against stress-related illness and depression. *Journal of Personality and Social Psychology* 52:663–676.

57. Swann, Tafarodi, and Pinel. *Personality and Social Psychology Bulletin* (under review).

58. R. A. Josephs, H. R. Markus, and R. W. Tafarodi (1992). Gender and self-esteem. *Journal of Personality and Social Psychology* 63:391–402.

Chapter 5: Romantic Self-Traps

1. M. M. Hunt (1959). *The Natural History of Love.* New York: Alfred A. Knopf.

2. G. Steinem (1992). *Revolution from Within: A Book of Self-Esteem.* Boston: Little, Brown.

3. Steinem (1992).

4. In the preface to her book, Steinem recounts how her editor correctly identified her self-esteem problem, noting that "I had felt drawn to the subject of self-esteem not only because other people needed it, but because I did." Steinem (1992), 6.

5. C. G. Hindy, J. C. Schwarz, and A. Brodsky (1989). *If This is Love, Why Do I Feel So Insecure*. New York: Atlantic Monthly Press, 19.

6. Hindy, Schwarz, and Brodsky (1989), 21.

7. A. Ellis (1962). *The American Sexual Tragedy*. New York: Lyle Stuart.

8. D. de Rougement (1940). *Love in the Western World*. M. Belgion, trans. New York: Harcourt & Brace, 13.

9. D. de Rougement (1959). The crisis of the modern couple. In R. N. Anshen, ed. *The Family: Its Function and Destiny*. New York: Harper, 453.

10. B. Thorpe, ed. (1840). *Ancient Laws and Institutes of England. Volume the First*. The Commissioners of the Public Records of the Kingdom, 407.

11. B. I. Murstein (1974). *Love, Sex, and Marriage through the Ages*. New York: Springer, 98.

12. Murstein (1974), 150.

13. Ulrich von Liechtenstein. *An Autobiography in Service of Ladies*. J. W. Thomas, trans. Chapel Hill: University of North Carolina Press (1969). Although there is no question that Ulrich wrote *An Autobiography in Service of Ladies*, historians have debated the authenticity of some of the assertions made in that document. Most of the account offered here was inspired by Morton Hunt's elegant treatment of the topic in *The Natural History of Love*. Although Hunt believed that the story should be taken at face value, others (including J. W. Thomas, who translated the autobiography) insist that many events were fabricated to amuse the audience.

14. A. Capellanus (1941). *The Art of Courtly Love*. J. J. Parry, trans. and ed. New York: Columbia University Press, 106–107.

15. For a further discussion, see Murstein (1974).

16. Murstein (1974).

17. E. K. Rothman (1984). *Hands and Hearts: A History of Courtship in America*. New York: Basic Books.

18. Rothman (1984).

19. Respondents could vote twice. A. Preston (1905). The ideals of the bride-to-be. *Ladies Home Journal* (June):26.

20. J. A. Simpson, B. Campbell, and E. Bersheid (1986). The association between love and marriage: Kephart (1967) twice revisited. *Personality and Social Psychology Bulletin* 12:363–372.

21. J. R. Averill and P. Booth-Royd (1977). On falling in love: In conformance with the romantic ideal. *Motivation and Emotion* 1:235–247.

22. See H. Fisher (1992). *The Anatomy of Love*. New York: W. W. Norton. W. R. Jankowiak and E. F. Fischer (1992). A cross-cultural perspective on romantic love. *Ethnology* 31:149–155.

23. Harter (1993), 98. S. Harter (1986). Processes underlying the construction, maintenance, and enhancement of the self-concept in children. In J. Suls and A. G. Greenwald, eds. *Psychological Perspectives on the Self*. Vol. 3. Hillsdale, N.J.: Erlbaum.

24. J. Austen (1813/1981). *Pride and Prejudice*. New York: New American Library.

25. C. Hendrick and S. Hendrick (1986). A theory and method of love. Journal of Personality and Social Psychology 50:392–402.

26. J. C. Babcock, J. Waltz, N. S. Jacobson, and J. M. Gottman (1993). Power and violence: The relation between communication pattern, power discrepancies, and domestic violence. *Journal of Consulting and Clinical Psychology* 61:40–50. Feelings of exclusivity and powerlessness have even been used to excuse murder. In one instance, a young man defended the murder of his girlfriend by claiming that he loved her too passionately to allow her to leave him. See D. Dunn (1984). Justice: A father's account of the trial of his daughter's killer. *Vanity Fair* (March):86–106. For a related discussion, see L. Sanford and M. E. Donovan (1984). *Women and Self-Esteem: Understanding and Improving the Way We Think and Feel about Ourselves*. New York: Anchor/Doubleday.

27. Although most of this research has focused on males, there is evidence that the findings apply to females as well. See G. V. Hamilton (1914). A study of sexual tendencies in monkeys and baboons. *Journal of Animal Behavior* 4:295–318. D. Symonds (1979). *The Evolution of Human Sexuality.* Oxford: Oxford University Press. J. R. Wilson, R. E. Kuehn, and F. A. Beach (1963). Modification in the sexual behavior of male rats produced by changing the stimulus female. *Journal of Comparative and Physiological Psychology* 56:636–644.

28. W. Griffitt (1981). Sexual intimacy in aging marital partners. In J. Marsh and S. Kiesler, eds. *Aging: Stability and Change in the Family.* New York: Academic. G. C. O'Neill and N. O'Neill (1970). Patterns in group sexual activity. *Journal of Sex Research* 6:101–112.

29. Z. Rubin (1973). *Liking and Loving.* New York: Holt, Rinehart & Winston. D. Byrne, and S. K. Murnen (1988). Maintaining loving relationships. In R. J. Sternberg and M. L. Barnes, eds. *The Psychology of Love.* New Haven: Yale University Press.

30. See T. L. Huston, S. McCale, and A. C. Crouter (1989). When the honeymoon's over: Changes in the marriage relationship over the first year. In R. Gilmore and S. Duck, eds. *The Emerging Field of Personal Relationships.* Hillsdale, N.J.: Erlbaum. See also K. J. Grover, C. S. Russell, W. R. Schumm, and L. A. Paff-Bergen (1985). Mate selection processes and marital satisfaction. *Family Relations* 34:383–386. H. J. Raschke. (1987). Divorce. In M. B. Sussman and S. K. Steinmetz, eds. *Handbook of Marriage and the Family.* New York: Plenum.

31. A. Pam (1970). A field study of psychological factors in college courtships. Doctoral dissertation, State University of New York at Buffalo. Cited on p. 34 of J. D. Cunningham and J. K. Antill (1981). Love in developing romantic relationships. In S. Duck and R. Gilmour, eds. *Personal Relationships.* Vol. 2. Developing Personal Relationships. London: Academic.

32. Not coincidentally, *Aladdin* was based on an Arabian epic that presumably helped sow the seeds of the romantic ideal in Europe.

33. E. Rapaport (1976). On the future of love: Rousseau and the radical feminists. In C. C. Gould and M. W. Wartofsky, eds. *Women and Philosophy: Toward a Theory of Liberation.* New York: Putnam, 199.

34. E. Berscheid (1982). Attraction and emotion in interpersonal relations. In M. S. Clark and S. T. Fiske, eds. *Affect and Cognition.* Hillsdale, N.J.: Erlbaum. See also E. Berscheid (1983). Emotion. In H. H. Kelley, E. Berscheid, A. Christensen, J. H. Harvey, T. L. Huston, G. Levinger, E. McClintock, L. A. Peplau, and D. R. Peterson, eds. *Close Relationships.* New York: W. H. Freeman. P. M. Blau (1964). *Exchange and Power in Social Life.* New York: Wiley. J. G. Holmes and J. K. Rmpel (1989). Trust in close relationships. In C. Hendrick, ed. *Review of Personality and Social Psychology: Close Relationships.* Vol. 10. Newbury Park, Calif.: Sage. S. S. Brehm (1985). *Intimate Relationships.* New York: Random House. C. T. Hill, Z. Rubin, and L. A. Peplau (1976). Breakups before marriage: The end of 103 affairs. *Journal of Social Issues* 43:147–168. E. Walster, G. W. Walster, and J. Traupmann (1978). Equity and premarital sex. *Journal of Personality and Social Psychology* 36:82–92.

35. P. M. Blau (1964). *Exchange and Power in Social Life.* New York: Wiley.

36. C. Hendrick and S. Hendrick (1986).

37. Berscheid (1983). Huston, McCale, and Crouter (1989). W. Waller (1938). *The Family: A Dynamic Interpretation.* New York: Dryden.

38. J. Levy and R. Monroe (1938). *The Happy Family.* New York: Alfred A. Knopf, 66–67.

39. Swann, De La Ronde, and Hixon (1994).

40. I say "apparent" when referring to this shift because the "cross-sectional" design of our study does not allow us to conclude that the same people who were seekers of positive evaluations when they were dating became seekers of negative evaluations when they were married; all we can say is that our particular dating and married participants showed this pattern.
    For related discussions, see Dymond, who concluded that "married love is not blind . . . the better each partner understands

the other's perceptions of himself and his world, the more satisfactory the relationship." See p. 171 of R. A. Dymond (1954). Interpersonal perception and marital happiness. *Canadian Journal of Psychology* 8:164–171. See also R. G. Tharp (1963). Psychological pattern in marriage. *Psychological Bulletin* 60:97–117. Similarly, Corsini reports that the congruence between self-perceptions and the perception by the spouse was particularly important in determining male happiness. See R. Corsini (1956). Understanding and similarity in marriage. *Journal of Abnormal and Social Psychology* 52:327–332. Luckey also discovered that the congruence of the husband's self-concept and the appraisal of the spouse were associated with satisfaction in marriage, although this was *not* true of wives. See E. B. Luckey (1960). Marital satisfaction and congruence self spouse concepts. *Sociological Forces* 39:153–157.

41. T. Huston and R. Houts (in press). The psychological infrastructure of courtship and marriage: The role of personal and compatibility in the evolution of romantic relationship. In T. Bradbuy, ed. *The Development of Marital Dysfunction.* Cambridge, Mass.: Cambridge University Press.

42. P. Berger and H. Kellner (1964). Marriage and the construction of reality: An exercise in the microsociology of knowledge. *Diogenes* 46:1–24. Quote is from p. 16.

Chapter 6: Esteem and the Pursuit of Competence

1. N. Seid (1994). Learning to live without a paycheck: How one mom gave up her job but kept her self-esteem. *Parents Magazine* 69:152.

2. Seid (1994).

3. See also Bellah et al. (1985). P. Marin (1975). The new narcissism. *Harper's Magazine* 251:45–50, 55–56. P. L. Wachtel (1989). *The Poverty of Affluence: A Psychological Portrait of the American Way of Life.* Santa Cruz, Calif.: New Society Publishers. D. Yankelovich (1981). *New Rules: Searching for Self-Fulfillment in a World Turned Upside Down.* New York: Random House.

4. S. Coontz (1992). *The Way We Never Were: American Families and the Nostalgia Trap.* New York: Basic Books, 169–170.

5. Coontz (1992), 170.

6. R. Marchand (1985). *Advertising the American Dream: Making Way for Modernity 1920–1940.* Berkeley, Calif.: University of California Press, 347–360.

7. P. Cushman (1990). Why the self is empty: Toward a historically situated psychology. *American Psychologist* 45:599–611. See p. 605.

8. Quoted in Wachtel (1989), 23.

9. T. Veblen (1992). *The Theory of the Leisure Class.* New Brunswick, N.J.: Transaction Publishers (original work published 1899), 61.

10. J. A. Russell and T. Branch (1979). Second Wind: *The Memoirs of an Opinionated Man.* New York: Ballantine Books, 98.

11. E. L. Deci and R. M. Ryan (1991). A motivational approach to self. In R. Deinstbier, ed. *Nebraska Symposium on Motivation.* Vol. 38. Lincoln: University of Nebraska Press. For a highly accessible account, see A. Kohn (1993). *Punished by Rewards.* Boston: Houghton Mifflin.

12. E. A. Locke and G. P. Latham (1990). *A Theory of Goal Setting and Task Performance.* Englewood Cliffs, N.J.: Prentice Hall.

13. D. Greene, B. Sternberg, and M. R. Lepper (1976). Overjustification in a token economy. *Journal of Personality and Social Psychology* 34:1219–1234.

14. The more money workers receive and the more equitably they believe it is distributed, for example, the more likely they will feel bonded to, and inclined to work for, the organization. For a discussion of relevant evidence, see D. Katz and R. L. Kahn (1978). *The Social Psychology of Organizations.* New York: Wiley. Also see D. Rosenfeld, R. Folger, and H. F. Adelman (1980). When rewards reflect competence: A qualification of the overjustification effect. *Journal of Personality and Social Psychology* 39:368–376. G. Pretty and C. Seligman (1984). Affect and the overjustification effect. *Journal of Personality and Social Psychology* 46:1241–1253. S. T. Fiske and S. E. Taylor (1984). *Social Cognition.* New York: Addison-Wesley.

15. A. J. Elliot and J. M. Harackiewicz (1994). Goal setting, achievement orientation, and intrinsic motivation: A mediational analysis. *Journal of Personality and Social Psychology* 66:968–980. J. M. Harackiewicz and C. Sansone (1991). Goals and intrinsic motivation: You can get there from here. In M. L. Maehr and P. R. Pintrich, eds. *Advances in Motivation and Achievement.* Vol. 7. Greenwich, Conn.: JAI Press.

16. Deci and Ryan (1991). For similar findings from the sociological literature, see C. L. Staples, M. L. Schwalbe, and V. Gecas (1984). Social class, occupational conditions, and efficacy-based self-esteem. *Sociological Perspectives* 27:85–109.

17. R. Bendix (1956). *Work and Authority in Industry.* New York: Wiley, 39. See also J. L. Hammond and B. Hammond (1925). *The Town Labourer.* London: Longmans, Green & Co., 13–16.

18. K. Marx (1964). *Early Writings.* T. B. Bottomore, trans. and ed. New York: McGraw Hill, 124–125.

19. For example, see K. Marx (1977). *Capital.* Vol. 1. B. Fowkes, trans. New York: Vintage, 356–357.

20. For a useful discussion of the scientific management movement and its limitations, see J. G. March and H. A. Simon (1993). *Organizations.* Cambridge, Mass.: Blackwell.

21. A. R. Hochschild (1983). *The Managed Heart: Commercialization of Human Feeling.* Berkeley: University of California Press, 4.

22. Hochschild (1983), 188.

23. D. R. Loseke and S. E. Cahill (1986). Actors in search of a character: Student social workers' quest for professional identity. *Symbolic Interaction* 9:245–258. Hochschild (1983). L. A. King and R. A. Emmons (1990). Conflict over emotional expression: Psychological and physical correlates. *Journal of Personality and Social Psychology* 58:864–877. B. Parkinson (1991). Emotional stylists: Strategies of expressive management among trainee hairdressers. *Cognition and Emotion* 5:419–434. D. R. Rutter and P. J. Fielding (1988). Sources of occupational stress: An examination of British prison officers. *Work and Stress* 2:291–299.

24. For accounts of Mary Kay's guidelines for emotional expression, see M. K. Ash (1984). *Mary Kay on People Management.* New York: Warner Books. For Disneyland's rules, see J. Van Maanen (1991). The smile factory: Work at Disneyland. In P. J. Frost, L. F. Moore, M. R. Louis, C. Lundberg, J. Martin, eds. *Reframing Organization Culture.* Newbury Park, Calif.: Sage Publishing. J. Van Maanen and G. Kunda (1989). "Real feelings": Emotional expression and organization culture. In L. L. Cummings and B. M. Staw, eds. *Research in Organization Behaviour.* Vol. 11. Greenwich, Conn.: JAI Press. For work in fast-food restaurants, see J. Komaki M. R. Blood, and D. Holder (1980). Fostering friendliness in a fast food franchise. *Journal of Organization Behavior Management* 2:151–164. Rafaeli, A. (1989a). When cashiers meet customers: An analysis of the role of supermarket cashiers. *Academy of Management Journal* 32:245–273. A. Rafaeli (1989b). When clerks meet customers: A test of variables related to emotional expressions on the job. *Journal of Applied Psychology* 74:385–393.

25. A. Zaleznik (1989). *The Managerial Mystique.* New York: Harper & Row, 110. D. L. Bradford and A. Cohen (1984). *Managing for Excellence: The Guide to Developing High Performance in Contemporary Organizations.* New York: Wiley. King and Emmons (1990). Parkinson (1991). A. Rafaeli and R. I. Sutton (1987). Expression of emotion as part of the work role. *Academy of Management Journal* 12:23–37. Rutter and Fielding (1988). R. I. Sutton (1991). Maintaining norms about expressed emotions: The case of bill collectors. *Administrative Science Quarterly* 36:245–268. R. I. Sutton and A. Rafaeli (1988). Untangling the relationship between displayed emotions and organizational sales: The case of convenience stores. *Academy of Management Journal* 31:461–487. A. S. Wharton (1993). The affective consequences of service work: Managing emotions on the job. *Work and Occupations* 20:205–232.

26. Although there is a sense in which actors playing a role are being "phony," such behavior is not necessarily inauthentic because both the actor and the audience know that the actor's behavior is constrained by the role.

27. H. Helson (1964). *Adaptation Level Theory.* New York: Harper & Row. See also A. Parducci (1968). The relativism of absolute judgments. *Scientific American* 219:84–90.

28. P. Brickman, D. Coates, and B. Janoff-Bulman (1978). Lottery winners and accident victims: Is happiness relative? *Journal of Personality and Social Psychology* 36:917–927. Also see C. Safran, (1974). All right! I won a million bucks. Now what do I do with it? *Today's Health* (Nov.):56–61.

29. Wachtel (1989).

30. H. Sklar (1995). Chaos or community: Seeking solutions, not scapegoats, for bad economics. Boston: South End Press, 5. During the Reagan years, there was a massive redistribution of wealth from the poor to the very rich. For example, from 1978 to 1988, there was an increase of more than three times in the number of millionaires in the United States (from 450,000 to 1,500,000) and an increase of 51 times in the number of billionaires (from 1 to 51). During this same period, the vast majority of Americans (those in the lowest 80th percentile) suffered a *decline* in real income, with those in the poorest 10th percentile incurring the worst losses (–14.8 percent). For a historical perspective on this redistribution of wealth, see K. Phillips (1990). *The Politics of Rich and Poor.*New York: Random House. F. Levy (1987). *Dollars and Dreams: The Changing American Income Distribution.* New York: Russell.

31. D. G. Myers (1994). *Exploring Social Psychology.* New York: McGraw Hill, 107.

32. Ironically, during the past two decades the rate of unemployment has also doubled, which means that while some people are working more, others are completely idle. This reflects the fact that employers have sought to increase their profits by extending the hours that employees work and hiring part-time employees (many of whom do not receive benefits) rather than additional full-time employees (who would require benefits). See Schor (1991).

33. Schor (1991). For example, Figure 3.1 on p. 45 suggests that the average worker today is putting in longer hours than the adult male peasants of the thirteenth century in the United Kingdom. See also the discussion on p. 163.

34. Schor (1991).

35. T. Kasser and R. M. Ryan (1993). A dark side of the American dream: Correlates of financial success as a central life as-

piration. *Journal of Personality and Social Psychology* 65: 410–422. T. Kasser and R. M. Ryan (1994). Further dismantling the American dream: The differential effects of intrinsic and extrinsic goal structures. Manuscript. University of Rochester, New York.

36. Schor (1991), 11–13.

37. C. Geertz (1979). From the natives' point of view: On the nature of anthropological understanding. In P. Rabinow, ed. *Interpretive Social Science: A Reader.* Berkeley, Calif.: University of California Press, 229.

38. M. Weber (1930/1958). *The Protestant Ethic and the Spirit of Capitalism.* New York: Charles Scribner.

39. R. Sennett and J. Cobb (1972). *The Hidden Injuries of Class.* New York: Knopf, 246.

40. Taken from S. Berglas (1986). *The Success Syndrome.* New York: Plenum, 191.

41. Bellah et al. (1985), 120.

42. R. D. Putnam (1995). Bowling alone: America's declining social capital. *Journal of Democracy* 6(1):65–78 . R. D. Putnam (1993). The prosperous community: Social capital and public life. *American Prospect* 13:35–42.

43. A. Etzioni (1993). *The Spirit of Community: Rights, Responsibilities and the Communitarian Agenda.* New York: Crown.

44. M. Lind (1995). To have and have not. *Harpers* 290:35–48. M. B. Katz (1995). *Improving Poor People: The Welfare State, the "Underclass," and Urban Schools as History.* Princeton, N.J.: Princeton University Press.

45. T. Gitlin (1995). *The Twilight of Common Dreams: Why America is Wracked by Culture Wars.* New York: Metropolitan Books/Holt, 35.

46. Yankelovich (1981), 251.

47. K. Patterson and P. Kim (1991). *The Day America Told the Truth: What People Really Believe about Everything that Really Matters.* New York: Prentice Hall, 66.

48. Karen (1994), 414.

49. Karen's assertions are extremely difficult to evaluate. In part this is because of the sheer number of changes that society has undergone over the last century; also, the diagnostic categories and the number of people seeking therapy have changed substantially over this period.

50. M. E. P. Seligman (1990). Why is there so much depression today? The waxing and waning of the commons. In R. E. Ingram, ed. *Contemporary Psychological Approaches to Depression*. New York: Plenum, 4–5.

51. J. D. Rockefeller (1907). John D. Rockefeller on opportunity in America. *Cosmopolitan* 43:368–372. The editor noted that "during a visit to Compiegne, France, last summer Mr. Rockefeller expressed himself freely in answer to a series of questions by a correspondent who was a companion of his leisure hours. From careful and accurate notes of these talks the following article has been transcribed." (Editor's note, p. 368.) The questions were not included in the article.

52. Alger admitted that he had been imprudent and resigned from the ministry. See R. M. Huber (1971). *The American Idea of Success*. New York: McGraw Hill, 451.

53. J. K. Galbraith (1992). *The Culture of Contentment*. Boston, Mass.: Houghton Mifflin.

54. From a scientific standpoint, attributing racial differences in intelligence to genetic factors is problematic for several reasons, including the substantial genetic overlap among races, which undercuts the meaning of race as a distinct category. In addition, even Herrnstein and Murray acknowledge that evidence that genes influence how well people within a group score on IQ tests does not mean that genes account for differences in the average scores of people in different groups. (Similarly, the fact that genes influence the relative heights of different pine trees within a forest does not explain why pine trees in lush regions grow taller than pine trees in arid regions.) See R. J. Herrnstein and C. Murray (1994). *The Bell Curve: Intelligence and Class Structure in American Life*. New York: The Free Press.

   Substantial evidence runs counter to the idea that genes are the primary cause of racial differences in intelligence. One study showed that black orphans adopted by white families had above average IQs. See S. Scarr and R. A. Weinberg (1976). IQ test performance of black children adopted by white families. *American Psychologist* 31:726–739. Similarly, studies have found no relationship between IQ scores and degree of African ancestry of African Americans estimated from analyses of blood groups. See J. C. Leohlin, S. G. Vandenberg, and R. T. Osborne (1973). Blood group genes and Negro-White ability differences. *Behavior Genetics* 3:263–270. S. Scarr, A. J. Pakstis, S. H. Katz, and W. B. Barker (1977). Absence of a relationship between degree of White ancestry and intellectual skills within a Black population. *Human Genetics* 39:69–86.

Also, a genetic argument cannot explain regional differences in IQ. During World War I, for example, black soldiers from Ohio, Illinois, New York, and Pennsylvania outscored white soldiers from Georgia, Arkansas, Kentucky, and Mississippi. See H. J. Butcher (1973). *Human Intelligence: Its Nature and Assessment.* New York: Harper & Row, 252.

And in a study of children fathered by American soldiers during the army of occupation after World War II, there were no clear differences in the IQs of those sired by black as compared to white soldiers. See K. Eyferth (1961). Leistungen verchiedener Gruppen von Besätzungskindern im Hamburg-Wechsler Intelligentztest für Kinder (HAWIK). *Archive für die gesamte Psychologie* 113:222–241. J. C. Loehlin, G. Lindzey, and J. N. Spuhler (1975). *Race Differences in Intelligence.* San Francisco: W. H. Freeman.

Conservative political economist Thomas Sowell at Stanford University's Hoover Institute has presented less direct but revealing evidence that is relevant to the origins of racial differences in IQ. He points out that the historical record shows that the IQ scores of various groups change as their conditions improve. When he examined changes in the IQ test scores of groups who immigrated to the United States from Europe in the twentieth century, he discovered that virtually all newly arrived immigrant groups began by scoring approximately 15 points below the average—the same margin of difference between blacks and whites—but that their IQ scores increased with improvements in their socioeconomic conditions. This pattern has characterized virtually every racial group that has set foot upon American shores, including ones that are now thought to have normal or above normal intelligence (for example Jewish, Japanese, Chinese, Italian, and Polish). Taken together, this evidence is consistent with the possibility that if the experiences of blacks and other members of the underclass improved, their scores on IQ tests would improve accordingly. See T. Sowell (1981). *Ethnic America.* New York: Basic Books, 216–220. T. Sowell (1978). Race and IQ reconsidered. In T. Sowell, ed. *Essays and Data on American Ethnic Groups.* Washington, D.C.: The Urban Institute. T. Sowell (1995). *Race and Culture: A World View.* New York: Basic Books. For a more general discussion of race and intelligence, see R. Jacoby and N. Glauberman (1995). *The Bell Curve Debate.* New York: Random House.

55. Kasser and Ryan (1993). Sroufe, Carlson, and Shulman (1993).

56. A. Burns, R. Homel, and J. Goodnow. (1984). Conditions of life and parental values. *Australian Journal of Psychology* 36:219–237. M. L. Kohn (1977). *Class and Conformity: A Study in Values.* 2nd ed. Chicago: University of Chicago Press.

57. S. Steele (1990). *The Content of Our Character.* New York: Harper Perennial, 54.

58. C. M. Steele (1992). Race and the schooling of Black Americans. *Atlantic Monthly* (April):68–78.

59. C. M. Steele and J. Aronson (1995). Contending with a stereotype: African-American intellectual test performance and stereotype vulnerability. Manuscript.

60. S. J. Spencer and C. M. Steele (1995). Under suspicion of inability: Stereotype vulnerability and women's math performance. Manuscript. Earlier researchers reported that the gender gap in performance on science tasks disappeared when the "I don't know" option was eliminated.

61. Katz (1995), 78–79.

62. It may, however, diminish people's faith that they will share in that dream. Robert Reich, President Clinton's secretary of labor, lamented that recognition of the stagnation of the lower class was eroding "the moral core at the heart of capitalism, the faith that if you work hard you can get ahead." From *New York*

Times news service; appeared in the June 18, 1995, *Austin American Statesman.*

63. Kasser and Ryan (1993).

64. H. B. Kaplan and R. J. Johnson (1991). Negative social sanctions and juvenile delinquency: Effects of labeling in a model of deviant behavior. *Social Science Quarterly* 72:98–122.

65. For a useful discussion of the mechanisms underlying the emergence of feelings of hostility toward the dominant group, see H. Tajfel and J. C. Turner (1986). The social identity theory of intergroup behavior. In S. Worschel and W. Austin, eds. *Psychology of Intergroup Relations.* Chicago: Nelson-Hall.

66. D. S. Kaplan, B. M. Peck, and H. B. Kaplan (1994). Structural relations model of self-rejection, disposition to deviance, and academic failure. *Journal of Educational Research* 87: 166–173.

67. M. Rosenberg, C. Schooler, and C. Schoenbach (1989). Self-esteem and adolescent problems: Modeling reciprocal effects. *American Sociological Review* 54:1004–1018.

68. Galbraith (1984).

69. The tendency for Americans to conclude that the actions of their compatriots reflect their dispositions rather than the situational forces that are impinging on them has been astutely and extensively documented by psychologists Edward Jones, Lee Ross, Daniel Gilbert, and others. Evidence that members of other cultures do not share this bias can be found in the work of anthropologists such as Richard Shweder and psychologists Joan Miller and Michael Morris and their colleagues. See E. E. Jones (1979). The rocky road from acts to dispositions. American Psychologist 34:107–117. D. T. Gilbert and P. S. Malone (1955). The correspondence bias. Psychological Bulletin 117:21–38. J. G. Miller (1984). Culture and the development of everyday social explanation. Journal of Personality and Social Psychology 46:961–978. M. W. Morris and K. Peng (1994). Culture and cause: American and Chinese attributions for social and physical events. Journal of Personality and Social Psychology 67:949–971. L. Ross (1977). The intuitive psychol-

ogist and his shortcomings: Distortions in the attribution process. In L. Berkowitz, ed. Advances in Experimental Social Psychology. Vol. 10. New York: Academic. R. A. Shweder and E. Bourne (1982). Does the concept of the person vary cross-culturally? In A. J. Marsella and G. White, eds. Cultural Concepts of Mental Health and Therapy. Boston: Reidel.

70. M. Lerner (1980). *The Belief in a Just World: A Fundamental Delusion.* New York: Plenum. M. Lerner and D. T. Miller (1978). Just-world research and the attribution process: Looking back and ahead. *Psychological Bulletin* 85:1030–1051.

Chapter 7: Raising Self-Esteem

1. T. S. Eliot (1974). *The Cocktail Party.* London: Faber & Faber Ltd., 130.

2. E. Kazan (1967). *The Arrangement.* New York: Stern & Day.

3. The self-esteem of some people is more stable than that of others. See M. H. Kernis and S. B. Waschull (1995). The interactive roles of stability and level of self-esteem: Research and theory. In M. P. Zanna, ed. *Advances in Experimental Social Psychology.* Vol. 27. New York: Academic. Overall, however, the level of self-esteem stability is fairly high over periods as long as 30 years. See J. Block and R. W. Robins, (1993). A longitudinal study of consistency and change in self-esteem from early adolescence to early adulthood. *Child Development* 64:909–923. J. Block, P. F. Gjerde, and J. H. Block (1991). Personality antecedents of depressive tendencies in 18-year-olds: A prospective study. *Journal of Personality and Social Psychology* 60:726–738. D. A. Blyth, R. G. Simmons, and S. Carlton-Ford (1983). The adjustment of early adolescents to school transitions. *Journal of Early Adolescence* 3:105–120. P. M. O'Malley and J. G. Bachman (1983). Self-esteem: Change and stability between ages 13 and 23. *Developmental Psychology* 19:257–268. For a related discussion, see L. A. Sroufe and D. Jacobvitz (1989). Diverging pathways, developmental transformations, multiple etiologies, and the problem of continuity in development. *Human Development* 32:196–203).

4. G. Steinem (1992). *Revolution from Within: A Book of Self-Esteem.* Boston: Little, Brown, 38.

5. E. Bass and L. Davis (1988). *The Courage to Heal: A Guide for Women Survivors of Child Sexual Abuse.* New York: Harper & Row, 62.

6. Sacks (1990), 97.

7. Sacks (1990), 99.

8. H. Markus and P. Nurius (1986). Possible selves. *American Psychologist* 41:954–969.

9. Ray eventually came to miss the spontaneity of his pre-Haldol self. He devised the compromise of taking Haldol only during the week, which allowed him to revert back to his old "witty ticcy Ray" on the weekends. See Sacks (1990), 100–101.

10. S. E. Finn and M. E. Tonsager (1992). Therapeutic impact of providing MMPI-2 feedback to college students awaiting therapy. *Journal of Psychological Assessment* 4:278–287. For a related conceptualization of the therapeutic process, see C. T. Fischer (1985). *Individualizing Psychological Assessment.* Monterey, Calif.: Brooks-Cole.

11. S. Hollon and A. T. Beck (1994). Cognitive and cognitive-behavioral therapies. In A. E. Bergin and S. C. Garfield, eds. *Handbook of Psychotherapy and Behavior Change.* 4th ed. New York: Wiley.
   Electroconvulsive shock therapy and antidepressant drugs seem to be about as effective as cognitive and interpersonal therapies in treating depression (and even more effective in treating severe depression and depression with biochemical origins). For a highly accessible discussion, see Seligman (1994).

12. See, for example, K. L. Howard, D. E. Orlinsky, and R. J. Lueger (1995). The design of clinically relevant outcome research: Some considerations and an example. In M. Aveline and D. A. Shapiro, eds. *Research Foundations for Psychotherapy Practice.* New York: Wiley.

13. For related discussions, see M. D. Evans, S. D. Hollon, R. J. DeRubeis, J. M. Piasecki, W. M. Grove, M. J. Garvey, and V. B. Tuason (1992). Differential relapse following cognitive therapy and pharmacotherapy for depression. *Archives of General Psychiatry* 49:802–808. S. A. Montgomery (1994). Antidepressants in long-term treatment. *Annual Review of Medicine* 45:447–457.

14. R. H. Vose (1981). *Agoraphobia*. London: Faber & Faber.

15. R. J. Hafner (1983). Marital systems of agoraphobic women: Contributions of husbands' denial and projection. *Journal of Family Therapy* 5:379–396.

16. D. T. Gilbert and E. E. Jones (1986). Perceiver induced constraint: Interpretations of self-generated reality. *Journal of Personality and Social Psychology* 50:269–280. W. B. Swann, Jr., B. W. Pelham, and D. Roberts (1987). Causal chunking: Memory and inference in ongoing interaction. *Journal of Personality and Social Psychology* 53:858–865.

17. For a useful discussion of interpersonal therapy, see Wachtel and Wachtel (1986).

18. M. Twain (1906). *What Is Man?* New York: De Vinne Press.

19. Bowlby (1973), 369.

20. Quoted in Karen (1994), 266.

21. Van den Boom (1994).

22. Sroufe (1983), 77. I have added the name "Joey."

23. Sroufe (1983).

24. J. E. Gillham, K. J. Reivich, L. H. Jaycox, and M. E. P. Seligman (1995). Prevention of depressive symptoms in school children: Two year follow-up. *Psychological Science* 6:343–351.

25. Harter (1993).

26. Linton goes on to extol the virtues of arranged marriages. He begins by noting that marriage serves several social functions: reproduction, child care, sexual gratification, and economic cooperation. He then argues that whereas family leaders are acutely sensitive to all these functions, romantic partners tend to focus exclusively on their personal needs and desires. For this reason, family leaders represent the needs of the larger society better than do persons who are contemplating marriage. To those who counter that arranged marriages ignore the preferences of children, Linton replies that the parents who engineer such marriages usually consult the children. See R. Linton (1936). *The Study of Man*. New York: D. Appleton-Century, 75.

27. Berscheid explains this phenomenon by noting that emotional distress occurs when important goals are blocked. As long as a companionate love relationship is functioning smoothly, partners will help each other to satisfy their mutual goals (raising children, maintaining the house, satisfying each other's emotional needs, and so forth), and arousal will remain low. When breakup occurs, however, both partners are forced either to give up hope of achieving some goals or to pursue them on their own. This transition will be quite disruptive, at least temporarily. The emotional arousal that such disruptions produce will be experienced as grief at the loss of the lover. Consistent with this analysis, Berscheid and her colleagues have found that length of time in relationships is directly related to emotional distress upon breakup. See Berscheid (1983). See also E. Berscheid, M. Snyder, and A. M. Omoto (1989). The relationship closeness inventory: Assessing the closeness of interpersonal relationships. *Journal of Personality and Social Psychology* 57:792–807.

28. U. Gupta and P. Singh (1982). Exploratory study of love and liking and type of marriages. *Indian Journal of Applied Psychology.* 19:19–97.

   In countries that began to abandon arranged marriages several decades ago, traditionalists still claim that marriages contracted by the partners "start out hot and grow cold," whereas arranged marriages "start out cold and grow hot." In the late 1950s, Robert Blood noted that in Japan there were a large number of both types of marriages. He saw a chance to compare the marital satisfaction of people in arranged marriages with that of those in love marriages.

   One of his findings was that both groups showed a *decline* in satisfaction over the nine-year duration of their relationships. In general, then, all marriages tended to "grow cold" over time, which contradicts the strong version of the traditionalist argument that arranged marriages "grow hot." But there was more. In the end, women expressed the most satisfaction with love marriages, and men were most satisfied with "hybrid" marriages. Hybrid marriages were arranged by the family but were modernized in that a courtship period was added to allow a love relationship to develop prior to marriage. See R. O. Blood (1967). *Love Match and Arranged Marriage.* New York: The Free Press.

Several years later, researchers followed up Blood's study with a similar study of Chinese women. The findings offer converging evidence for the salutary effects of love marriages, even 25 years after the wedding. On the surface, this evidence seems to support the romantic ideal. A closer look at the Chinese study weakens this conclusion, however. It turns out that the phrase "love marriage" is a misnomer here. Although the people in such marriages freely chose their mates, they typically did so on the basis of pragmatic characteristics such as income or the type of housing the man would probably provide—romance was rarely an issue. In fact, during this period in China, using the term *love* to describe a relationship between a man and a woman typically connoted an illicit relationship rather than a socially sanctioned one. One Chinese woman summarized this idea by noting, "While our impressions of each other deepened, we remained on the level of platonic friendship. We never talked about the word love when we saw each other; therefore I trust him deeply and respect him very much." See X. Xiaohe and M. K. Whyte (1990). Love matches and arranged marriages: A Chinese replication. *Journal of Marriage and the Family* 52:709–722. F. L. K. Hsu (1981). *Americans and Chinese: Passage to Differences.* Honolulu: University Press of Hawaii, 52.

Furthermore, Chinese women seldom have the extensive dating experiences that Americans do. More than 90 percent of the sample of Chinese women never considered marrying anyone other than their eventual husbands, and close to half the women never dated their future husbands before the marriage. So although these women did indeed choose their husbands, they had little or no experience with the Western version of love and romance when they did so. As a result, their experiences are far removed from those of people who grow up in a country in which love and romance are national obsessions.

29. See H. Fisher (1992). *The Anatomy of Love.* New York: W. W. Norton. W. R. Jankowiak and E. F. Fischer (1992). A cross-cultural perspective on romantic love. *Ethnology* 31:149–155.

30. D. Leonard-Barton (1992). The factory as a learning laboratory. *Sloan Management Review* (Fall):28.

31. Several years later, researchers reported similar findings based on a study at a new automobile factory in Kalmar, Sweden. For overviews of the Scandinavian experiments and related studies, see D. Katz and R. L. Kahn (1976). *The Social Psychology of Organizations.* New York: Wiley.

The movement to empower workers has a downside, however. James Barker has pointed out that when workers are responsible to one another rather than to a single supervisor, they may feel (with good reason) that they are under more or less constant scrutiny. The pressure of work thus becomes even stronger. See J. R. Barker (1993). Tightening the iron cage: Concertive control in self-managing teams. *Administrative Science Quarterly* 38:408–437.

32. J. Schor (1991). *The Overworked American.* New York: Basic Books, 152–157.

33. Katz (1995), 72.

34. Katz (1995), 74.

35. Lind (1995).

36. See the discussion of Claude Steele's work on disidentification in Chapter 6. Also see T. I. Chacko (1982). Women and equal employment opportunity: Some unintended effects. *Journal of Applied Psychology* 67:119–123. R. J. Summers (1991). The influence of affirmative action on perceptions of a beneficiary's qualifications. *Journal of Applied Social Psychology* 21:1265–1276.

37. J. Sander (1991). *Before Their Time: Four Generations of Teenage Mothers.* New York: Harcourt Brace Jovanovitch, 178.

38. S. B. Heath and M. W. McLaughlin (1993). *Identity and Inner-City Youth: Beyond Ethnicity and Gender.* New York: Teacher's College Press.

39. Damon (1995).

40. W. Kaminer (1993). *I'm Dysfunctional, You're Dysfunctional: The Recovery Movement and Other Self-Help Fashions.* New York: Addison-Wesley.

41. See the preface to the paperback edition of Kaminer's book.

42. Burns (1993).

43. Burns cites one study conducted by Scogin as support for the effectiveness of reading self-help books to improve self-esteem. At the very best, Scogin's study provides suggestive evidence for the efficacy of such treatments in ameliorating depression and no evidence whatsoever that they are effective in increasing self-esteem. See F. Scogin, C. Jamison, and K. Gochneaur (1989). Comparative efficacy of cognitive and behavioral bibliotherapy for mildly and moderately depressed older adults. *Journal of Consulting and Clinical Psychology* 57:403–407. F. Scogin, C. Jamison, and N. Davis (1990). Two-year follow-up of bibliotherapy for depression in older adults. *Journal of Consulting and Clinical Psychology* 58: 665–667.

There is no reason to expect that cognitive therapy should lead to permanent increases in self-esteem, because it focuses on changing the way people view themselves here and now but does nothing to alter the many variables that determine how they will feel about themselves down the road. For this reason, when people set down Burns's book, they may feel better about themselves, but unless they do something about the behaviors that caused them discomfort in the first place, their negative feelings about themselves will come back to haunt them. It is certainly conceivable that people will maintain their positive feelings about themselves for a while. It is also possible that they will develop new relationships that confirm their newly developed positive self-views. And it is even plausible that people will discard deeply entrenched cultural beliefs about how to bolster their self-esteem or that those who have been disadvantaged by society may benefit from social changes that allow them to pursue self-worth that is compatible with leading happy and productive lives. Yet for all the reasons spelled out in this book, none of these happy outcomes is guaranteed. Thus, any gains in "self-esteem" produced by these programs may be fleeting.

44. Seligman (1994).

45. The techniques favored by the self-esteem movement may also appear to work, not because they are inherently effective but because people *believe* that they will work. This phenomenon is called the *placebo effect*, a name that emerged when

doctors who were doing drug trials noticed that simply administering a pill tended to produce the desired effect even if it contained no active ingredients. The power of the placebo effect could make it appear that even the silliest affirmation exercise was raising self-esteem. Perhaps recognizing this, writers of self-help books are typically careful to cultivate the perception that their techniques really do work. Here is what one set of authors said in an effort to counter skepticism about the effectiveness of "visualization" techniques:

> *Whether or not you believe in the effectiveness of visualization doesn't matter. Faith in the technique may help you achieve results faster than a "nonbeliever" but faith isn't essential to the process. Your mind is structured in such a way that visualization works no matter what you believe. Skepticism may keep you from trying visualization, but it won't stop the technique from working once you try it.* (From M. McKay and P. Fanning, 1992. *Self-Esteem.* Oakland, Calif.: Harbinger Publications, 171.)

The placebo effect may be one reason that programs such as Alcoholics Anonymous work reasonably well for people who choose to enter them but not well at all for people who are forced to attend them. In fact, there is some evidence that those who are compelled to attend AA meetings because they have been arrested for drunk driving or because their company wishes them to do so do *worse* than those who are left to their own devices. See G. E. Vaillant (1983). *The Natural History of Alcoholism: Causes, Patterns, and Paths of Recovery.* Cambridge, Mass.: Harvard University Press, 61.

APPENDIX:
SELF-ATTRIBUTES
QUESTIONNAIRE

The index of self-views used in the marital bliss study discussed in Chapter Two was the Self-Attributes Questionnaire (SAQ), a portion of which is reproduced here. To discover how you would have scored in the marital bliss study, follow the directions below. An explanation of the results follows the questionnaire.

—Self-Attributes Questionnaire from B. W. Pelham and W. B. Swann, Jr. (1989). From self-conceptions to self-worth: On the sources and structure of global self-esteem. *Journal of Personality and Social Psychology* 57: 672–680.

Rate yourself compared to other people your own age and sex by using the following scale:

1	2	3	4	5	6	7	8	9	10
Bottom 5%	Lower 10%	Lower 20%	Lower 30%	Lower 50%	Upper 50%	Upper 30%	Upper 20%	Upper 10%	Top 5%

Here is an example of how the scale works. If one of the attributes listed below were "height," a woman who is just below average height would choose "5" for that question. A woman who is taller than 80% (but not taller than 90%) of other women for her age would mark "8," indicating that she is in the top 20% (but not in the top 10%) on this dimension. If you have a question about how the scale works, please do not hesitate to ask the researcher. You will answer each item using the same scale (always circle one number).

Intelligence:

1	2	3	4	5	6	7	8	9	10
Bottom 5%	Lower 10%	Lower 20%	Lower 30%	Lower 50%	Upper 50%	Upper 30%	Upper 20%	Upper 10%	Top 5%

Social skills/social competence:

1	2	3	4	5	6	7	8	9	10
Bottom 5%	Lower 10%	Lower 20%	Lower 30%	Lower 50%	Upper 50%	Upper 30%	Upper 20%	Upper 10%	Top 5%

Artistic and/or musical ability:

1	2	3	4	5	6	7	8	9	10
Bottom 5%	Lower 10%	Lower 20%	Lower 30%	Lower 50%	Upper 50%	Upper 30%	Upper 20%	Upper 10%	Top 5%

Athletic ability:

1	2	3	4	5	6	7	8	9	10
Bottom 5%	Lower 10%	Lower 20%	Lower 30%	Lower 50%	Upper 50%	Upper 30%	Upper 20%	Upper 10%	Top 5%

Physical attractiveness:

1	2	3	4	5	6	7	8	9	10
Bottom 5%	Lower 10%	Lower 20%	Lower 30%	Lower 50%	Upper 50%	Upper 30%	Upper 20%	Upper 10%	Top 5%

To discover how you would have been classified had you participated in the marital bliss study, answer each of the foregoing questions and add your responses. A total score ranging from 5 to 27 would have put you in the negative self-concept group, a score ranging from 28 to 32 would have put you in the moderate self-concept group, and a score above 32 would have put you in the positive self-concept group.

What does it mean to have positive, negative, or moderate self-views? First, your group assignment is based on how you scored relative to the people who took part in our initial studies—people from central Texas who happened to participate in our study at the horse ranch or shopping mall. Although these scores are fairly typical of the scores of thousands of people who have completed our scale, I should point out that most of these people have been white, middle-class college students. Because self-views may differ somewhat across racial and socioeconomic groups, the category you fall into could be influenced by the group to which you compare yourself. The same absolute score will seem lower when compared against a group of people who think extremely well of themselves than it would when compared against a group of people who tend to think badly of themselves.

Note also that the SAQ is not an index of global self-esteem. Rather, it focuses primarily on the perceived competence component of self-esteem—how capable people think they are of achieving various goals. People can be low on the perceived competence component of self-esteem but be high on the other major component, perceived lovability. This means that even if you scored low on the SAQ, you might still be high in perceived lovability, which would give you reasonably high global self-esteem.

There are two additional points to bear in mind when considering scores on the SAQ. First, thinking that you have lots of certain qualities such as intelligence, sociability, or athletic ability is not the same as actually having those qualities. Many of the self-views that we care about most—such as those related to self-esteem—are only loosely associated with "objective reality." Some people may conclude erroneously that they are totally incompetent when in reality they are quite capable. Second, although people sometimes experience dramatic changes in their self-views, self-views tend to remain stable, for reasons that are spelled out in this book.

INDEX

References not listed here may be found in the Notes.